Rethinking California:
Politics & Policy
in the Golden State

Matthew Alan Cahn
California State University, Northridge

H. Eric Schockman
University of Southern California

David M. Shafie
Ohio University

Prentice
Hall

Upper Saddle River, New Jersey 07458

Library of Congress Cataloging-in-Publication Data

Cahn, Matthew Alan.
    Rethinking California: politics and policy in the golden state/Matthew Alan Cahn,
    H. Eric Schockman, David M. Shafie.
      p. cm.
    Includes bibliographical references and index.
    ISBN 0-13-467912-1
      1. Political planning—California. 2. Political culture—California. 3. California—Politics
    and government. I. Schockman, H. Eric. II. Shafie, David M. III. Title.

    JK8749.P64 C34 2000
    320.9794—dc21
                                                  00-053054

VP, Editorial director: Laura Pearson
Assistant editor: Brian Prybella
Editorial assistant: Jessica Drew
Director of marketing: Beth Gillett Mejia
Editorial/production supervision: Kari Callaghan Mazzola
Prepress and manufacturing buyer: Ben Smith
Electronic page makeup: Kari Callaghan Mazzola and John P. Mazzola
Interior design: John P. Mazzola
Cover director: Jayne Conte
Cover photo: Corbis Digital Stock

This book was set in 10/12 Times by Big Sky Composition
and was printed and bound by Courier Companies, Inc.
The cover was printed by Phoenix Color Corp.

© 2001 by Prentice-Hall, Inc.
A Division of Pearson Education
Upper Saddle River, New Jersey 07458

Printed in the United States of America
10 9 8 7 6 5 4

ISBN 0-13-467912-1

PRENTICE-HALL INTERNATIONAL (UK) LIMITED, *London*
PRENTICE-HALL OF AUSTRALIA PTY. LIMITED, *Sydney*
PRENTICE-HALL CANADA INC., *Toronto*
PRENTICE-HALL HISPANOAMERICANA, S.A., *Mexico*
PRENTICE-HALL OF INDIA PRIVATE LIMITED, *New Delhi*
PRENTICE-HALL OF JAPAN, INC., *Tokyo*
PEARSON EDUCATION ASIA PTE. LTD., *Singapore*
EDITORA PRENTICE-HALL DO BRASIL, LTDA., *Rio de Janeiro*

This book is dedicated to the legacy of Governor Edmund G. "Pat" Brown, whose vision of a great state and whose passion for elevating everyday people provided the leadership to build California's robust infrastructure, which sees us through both good times and bad.

Contents

CHAPTER 11
NON-INSTITUTIONAL PLAYERS: THE MEDIA, POLITICAL PARTIES, AND INTEREST GROUPS 109

CHAPTER 12
THE ELECTORATE AS PLAYERS: ELECTIONS AND POLITICAL PARTICIPATION 121

PART IV: POLICY

CHAPTER 13
EDUCATION POLICY 133

CHAPTER 14
ENVIRONMENTAL POLICY 144

CHAPTER 15
IMMIGRATION POLICY   163

CHAPTER 16
CIVIL RIGHTS POLICY   176

PART V: CONCLUSION

CHAPTER 17
RETHINKING CALIFORNIA   191

APPENDIX A
CALIFORNIA COUNTIES   197

Acknowledgments

No book is the work of its authors alone. We would like to thank several people for their insights into the California experience. They include Tim Hodson at the Center for California Studies (CSU, Sacramento), Jaime Regalado at the Pat Brown Institute (Cal State, Los Angeles), Michael Dear at the Southern California Studies Center (USC), Fernando Guerra at the Center for the Study of Los Angeles (Loyola Marymount), and the entire Faculty Advisory Board at the Center for Southern California Studies (CSUN).

We thank Teodora Manolova and Shervin Boloorian at the Center for Southern California Studies (CSUN) and Scott and Gilda Sveslosky at the University of Southern California for tirelessly providing research assistance and staff support. We also thank Ms. Clare Walker (USC) for her superb production skills in helping to prepare the manuscript. Their supportive friendships were as helpful as their skills and commitment.

We also thank the following reviewers: Steven Alan Holmes, Bakersfield College; Mark Somma, California State University, Fresno; Richard L. Palmer, California State University, Dominguez Hills; and Richard G. Randall, Merced College.

On a personal level we would like to thank our families, including Diane, Jonah, and Tobin; Steven H. Crithfield, who is a partner in life and an essential moral component in building a long-term, loving relationship; and Ann Gordon.

About the Authors

MATTHEW ALAN CAHN is Director of the Center for Southern California Studies and Professor of Public Policy at California State University, Northridge. His research interests include California politics, urban environmental policy, and resource management. Dr. Cahn has been involved in several applied policy areas, ranging from transportation issues in metropolitan Los Angeles to the question of marine protected areas in the Channel Islands National Marine Sanctuary. He is the author or co-author of several books, including *Environmental Deceptions*; *Thinking about the Environment*; and *California: An Owner's Manual*. Over the years Dr. Cahn has taught at San Francisco State, San Jose State, the University of Southern California, and UC Santa Barbara.

H. ERIC SCHOCKMAN is Associate Dean and Associate Professor of Political Science at the University of Southern California. He has headed up numerous policy "think-tanks" and served as a high level consultant to the California Legislature and the City Council of Los Angeles. Dr. Schockman is the author of numerous academic manuscripts, articles, and books, including *Rethinking Los Angeles* and *California: An Owner's Manual*. He served as pro-bono Policy Director for the Elected Los Angeles Charter Reform Commission, and he currently sits as a Commissioner on the State of California's Little Hoover Commission, a government oversight and efficiency commission.

DAVID M. SHAFIE is Assistant Professor of Political Science at Ohio University. His research interests include state and local politics, environmental policy, and media and politics. He has also been a journalist and has taught at California State University, Long Beach and California State University, Fullerton.

CHAPTER 1

The Three States of California: An Introduction

Featured Reading / Pages 7–9
Joan Didion
Notes from a Native Daughter

[Many people] have been to Los Angeles or to San Francisco, have driven through a giant redwood and have seen the Pacific glazed by the afternoon sun off Big Sur, and they naturally tend to believe that they have in fact been to California. They have not been, and they probably never will be, for it is a longer and in many more ways a more difficult trip than they might want to undertake, one of those trips on which the destination flickers chimerically on the horizon, ever receding, ever diminishing.

—Joan Didion, from *Notes from a Native Daughter*

California has always been considered somewhat different from the rest of the nation. It is, as Theodore Roosevelt pointed out, "west of the West." Yet California has emerged as a dominant trendsetter, establishing models and approaches that are emulated throughout the nation. California may be west of the traditional centers of power, but its size and influence have surpassed all other states. Stretching 825 miles from Crescent City to San Diego and 215 miles from Monterey to Mono Lake, California comprises 164,000 square miles and 32 million people—12.3 percent of the total U.S. population.[1]

Captured by the United States in 1846, with statehood bestowed in 1850, California was a latecomer to national politics. As a consequence of both its distance from the established power centers of the East and its "frontier" culture, California was seen more as a repository of rich natural resources than as a partner in policy. California was a terrain contested by three nations and dozens of Native-American communities. Between Cabrillo's claims on the Pacific Coast in 1542 and the Mexican-American War in 1846, Spain, Mexico, and the United States maneuvered, battled, and manipulated to gain control.

Spanish colonization of California began in 1769 when Junipero Serra established El Camino Real, the Mission Trail—nine missions whose central function was to control Indian land on behalf of Spain and convert native civilizations to Christianity. Spain actively recruited settlers from Mexico, drawing fundamentally from the poorest *mestizo* communities.[2] Spain's hold on California was weak, with only 3,000 settlers—most of whom were Mexican. When Mexico became independent of Spain in 1821, California became a Mexican territory. City names like Mendicino, Sonoma, San Francisco, San

1

Jose, Santa Cruz, Monterey, San Luis Obispo, Los Angeles, and San Diego reflect its Native-American, Spanish, and Mexican heritage—and its ethnic ambivalence. The 46 original settlers of Los Angeles, for example, were *mestizos* of Indian, African, and Spanish ancestry.[3] This ambivalence runs deep in part because the U.S. claim on California was pushed by American squatters in what was then Mexico.[4]

THE THREE STATES OF CALIFORNIA

Many observers have noted that California, with its complex network of communities and regional resources, may in fact be composed of three states. If one were to explore how California's many communities related to each other, it would be possible to identify clear regional cultures within which unique subcultures interacted. Politically, economically, socially, philosophically, even ethnically, California is actually three different places: Southern California (San Diego north to San Luis Obispo County); Northern California (Monterey County up through Humboldt County); and the Central Valley (Kern and Inyo Counties north to Oregon). Each of these regions maintain unique economies, idiosyncratic political cultures, unique microclimates, even distinct language patterns and cultural reference points. To fully understand California one must understand its separate regional identities.

SOUTHERN CALIFORNIA

Southern California may be characterized as densely populated urban coastline, particularly between Ventura and Orange Counties. With the notable exception of Los Angeles and Santa Barbara Counties, Southern California tends to vote Republican. As a consequence of the large metropolitan areas, Southern California remains ethnically and religiously diverse. Traditional Southern California economic engines have been manufacturing and light industry. Since the 1970s, however, the Southern California economy has become more service oriented and corporate in nature. The archetypal Southern California job in the 1950s was industrial (shipyards, tire manufacturing). The archetypal Southern California job in the 1990s is service sector (low paying jobs include food service and retail; high paying jobs include international banking and consulting).

Add to these structural phenomena the unique architectural and cultural edifices and the Southern California character is complete. Since the region grew extremely quickly—exponentially increasing in population between 1940 and 1990—effectively planning the infrastructure was impossible. The result is evident in both land planning and transportation. The mini-mall, a Southern California invention, has come to dominate the landscape. These strip malls, which typically include some combination of convenience store, donut shop, dry cleaners, and hair & nail shop, were in many ways predetermined by Southern California's geography. Quick growth and conservative politics tend to preclude land and architectural planning; warm weather encourages convenience shopping in open air storefronts; the reliance on cars makes parking lots a necessity; and the relatively cheap land in outlying areas encourages the construction of multi-unit retail space (e.g., mini-malls) on speculation by small investors.

Southern California is defined in many ways by its freeways. This, however, was not always the case. As early as 1924, Southern California's Red Car system carried 100 million riders annually between San Fernando, Newport Beach, Pasadena, and San Bernardino—covering an area from Los Angeles and out some 75 miles in all directions. The fate of mass transit in Southern California was doomed, however, for two reasons. First, the short-term success of the Red Car actually prevented long-term success because the system encouraged building out rather than building up, as in most cities. Home builders built large tracts on cheap land, advertising "live in the country, work in the city." The Red Car made it possible to buy a house in an inexpensive area, while commuting into the city. However, as development grew beyond train stations in outlying areas, mass transit became less attractive. By the 1940s, home builders were advertising garages with driveways rather than proximity to train stations.

Second, as a relatively new urban area, Southern California's major investment in its transportation infrastructure came at a time when cars were increasingly inexpensive and roads were relatively uncongested. Related issues such as energy and air quality were not yet significant concerns. In 1926, when Angelenos were asked to vote on bond measures that would define Southern California's transportation infrastructure for the next century, rail construction lost out to freeway construction. This was perhaps preordained. Who in 1926 could have predicted the growth Southern California would achieve over the next half century?

In addition, Southern California's weather—with a year-round median temperature in the mid-70s and little rainfall—encourages an outdoor lifestyle. The architecture reflects this, as does the fashion and the vernacular. Housing tracts—with two-bedroom Spanish-style bungalows in the 1920s and 1930s, larger "modern" ranch-style houses boasting three bedrooms and two bathrooms in the 1940s, 1950s, and 1960s, and even larger Mediterranean styles in the 1970s, 1980s, and 1990s—suggest a Southern California style. Front yards are dominated by garages and driveways, with the notable absence of porches, suggesting a space of utility rather than socializing with neighbors. Backyards are dominated by "family space," including BBQ areas, swingsets, and dog runs.

The warm weather and proximity to a swimmable coastline ensures an enduring relationship with the beach and ocean. While the Aloha shirt may or may not be fashionable throughout the state, it has never lost favor in Southern California. Southern California vernacular has consistently included outdoor references. From the Annette Funicello/ Frankie Avalon beach party movies to "Baywatch," Southern Californians have long had to balance externally imposed stereotypes with organic, homegrown lifestyles. This hasn't been easy, in large part because the Southern California media persists in celebrating the "Baywatch" ideal and because of the high number of transplants who have flocked to Southern California in search of this idealized lifestyle. While many outsiders see Malibu or Santa Monica as quintessential Southern California, the real Southern California is a quilt of cultures, alive and well in places like Ventura and Oxnard, San Fernando, Inglewood, Monterey Park, San Pedro, Long Beach, San Clemente, and Oceanside.

NORTHERN CALIFORNIA

Mark Twain once commented that the coldest winter he ever spent was a summer in San Francisco. Where Southern California is often warm and dry, Northern California is often cold and damp. But the differences go far beyond weather. Northern California tends to vote Democratic, albeit with distinct enclaves of conservative voters. While architecture dominates the Southern California landscape, in Northern California landscape dominates architecture. The "Little Boxes" that dot Daly City's residential tracts are necessitated by the urban density of the San Francisco peninsula. Bordered by the bay and the ocean, the available space to build is severely limited.

The earth tones of Marin architecture and the unobtrusive style of Big Sur architecture reflect the region's comfort with nature. This is a function of lower density and cooler weather. Southern Californians spend much of the year indoors to avoid the heat. Northern Californians spend much of the year indoors to avoid the rain. Each climate requires different architecture. Functional fashion may also be a result: Hiking boots and flannel make more sense in Humboldt than in San Diego.

Northern California may itself represent two different places. The Bay Area is distinctly different from the northern coast. The high-tech industries along the San Jose-San Francisco corridor lead the nation in new technology research and development and in high-tech manufacturing. The income generated in Silicon Valley is illustrated by a local housing market that is two to three times higher than in the Bay Area generally. At the same time, the timber-based economy of the North is extremely vulnerable. Median income in Santa Clara County (including Silicon Valley) is $54,672. Median income in Glenn County is $25,648.[5]

In the same way, Northern California's urban centers mirror the diversity of Southern California, but its rural northwest does not. The Bay Area is extremely diverse, incorporating strong and politicized black, Latino, Asian, and Native American communities. Cities like Oakland, San Francisco, and San Jose are among the nation's premier multicultural centers. At the same time, the northwest coast from Mendicino to Crescent City looks more like Oregon than California—predominantly white, modest incomes, and largely Christian.

If there is a Northern California vernacular it may be due to politicized university students from Santa Cruz, Stanford, Berkeley, San Francisco, San Jose, Hayward, Sonoma, and Humboldt State. These institutions have a long history of activism, particularly with regard to environmental issues and civil rights. A case in point: The tired phrase "politically correct" originated on Northern California campuses as an affectionate jab by campus leftists at their more programmatic colleagues. In a bit of Orwellian doublespeak, it has since been highjacked by conservatives to marginalize progressive concerns.

THE CENTRAL VALLEY

The Central Valley is California's Heartland. It is primarily agricultural, with small cities separated by miles of farmland. Density is low outside of its major cities. It is the home of the Central Valley Project, the primary delivery system for agricultural water diverted from the Sacramento Delta. The relatively narrow valley, bordered east and west by mountains, is home to a thick fog every winter. This Tule fog is both an institution and a hazard. Most Californians know the Central Valley at 70 mph as they drive between the Bay Area and Southern California along Interstate 5. Relatively few travel off the interstate, making the Valley unknown to most Californians.

The Central Valley includes vast rural areas, with growing urban areas in Bakersfield, Fresno, and, of course, the greater Sacramento area. Fresno and Sacramento are among the state's ten largest cities, with populations of 405,100 and 396,000, respectively. Fresno County is one of the state's fastest growing areas, predicted to grow from its current population of 765,000 to 2.5 million over the next 40 years.[6] And, while many small cities in the Central Valley are predominately white and Latino, the larger cities are extremely diverse. Bakersfield, Fresno, Stockton, and Sacramento reflect the diversity of the rest of the state. Stockton, for example, is 23 percent Asian, compared to San Francisco's 29 percent, and Los Angeles' 9.6 percent. Fifty-five percent of Stockton's 48,000 Asians are Vietnamese, Cambodian, Hmong, and Laotian.[7]

Politically, the Central Valley tends to be split. The agricultural counties tend to vote Republican, the urban counties vote Democratic. The Central Valley's economic engine is primarily agricultural, from the farms in Kern, Kings, and Fresno Counties in the south up to the northern counties that unfold along the Sacramento River—Colusa, Butte, and Tehama Counties. Stockton and Sacramento remain active port cities, with light industry and related services. The Sacramento, American, and Feather Rivers spill into the Sacramento Delta, a vast maze of bayous and tributaries, invoking the flavor of Louisiana in California.

If there is a "beltway" in California, it is Sacramento. With the high number of state offices and the influx of representatives, staff, lobbyists, and the public, Sacramento at times looks more like Washington than the sleepy Central Valley river town it once was. As the political nexus of the state, downtown Sacramento has been able to remake itself in the image of every Californian. This is remarkable considering how different Californians are from one another. The warm weather and urban sprawl are familiar to Southern Californians, the heavy tree covering and lush gardens are familiar to Northern Californians, and to the Central Valley, Sacramento is—well, home.

How Many Californias?

Some observers see even more than three states within California's borders. Philip Fradkin, for example, identifies seven.[8] Fradkin sees differing landscapes as critical determinants of cultural expression. Fradkin's first California is the deserts, along the southeastern corridor of the state from Mono Lake south to the Salton Sea. The deserts are defined by drought, little population, untamed open space, and ghosts of past civilizations. His second California is the Sierra, encompassing the Sierra Nevada from Donner Pass to Bakersfield. This 430-mile-long mountain region is distinguished by vast wilderness, even fewer people, and characterized by a pioneer past. The Sierra Nevadas, while never tamed, had to be understood to allow westward immigration. The hard lessons of the Donner Party[9] underscore life in this California.

Fradkin's third California, "the Land of Fire," is the volcanic Cascade region in the northeasternmost section of the state. His fourth California, "the Land of Water," is the northwest coastal area from Crescent City to Point Arena. This California is dominated by forests, wind, fog, and rain. The population is centered in Crescent City, Arcata, Humboldt, and Eureka. Separated by thick forests from the rest of the state, there is a palpable sense of isolation. California number five is the "Great Valley." The central valley between Redding and Bakersfield is the state's bread basket, making up one of the largest regions of sustained agriculture in the nation. Population is greatest in the greater Sacramento area, inclusive of Stockton, and in the Fresno/Bakersfield area, which is the fastest growing region of the state, but is distributed throughout the region. California number six includes the northern California coastline from Point Reyes to Point Conception. The "Fractured Province" is defined in large measure by the frequency of earthquake fault lines.

Finally, California number seven, Southern California from Point Conception to San Diego, is Fradkin's "Profligate Province." This region is the most populated and, in Fradkin's view, the most wildly extravagant. The cycle of earthquake, fire, and flood is somehow a function of Southern California's hubris. In this Fradkin anticipates Mike Davis' *Ecology of Fear.*[10] Whether one accepts the notion of multiple Californias or not, it is clear that regional differences have emerged as important to California's diversity.

URBAN CALIFORNIA, URBAN PERIPHERIES, AND RURAL CALIFORNIA

Some observers note that while there are different Californias, it is not geography that distinguishes them. Rather, the very different types of cities and towns throughout the state can be delineated by economic base, demographics, and size. More specifically, communities throughout the state can be divided into Urban California, Urban Peripheries, and Rural California. According to this analysis, cities of like size, demography, and structure have more in common than those cities that share a geographic region. San Francisco, for example, has much more in common with Los Angeles than with Willits, a small lumber town in Mendicino. Similarly, Vista, in northern San Diego County, has much more in common with Concord, in the Bay Area, than with San Diego.

Urban centers tend to share common concerns, as do urban peripheries and rural areas. Urban cores are concerned with race relations, economic revitalization, international commerce, crime, and crumbling school districts. Urban peripheries, those suburbs that ring urban cores, depend on the central city for economic sustenance, but struggle with issues of open space, zoning, and the retail "flavor" of boutique downtown areas. Crime is a major preoccupation, but typically in the context of containing "city crime" from spreading into the periphery neighborhoods. Rural areas share a concern for agricultural and timber resources, tend to oppose environmental restrictions, and fear "urban sprawl," where urban peripheries begin to extend into agricultural areas. At the same time, rural communities battle periphery cities over open space issues. Newly incorporated cities in outlying areas hope to preserve open space in perpetuity, while rural communities often assert a right to develop open space as the market dictates.

CALIFORNIA DIVIDE

Whether one agrees with Fradkin's borders or a more modest set of borders, there clearly are significant regional differences within the state. With 58 distinctive counties this is, perhaps, no surprise. How these different communities interact as a common state, however, often is. Intraregional relations, interregional relations, and region-to-state relations all depend on the unique cultures and politics that dominate the region. As we explore these relationships we must keep an eye toward the regional idiosyncrasies that make California unique.

Notes from a Native Daughter   Joan Didion

It was very easy to sit at the bar in, say, La Scala in Beverly Hills, or Ernie's in San Francisco, and to share in the pervasive delusion that California is only five hours from New York by air. The truth is that La Scala and Ernie's are only five hours from New York by air. California is somewhere else.

Many people in the East (or "back East," as they say in California, although not in La Scala or Ernie's) do not believe this. They have been to Los Angeles or to San Francisco, have driven through a giant redwood and have seen the Pacific glazed by the afternoon sun off Big Sur, and they naturally tend to believe that they have in fact been to California. They have not been, and they probably never will be, for it is a longer and in many more ways a more difficult trip than they might want to undertake, one of those trips on which the destination flickers chimerically on the horizon, ever receding, ever diminishing. I happen to know about that trip because I come from California, come from a family, or a congeries of families, that has always been in the Sacramento Valley.

You might protest that no family has been in the Sacramento Valley for anything approaching "always." But it is characteristic of Californians to speak grandly of the past as if it had simultaneously begun, *tabula rasa*, and reached a happy ending on the day the wagons started West. *Eureka*—"I Have Found It"—as the state motto has it. Such a view of history casts a certain melancholia over those who participate in it; my own childhood was suffused with the conviction that we had long outlived our finest hour. In fact that is what I want to tell you about: what it is like to have come from a place like Sacramento. If I could make you understand that, I could make you understand California and perhaps something else besides, for Sacramento *is* California, and California is a place in which a boom mentality and a sense of Chekhovian loss meet in uneasy suspension; in which the mind is troubled by some buried but ineradicable suspension that things had better work here, because here, beneath that immense bleached sky, is where we run out of continent.

In 1847 Sacramento was no more than an adobe enclosure, Sutter's Fort, standing alone on the prairie; cut off from San Francisco and the sea by the Coast Range and from the rest of the continent by the Sierra Nevada, the Sacramento Valley was then a true sea of grass, grass so high a man riding into it could tie it across his saddle. A year later gold was discovered in the Sierra foothills, and abruptly Sacramento was a town, a town any moviegoer could map tonight in his dreams—a dusty collage of assay offices and wagonmakers and saloons. Call that Phase Two. Then the settlers came—the farmers, the people who for two hundred years had been moving west of the frontier, the peculiar flawed strain who had cleared Virginia, Kentucky, Missouri; they made Sacramento a farm town. Because the land was rich, Sacramento became eventually a rich farm town, which meant houses in town, Cadillac dealers, a country club. In that gentle sleep Sacramento dreamed until perhaps 1950, when something happened. What happened was that Sacramento woke to the fact that the outside world was moving in, fast and hard. At the moment of its waking Sacramento lost, for better or for worse, its character, and that is part of what I want to tell you about.

But the change is not what I remember first. First I remember running a boxer dog of my brother's over the same flat fields that our great-great-grandfather had found virgin and had planted; I remember swimming (albeit nervously, for I was a nervous child, afraid of sinkholes and afraid of snakes, and perhaps that was the beginning of my error) the same rivers we had swum for a century: the Sacramento, so rich with silt that we could barely see our hands a few inches beneath the surface; the American, running clean and fast with melted Sierra snow until July, when it would slow down, and rattlesnakes would sun themselves on its newly exposed rocks. The Sacramento, the American, sometimes the Cosumnes, occasionally the Feather. Incautious children died every day in those rivers; we had read about it in the paper, how they had miscalculated a current or stepped into a hole down where the American runs into the Sacramento, how the Berry Brothers had been called in from Yolo County to drag the river but how the bodies remained unrecovered. "They were from away," my grandmother would extrapolate from the newspaper stories. "Their parents had no *business* letting them in the river. They were visitors from Omaha." It was not a bad lesson, although a less than reliable one; children we knew died in the rivers too....

Later, when I was living in New York, I would make the trip back to Sacramento four and five times a year (the more comfortable the flight, the more obscurely miserable I would be, for it weighs heavily upon my mind that we could perhaps not make it by wagon), trying to prove that I had not meant to leave at all, because in at least one respect California—the California we are talking about—resembles Eden: It is assumed that those who absent themselves from its blessings have been banished, exiled by some perversity of heart. Did not the Donner-Reed Party, after all, eat its own dead to reach Sacramento?

I have said that the trip back is difficult, and it is—difficult in a way that magnifies the ordinary ambiguities of sentimental journeys. Going back to California is not like going back to Vermont, or Chicago; Vermont and Chicago are relative constants, against which one measures one's own change. All that is constant about the California of my childhood is the rate at which it disappears. An instance: on Saint Patrick's Day of 1948 I was taken to see the legislature "in action," a dismal experience; a handful of florid assemblymen, wearing green hats, were reading Pat-and-Mike jokes into the record. I still think of the legislators that way—wearing green hats, or sitting around on the veranda of the Senator Hotel fanning themselves and being entertained by Artie Samish's emissaries. (Samish was the lobbyist who said, "Earl Warren may be the governor of the state, but I'm the governor of the legislature.") In fact, there is no longer a veranda at the Senator Hotel—it was turned into an airline ticket office, if you want to embroider the point—and in any case the legislature has largely deserted the Senator for the flashy motels north of town, where the tiki torches flame and the steam rises off the heated swimming pools in the cold Valley night.

It is hard to *find* California now, unsettling to wonder how much of it was merely imagined or improvised; melancholy to realize how much of anyone's memory is no true memory at all but only the traces of someone else's memory, stories handed down on the family network. I have an indelibly vivid "memory," for example, of how Prohibition affected the hop growers around Sacramento: The sister of a grower my family knew brought home a mink coat from San Francisco, and was told to take it back, and sat on the floor of the parlor cradling that coat and crying. Although I was not born until a year after Repeal, that scene is more "real" to me than many I have played myself.

I remember one trip home, when I sat alone on a night jet from New York and read over and over some lines from a W. S. Merwin poem I had come across in a magazine, a poem about a man who had been a long time in another country and knew that he must go home:

... But it should be
Soon, Already I defend hotly
Certain of our indefensible faults,
Resent being reminded; already in my mind
Our language becomes freighted with a richness
No common tongue could offer, while the mountains
Are like nowhere on earth, and the wide rivers.

You see the point. I want to tell you the truth, and already I have told you about the wide rivers.

It should be clear by now that the truth about the place is elusive, and must be tracked with caution. You might go to Sacramento tomorrow and someone (although no one I know) might take you out to Aerojet-General, which has, in the Sacramento phrase, "something to do with rockets." Fifteen thousand people work for Aerojet, almost all of them imported; a Sacramento lawyer's wife told me, as evidence of how Sacramento was opening up, that she believed she had met one of them, at an open house two Decembers ago. ("Couldn't have been nicer, actually," she added enthusiastically. "I think he and his wife bought the house next *door* to Mary and Al, something like that, which of course was how *they* met him.") So you might go to Aerojet and stand in the big vendors' lobby where a couple of thousand components salesmen try every week to sell their wares and you might look up at the electrical wallboard that lists Aerojet personnel, their projects and their location at any given time, and you might wonder if I have been in Sacramento lately. MINUTEMEN, POLARIS, TITAN, the lights flash, and all the coffee tables are littered with airline schedules, very now, very much in touch.

But I could take you a few miles from here into towns where the banks still bear names like The Bank of Alex Brown, into towns where the one hotel still has an octagonal-tile floor in the dining room and dusty potted palms and big ceiling fans; into towns where everything—the seed business, the Harvester franchise, the hotel, the department store and the main street—carries a single name, the name of the man who built the town. A few Sundays ago I was in a town like that, a town smaller than that, really, no hotel, no Harvester franchise, the bank burned out, a river town. It was the golden anniversary of some of my relatives and it was 110° and the guests of honor sat on straight-backed chairs in front of a sheaf of gladioluses in the Rebekah Hall. I mentioned visiting Aerojet-General to a cousin I saw there, who listened to me with interested disbelief. Which is the true California? That is what we all wonder.

THE STRUCTURE OF THIS BOOK

This book explores the evolving role of politics and policy in California. To achieve this the book seeks to do the impossible: to convey the taste, smell, and feel of the state at the dawn of the twenty-first century. As the most populous state, California has emerged as a leader of national and international politics, economics, and culture. The following chapters review California's unique institutional structure on both the state and local levels, as well as California's unique cultural legacy.

Part I provides an overview of California's unique history and culture, with special attention paid to political culture, people and diversity, and politics and economics. Part II introduces the institutional infrastructure. These chapters explore the constitutional makeup of California, the governor, state legislature, and state judiciary, as well as local governments. Part III focuses on the policy players—those individuals and organizations who work to influence politics and policy throughout the state, including interest groups, the media, parties, campaigns, and elections. Part IV assesses the major policy issues affecting the state, including education, environment, immigration, and civil rights. California's political culture is as vast and complicated as its terrain. It is its people that make it special and its natural resources that make it unique. The following pages will introduce you to the personalities and ideas that are essential to an understanding of the Golden State, from its early history to the controversies that shape political conflict in the present day.

NOTES

1. California Department of Finance, Population Research Unit, *California Statistical Abstract Report 95 E-1.*
2. Mestizos were subsistence farmers of mixed native and European ancestry.
3. Ronald Takaki, *A Different Mirror: A History of Multicultural America* (Boston: Little, Brown and Company, 1993) and Clyde Milner II, Carol O'Connor, Martha Sandweiss, eds., *The Oxford History of the American West* (New York: Oxford University Press, 1994).
4. Takaki, *A Different Mirror.*
5. California Franchise Tax Board, 1995; California Department of Finance, Population Research Unit, *California Statistical Abstract Report 95 E-1, 95 E-2.*
6. California Department of Finances, Population Research Unit, *Reports 92-E-2 and 95 E-1.*
7. U.S. Census Bureau. 1990 Census.
8. Philip Fradkin, *The Seven States of California: A Natural and Human History* (Berkeley: University of California Press, 1995).
9. The Donner Party were a group of California pioneers who were trapped in a blizzard in the winter of 1846 while transiting what is now Donner Pass in the Sierra Nevada range. Members of the party were reduced to cannibalism in order to survive.
10. Mike Davis, *Ecology of Fear: Los Angeles and the Imagination of Disaster* (New York: Metropolitan Books, 1998).

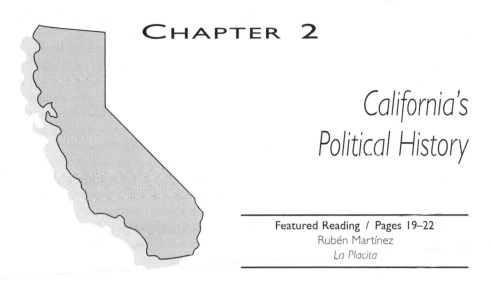

CHAPTER 2

California's Political History

Featured Reading / Pages 19–22
Rubén Martínez
La Placita

What surrounds me is my history, I repeat to myself. The words become my mantra: I must have a history.

—Rubén Martínez, from *La Placita*

California has always been viewed as unique. Historian Carey McWilliams argues that the state is "exceptional" in its evolution—different from any other region of the globe and inhabited by a different cabal of individuals. For McWilliams, California is "no ordinary state. It is an anomaly, a freak, the great exception among the American states."[1] The novelist Christopher Isherwood once called California "a tragic land—like Palestine, like every promised land."[2] Isherwood's comparison of California to the metaphoric New Jerusalem suggests both a biblical utopia, a cornucopia of natural resources and yet an unsettled and tragic land, consumed by the turmoil of its people. It may be the earthly representation of the garden of Eden or the twisted torment of paradise. Critics may deride California, its unique culture, its diversity and unconventional politics. But dismissing California belies its cultural and political significance. The Golden State is a dominant exporter of ideas. California's popular culture is emulated from rural West Africa to the crowded capitals of the Pacific Rim. The state's policy debates—ranging from the sublime to the surreal—are exported to the rest of the United States as grassroots movements and policy innovations. Thus from tax revolts to gay rights, from affirmative action to immigration, from term limits to welfare reform, California is widely viewed as a cradle of cutting-edge social and political movements.

A DIVERSE HERITAGE

To understand California it is necessary to place the state into historical perspective. There is evidence of human settlements in California dating back some 12,000 years. Nomadic tribes crossed the Bering Strait from Asia when the land bridge connected the two continents. The origins of California's diversity trace its roots back to these indigenous peoples. James Rawls points out that the construct of the California Indian is a white invention: "It was created for the purposes of description and analysis, but it was also useful as a stereotype for whites overwhelmed by the diversity of the peoples encountered in the area."[3] The terminology also encapsulated an underlining assumption that all these diverse tribes were homogeneous and of one culture, language, and philosophy.

In reality, California's indigenous peoples were autonomous, nomadic, and diverse. Nearly 300,000 people lived in California before the first European explorers arrived. There were over 100 tribes, or "tribelets," averaging only 250 individuals; together they spoke over 80 distinct dialects. California's indigenous peoples may have had the greatest linguistic diversity in the world.[4] The Tolowa Modoc, Shasta, and Kavok tribes (of the Athabascan Family), for example, lived on the border between Oregon and California; the Kawaiisu, Vanyume, Kitanemuk, Serrano, Tubatulabal, Miwok, and Monache tribes (of the Penutian and Shoshonean Families) inhabited California's vast Central Valley region; and the Diegueno, Kamia, and Yuma tribes (of the Hokan Family) dominated the southernmost part of the state, bordering Mexico.

These indigenous peoples evolved quite distinctly from their pre-Columbian cousins to the south. There was no common language, no regional confederation and no permanent settlements—except for a handful of tribes like the Mohave and Yuma that practiced agriculture. Nor were there great empires built like those of the Aztecs or Incas. California's earliest inhabitants were hunter-gatherers who roamed their territories living off the abundant plants and wildlife. This was both a blessing and a curse. For while these communities were empowered with their own self-government and autonomy, they were too small to collectively withstand the onslaught of Spanish conquest and colonization.

CONQUEST AND COLONIZATION

In 1542, fifty years after Christopher Columbus first came to the "New World," Spain claimed California as one of its possessions during the voyage of the Portuguese navigator Juan Rodriguez Cabrillo. The Spanish quickly lost interest in their new find, however. For almost two centuries, until the mid 1700s, Spain's western Pacific territory remained an outpost of limited commerce and settlement. By this time other European powers, notably France, Russia, and England, were exploring the region for potential new trading and commerce opportunities. Russian fur-trading posts were being established along the northern coastline above San Francisco (hence the name of Sonoma County's Russian River) and nearby Fort Ross.

In 1769 the Spanish ordered a small expedition headed by Gaspar de Portola as its military advisor and Father Junipero Serra as its Catholic missionary to move into "Alta California" to establish a series of missions, presidios (military bases), and pueblos in order to control the territory and convert the native population to Christianity. This process of "Hispanicizing" the indigenous population was a unique settlement plan, in blunt contrast to the forced displacement of Indians by land-hungry immigrants common in other areas of the Spanish Empire.[5]

For the next half-century the Spanish colonizers built a string of missions running the length of California. They established California's first civilian settlements, or pueblos, in San Jose in 1777, and on September 4, 1781, founded El Pueblo de Nuestra Señora la Reina de Los Angeles. Due in part to the Napoleonic wars and the remoteness of the colony itself, Spain was unprepared to devote much, if any, of its resources towards full colonization. It ruled the colony by proxy via its royal viceroy in Mexico City and at the height of its conquest had only about 3,000 subjects loyal to Spain living in California. Instead it used Hispanicization and the indentured servitude of the native people to develop its missions. The Franciscan padres were used as the principle instrument of colonization. Accounts by the Spanish military troops housed in the presidios adjacent to the missions describe unusually harsh treatment by the Franciscans—surpassing even the cruelty of latter-day institutional slavery. By the end of the eighteenth century, some 13,000 Indians were held in 18 missions across California.[6]

The Spanish empire began to unravel by 1822 when Mexico broke from its colonial orbit. As Mexico moved to shed its clerical ties to the Church, it secularized the California missions, giving civilian authority to its pueblos and introducing economic reforms. Mexico awarded large land grants for the development of *ranchos*—some up to a quarter of a million acres—as patronage to settlers strongly connected to governors sent from Mexico City. Emboldened by Mexico's weak administration, the rumors of a potential war between the United States and Mexico, and the onslaught of new American migrants flooding into California between 1830 and the mid-1840s, a short Yankee insurrection known as the Bear Flag Revolt began in 1846, led by John C. Fremont. The insurrection was soon to be overshadowed by the Mexican-American War.

THE MEXICAN-AMERICAN WAR

Following the Missouri Compromise, Texas applied for admission into the Union—as a slave state. This magnified the ongoing border dispute Texas had with Mexico, dating back to the 1830s. Against the backdrop of President James Polk's desire to fulfill "manifest destiny"—not only for the annexation of Texas, but also much of Utah, Colorado, Nevada, and all of California, Arizona, and New Mexico—the Texas boundary dispute was enough to launch the Mexican-American War of 1846. By January 1847, the U.S. military was in control of much of this territory, encountering little resistance and eventually capturing Mexico City itself. The provisional government signed the Treaty of Guadalupe Hidalgo in 1848 to cede these territories to the United States in exchange for a payment of $15 million and the recognition that Mexican Californians could become U.S. citizens if they so wished and that land titles issued by Mexico and Spain would be honored. One interesting provision of the treaty, later repealed in the state's second constitution, was the assurance that Spanish would remain one of California's official languages along with English.

CALIFORNIA'S BOOM

California's status as a sleepy possession of the United States under military rule ended three years later with the discovery of gold at Sutter's Mill in January 1848. The gold rush brought in a quarter million settlers to the state between 1848 and 1853. Gold made California and the West a new promised land, first for miners, then for their suppliers, then for those who followed: ranchers, railroad tycoons, and land developers. Later, "black gold"—discovered in the form of oil—fueled an economic boom in Southern California. Offshore drilling of oil started as early as the 1920s off the coast of Santa Barbara. By the 1870s "green gold," or agricultural land, was to the Central Valley what gold was to Northern California and oil was to Southern California. By 1935 the great Central Valley, 100 miles wide and 500 miles long, thrived as the Central Valley Water Project delivered a grid of dams and channels to bring water to California's fertile fields.

As each of these "booms" hit, so did the arrival of new settlers armed with their own set of Yankee prejudices. They eventually outnumbered the original Californians, most with pure or mixed Mexican blood. Land grants were compromised, businesses stolen outright, and quasilegal maneuvers forced many into squalor. The native Indian population fared even worse. A defacto genocide was conducted against them from the time of the mission period. Ravaged by Western diseases, embattled by each wave of new colonizers, whole tribes became extinct: By the census of 1880 only 6 percent of the original 300,000 native Americans remained.

A smattering of symbols constantly remind us of a previous civilization swept aside in the crush of Americanization. They are emblazoned on the street names as directional icons: Pico Boulevard and Olvera Street. They are assigned as names to jurisdictional cities or counties as if they were some trophy snatched away in the victory of a war: Modoc County, Shasta County, Mono County, or such city names as San Francisco, Monterey, Santa Ana, and San Bernardino. They are evident in such architectural facades as Spanish Colonial and in the romance of the Old West celebrated in museums and festivals, symbolically preserving relics of a displaced culture even as its legacy was erased.

√ RAILROAD POLITICS

The Americanization of California could not have been accomplished without the arrival of the era's new technology: the railroad. The railroad transformed the demographics, commerce, and politics of the state. The Central Pacific Railroad, founded by Leland Stanford, Collins Huntington, Charles Crocker, and Mark Hopkins—the "Big Four"—transformed California during the 1860s from a remote island across the Sierra Nevada to an accessible destination. In six years California was linked by rail to virtually every major city in the United States. The heavy labor of building the rail lines and tunneling through the Sierras was done by a predominantly Chinese workforce, imported for their skill and willingness to work for a subsistence wage.

Their impact on California's emerging commercial infrastructure is surpassed only by their impact on California's expanding cultural diversity.[7]

The Big Four's monopolization of the railroads and their commensurate control of the early political process would come to dominate California's economy and politics for the next 50 years. With shrewd politicking they were able to convince state and federal taxpayers to fund their transcontinental railroad in the name of the "public interest." After Stanford became governor of California in 1862, he persuaded the state legislature to provide public subsidies and low interest loans to the Central Pacific Railroad project, which was to be built from two directions simultaneously east and west. Another flow of funding came "voluntarily" from local cities and counties in the state, who were reasonably concerned that if they did not ante up the railroad would simply be built around or away from their community. When the city of San Bernardino refused to subsidize the Southern Pacific Railroad,[8] the company simply moved its proposed depot to a small town just southwest of the city –the town of Colton—where it served as the regional hub to move cargo and people in and out of the area.[9]

The last subsidy of the funding mosaic came from the federal treasury. For this the Big Four relied on one of their own, Collins Huntington,[10] to be their point person and advocate back in Washington. Through Huntington's East Coast political connections and his corporate position as vice president of the railroad, he was successful in getting Congress to pass the Pacific Railway Act in 1862. The federal government's financial largess was the final link: It provided large land grants from the public domain. Over the next century, Southern Pacific would become the largest landholder in the state, controlling over 11.5 million acres, or approximately 12 percent of all the state's land. The law also provided millions of dollars in long-term loans to subsidize the railroad.

Upon completing the transcontinental railroad in 1869, the Big Four moved on to monopolize the state's entire transportation system. By the 1880s these four men controlled 85 percent of all transportation in the state.

Business development closely followed the state's transportation growth. As a result of the Southern Pacific's deep ties to the state's economy, a vast political machine emerged on all levels of government in California. Political leaders, the state's major newspapers, and even the judiciary had a strong pro-railroad bias. When it came to the state's economic development, what was good for Southern Pacific was good for California. However, this marriage of corporate convenience was short-lived. The depression of the 1870s brought serious economic shifts to the state and consequently ushered in a more pessimistic mood, fueled by economic anxiety and manifesting in political activism and anti-Chinese xenophobia. The political empire built by the Big Four began unraveling, though the sustained power of Southern Pacific remained.

Xenophobia has been a common political feature in California since 1877. In September 1877, Dennis Kearney formed the Workingmen's Party in San Francisco, which was not only the first official opposition to the railroads but also one of the first organized xenophobic movements. The Kearneyites turned to the streets for mob action, denouncing not only the Big Four cartel, but invoking the more potent rallying cry that "the Chinese must go." Later, through more placid and traditional means of democratic change, they used the foil of the Workingmen's Party to organize a united front at the constitutional convention of 1878, which ultimately produced the second of California's two constitutions—the one in force today.

CALIFORNIA'S CONSTITUTION

The usual definition of a constitution alludes to some framework of orderly systems and principles by which a diverse mass of citizens consent to be governed. They embody not only "timeless" principles but also practical political compromises to resolve the power conflicts of the time in which they were written. California's two constitutions (1849 and 1879) are both lofty, visionary, and inspirational documents—as well as windows to the political currents of the historical periods during which they were drafted and ratified.

THE FIRST CONSTITUTION

To prepare California for admission into the Union in 1850, a constitutional convention was held in the fall of 1849. Nationally, the debate over California's admittance hung over the slavery controversy. Under the Missouri Compromise, California would be admitted as a free (non-slave) state. With this decided the convention went about drafting the state's first constitution. The 48 delegates borrowed heavily from constitutions of other states, notably New York and Iowa, two states where many of the delegates had previously lived.

The structure of government was to have a divided framework whereby the governor, lieutenant governor, controller, superintendent of public instruction, attorney general, and surveyor general would all be elected directly by the voters. The legislature was bicameral. The judiciary would be composed of lower courts and a supreme court. San Jose was chosen as the state capital. Perhaps most noteworthy, however, was the state constitution's explicit emphasis on basic civil liberties for its citizens. Article I, Section 1 of California's first constitution asserts: "All people are by nature free and independent and have inalienable rights. Among these are enjoying and defending life and liberty, acquiring, possessing, and protecting property, and pursuing and obtaining safety, happiness, and privacy." The U.S. Congress accepted the constitution and on September 9, 1850, California was admitted as the thirty-first state in the Union.

THE SECOND CONSTITUTION

The economic and social turmoil of the 1870s brought about the call for a new constitutional convention. The convention had a strong presence of Kearneyites and small farmers (represented by the Grange) who were allied in their pursuit to constitutionally limit the power of large corporations, banks, utilities, and the railroads. The delegates included strict regulatory oversights for these entities—although these have been gradually amended out of the constitution over the years. At the same time, there were other structural overhauls to the constitution. These included setting limits on taxing and spending by the legislature, refinement of the judicial branch, and the extension of civil liberties for some Californians. At the same time the pronounced anti-Asian (Chinese, in particular) exclusionary provisions worked to maintain a system of race-based employment, and later, housing discrimination. These were encrusted in the state constitution and only repealed as late as 1952. Furthermore, the revised constitution took away the provision guaranteed in the Treaty of Guadalupe Hidalgo to place Spanish as one of the two "official" languages of California. The debates we have seen in California in the 1990s over English as the state's "official language" and over immigration reform are in fact longstanding political schisms that have challenged California's collective character for the past 120 years.

THE PROGRESSIVE MOVEMENT'S LEGACY

The Progressive movement emerged in California in the early 1900s following a national trend and brought about significant reforms in the way Californians viewed government. Every time we enter the voting booth to exercise our right to direct democratic initiatives to improve the living, working, and environmental conditions brought on by industrial and postindustrial society, we are participating in political reforms brought about by the Progressive movement. The Progressives were a professional, mostly white, middle-class reform movement that emerged as a response to the political corruption and excessive special-interest power that had been commonplace in major urban cities throughout the second half of the nineteenth century. They sought "progressive" reform, greater access to government, and greater control over "undesirable" classes—specifically working-class and immigrant populations.

In California, that meant taking on the Southern Pacific Railroad. As the dominant corporation of its day, the Southern Pacific Railroad heavily influenced the legislature, courts, and most local and county offices. The Progressives also fought for increased citizen participation and more accountability of elected officials. One of the defining variables that distinguished the California Progressives was their common distrust for centralized power and their desire to democratize every aspect of the decision-making process in order to incorporate greater voices. As Chapter 6 discusses, the tools of "direct democracy" favored by the Progressives are still used today as an essential part of the electoral arsenal. The most significant policy questions of the 1970s, 1980s, and 1990s used the initiative process brought about by the Progressive movement. Proposition 13 (property tax reform), Proposition 187 (cutting basic services to undocumented immigrants), and Proposition 227 (banning bilingual education) owe their existence to the Progressive legacy.

The Progressives first organized the larger urban centers of California, and by 1907 created the Lincoln-Roosevelt League within the Republican Party. The League was successful in fielding their own slate of reform candidates to the state legislature and by 1908 were in the statehouse pushing for the dismantling of machine politics. They ended party nominations of future candidates by introducing the direct primary, allowing voters to directly choose their candidates. In 1910 Progressive Republican Hiram Johnson was elected governor, clearing the way for significant Progressive reform. His campaign theme was simple but effective: "Kick the Southern Pacific out of politics."

Between 1911 and 1913 the Progressives put into constitutional or statutory law the following reforms:

- The establishment of the Public Utilities Commission to regulate the railroads and utilities (electricity, gas, and telephones)
- Women were extended the right to vote
- Child labor laws were enacted
- Worker compensation laws were enacted
- Conservation and environmental regulations were passed
- The removal of party labels to make local city, county, and special district elections nonpartisan (this also applied to judicial and school board elections)
- They introduced "cross-filing" by candidates, which permitted them to seek nomination by any party
- The institutionalization of the civil service system for government workers to break the old patronage system
- Perhaps most enduring, the direct democracy tools of the initiative, referendum, and recall

THE PROGRESSIVES SOCIAL AGENDA

The Progressives were interested in more than political reform. They also pursued a nativist social agenda that sought to regulate class, cultural, and racial deviation from what they considered a white, middle-class norm. The Progressives' message found saliency against a backdrop of large waves of immigration from western and southern Europe. The Progressive agenda became a national blueprint for business and upper-middle-class elites to close ranks against emerging ethnic constituencies and reframe the cultural debate in the language of electoral reform and government efficiency.[11] The Progressives led the national debate on more restrictive immigration reforms driven by the racism of "yellow-peril" hysteria. California was their testing ground. Noncitizens were forbidden to own land in the state. Chinese immigration was cut off by 1882; Japanese immigration by 1924. Soon new "aliens" came from the South (Mexico) to feed the need of California growers for cheap agricultural workers. In this context one can see that the current fight over California's social and cultural soul is only the latest onslaught in a century-long debate on what it means to be a Californian.

La Placita
Rubén Martínez

Newspapers, photos, diary notes, articles, stat sheets, and books—Christopher Isherwood's *A Single Man*, Rudy Acuña's *Occupied America*, Raymond Chandler's *The High Window*, Susan Kelly's *Mastering Word Perfect 5*—and family heirlooms surround me in a pile across what was once my father's bedroom. He stood at the picture window to my right during the air-raid blackouts of World War II, watching searchlights crisscross skies just like tonight's when a rusty-gray blanket hides the handful of stars that can survive the city glare.

And I begin by lighting a votive candle emblazoned with the image of San Martín de Porres at the altar where I've gathered together the objects of the living and the dead: grandmother's finely molded hand mirror with the Deco engraving on the back (if I look into it now will I see her face instead of mine?); the wallet-sized photo of my girlfriend, her stare questioning my soul from three thousand miles away in Guatemala City where maybe I'd rather be; the brittle yellowed leaf from Palm Sunday at the Old Plaza Church, where Father Luis Olivares showered the thousands of Mexicanos and Centroamericanos surrounding him with holy water; the calling card that Hector Oqueli handed me three months before he was kidnapped and assassinated in Guatemala City; the cassette sleeve with the red-black-yellow slogans that Dago the ardent revolutionary gave me a month before a Salvadorian army bullet pierced his lung and he convulsed into his final breath during the FMLN guerrilla offensive of 1989 in downtown San Salvador.

I continue by turning off the overhead light so that the candle flame transforms the shadow of the crucifix into a pair of outstretched arms. The faint, wavering light glows upon the photos of my late grandparents.

I do this alone, in my grandparents' house in the L.A. neighborhood north of downtown known as Silver Lake. I do it because my grandmother once did it, each night with me before I said my prayers. I do this and many other things like it, here in this house, because I feel as if somehow my grandparents were living through me when I do. This is important—it is my history. There is much else that is my history, too; the things that pertain to my particular generation, which I experienced directly or indirectly and that make up my cultural and political vocabulary. Everything from Watergate to the Flintstones to Robert Kennedy's assassination and the time the white hippie from Marshall High spit on me, the brown scrub, while I walked home from Franklin Elementary; to the earthquakes and dozens of *noir* and war movies I watched with my father; to Rubén Salazar's death at the Chicano Moratorium and later on my own belated encounter with Revolution via Nicaragua and El Salvador and the subsequent disillusionments, and the sex, lies, and performance art of the eighties, and now The Walls Coming Down.

And this is as close as it gets to home, right here in Silver Lake on this cool L.A. summer night looking down on a deserted Glendale Boulevard, a block above where my grandparents worked themselves into alcoholism and heart attacks at La Ronda, the Mexican restaurant they owned in the fifties and sixties and that now is a gay bar. "As close as it gets," because my home is L.A. and L.A. is an anti-home. So, this journal is an attempt to gather together the strewn shards of my identity scattered like the beads of broken glass across the Golden State Freeway three miles north of here, where a few days ago a big rig hauling fifty thousand pounds of tomatoes crushed a trailer home, killing three of four members of a tourist family who'd come all the way from Canada to visit Disneyland.

What surrounds me is my history, I repeat to myself. The words become my mantra: I must have a history.

"Baptism Souvenir," it says, in badly printed, kitschy cursive on the cardboard frame. "Our Lady Queen of the Angels (Old Mission Plaza)." A smiling kid swathed in virgin white, laid out horizontally before the silver-haired priest (horn-rimmed glasses, lips pursed), who the frame catches right at the moment he's letting the water fall on my head.

Our Lady Queen of the Angels Church, popularly known as La Placita, is the historic center of the city: where the city began, where I began. Every Sunday, at this modest mission founded in 1781, an average of 250 Mexicanos, Chicanos, and, increasingly, Centroamericanos, bring their babies to be baptized in the chapel christened Nuestra Señora la Reina de Los Angeles de Porciúncula—the original, overwrought Catholic name for L.A. They come, dressed to kill in rented suits and home-stitched silk dresses, and the photographers swarm around them, exactly as one George A. Pérez (whose name is printed on the back of the cardboard frame) accosted my family one Sunday twenty-eight years ago. I am cradled by my grandfather, whose hair is just beginning to turn gray. His aquiline, northern Mexican nose gives him an air of dignified *mestizo*-ness, right on the border between the *indígena* and the Spaniard; my grandmother (softer feathers, light-complected, large eyes, less *indígena*) holds my hand.

It is 1962, just before the October Missile Crisis. My grandparents' restaurant has taken shape on Glendale Boulevard. Elvis Presley stopped by not long ago (my grandparents had no idea who he was) and wrote, "Nice place, great food. Elvis Presley," on a napkin that is now my younger sister's prized possession.

My father is doing litho work at a place called Rapid Blue Print, making very good money ($1.50 an hour) for a first-generation Mexican. He likes to slick his hair but he is not a *pachuco*—he's proud to speak an accentless English as well as a perfect Spanish. And, as he will still say thirty years later, is proud to be better off than the *chusma*, the recently arrived immigrants who gather in squalor in the barrios to the south and to the east of La Placita. My mother's English is still awkward and heavily accented; she's doing her best at playing the classic housewife, watching a lot of TV (which inspires her to do her hair up Jackie Kennedy-style), singing nursery rhymes to me in Spanish in the afternoons, and probably still thinking a lot about her native El Salvador, which she left only a few years before.

My parents live in their newly built house in Silver Lake (only five minutes away from my grandparents). It's all very idyllic and I'm the model firstborn son; my parents have representatives of the fledgling Latino middle class over to the house often for martinis and cha-cha dancing, the men with Brylcreamed hair wearing sharp suits and thin ties and the women with knee-length solid-colored or polka-dotted dresses and teased, Roman-arched hair.

Father must work eighteen, sometimes twenty hours a day, and this begins to take its toll on my mother. Late one night, alone in the house with her son fast asleep, the isolation, her longing for the comfort of the large family she left behind in El Salvador and the vastness of a city she doesn't understand bring her to the verge of a breakdown. She locks herself in the bathroom. My father comes home and finds her still there, shaken and wordless, in the early morning hours. From this moment on, I begin to have nightmares about monsters lurking outside in the darkness of the city, poised to leap out and tear my family apart.

Nearly thirty years later, I'm still hanging out at La Placita. Something in or about that baptism water.

Today, a pierced blue sky. The famous "Santa Ana winds" have returned with their dry cowboy heat and blown the smog out to sea. Y.—who is here for a month before she returns to Guatemala—and I awake, slightly hungover, in my father's old bedroom. (Father told me recently that sleeping with a woman who is not my wife in my grandmother's house is probably enough to make her turn over in her grave.) …

We straggle out of bed and arrive at La Placita just in time for the eleven-thirty mass. La Placita today is not the church it was before the arrival in 1981 of Father Luis Olivares. Back then, it still leaned toward a touristy quaintness and was mainly attended by the Chicano and Mexicano middle class. Today, shrines paying tribute to the various Latino communities that make up the parish adorn the walls of the church—*El Cristo Negro de Esquipulas* (Guatemala), *El Santo Niño de Atocha* (El Salvador), *El Señor de los Milagros* (Peru), and, Olivares's favorite, the expressionistic lithograph depicting the assassination of Salvadorian archbishop Oscar Arnulfo Romero. Surrounding the church and in the internal patio, Olivares has allowed dozens of Latino street vendors to sell their wares, everything from bootlegged cassettes, tamales and *champurrados* to blinking plastic roses. The vast majority of the parishioners are recent arrivals—Mexicanos and Centroamericanos who came to La Placita because they already knew of the church and its controversial pastor long before they began their dangerous journeys north. La Placita has become a mythic haven on the well-trodden path to the American Dream; hundreds sleep in the church's shelter every night. In 1985, Olivares declared La Placita—in public defiance to the Immigration Reform and Control Act—a "sanctuary" for Central American refugees and the destitute undocumented from Mexico.

Whether or not La Placita will remain a haven for the poor is now in question, however. Months ago, Olivares's superiors of the Claretian Order announced that he would be transferred to a Fort Worth parish. And then, only two weeks before his scheduled departure, he fell gravely ill with what was initially diagnosed as meningitis with complications.

This Sunday was to have been his farewell. We enter the church, squeezing in with the typical overcapacity crowd. To everyone's surprise, Olivares is at his usual post, beneath the large image of the Vírgen de Guadalupe to the left of the altar. His head is bowed with exhaustion, and he is still wearing a hospital I.D. bracelet (his condition is listed as "serious" at Cedars-Sinai Hospital, and he will be rushed back immediately after the service). All eyes are fixed upon the now-fragile Olivares, whose voice once boomed out from the pulpit, challenging his parish to confront its enemies: the *migra*—the Immigration and Naturalization Service agents who flash their badges and ask for green cards—the LAPD, the U.S. government. He cradles his head in pain.

Associate pastor Michael Kennedy officiates the mass, but when it comes time for the homily, he hands the microphone to Olivares, who is so weak he can barely hold it. His voice begins in a weak whisper, but soon he is weaving a powerful and emotional sermon. He confides that the doctors have given him one or two years of life. "But I do not fear my death, my brothers and sisters. One must accept the will of God. If He wants me to stay on in this, this," he says, summoning a weak somewhat ironic smile before going on, "vale of tears, then I will stay. If He wishes me to leave, I will leave."

Father Luis Olivares bids La Placita farewell with these words: "Like John the Baptist called ... so each of us, upon being baptized, is called to be a prophet of love and justice. I ask the Lord for a special blessing for this community that has fought so hard for justice, not only here and in Central America, but all over the world. May it continue to do so, to live out the true meaning of the Gospel." After saying this, he sinks back into the wheelchair, exhausted.

After the recitation of the Lord's Prayer, and during the traditional mutual offering of peace, an old Mexicana painfully canes her way up to the altar to touch Olivares. Next, a communion-aged boy does the same. Soon, a steady stream of parishioners is tearfully laying hands upon him. But suddenly a tall, attractive blond woman who has been standing near Olivares ... puts a stop to this. Towering over the children and *ancianos* with tears in their eyes, she tells them to go back, "No más, no más," in a thickly accented Spanish.

Five days later, during my morning ritual at the Silver Lake house, I open the front door and pick up the morning edition of the *L.A. Times*. I scan the Metro section.... That page is now torn out, gathering dust on the floor along with all the other clippings:

Activist Priest Says He Has Aids

Father Luis Olivares, the activist Roman Catholic priest and long-time champion of Central American refugees who had been hospitalized for the past month with meningitis, revealed Thursday that he has AIDS. Doctors said they believe that he contracted the disease from contaminated needles while undergoing treatment for other ailments while traveling in Central America....

L.A. history begins at La Placita, and ends at La Placita....

SUMMARY

California is no ordinary state. Its politics stem from the unique blend of circumstances and personalities that molded its history. Diverse groups—from California's original inhabitants to the early Europeans, to the Mexican conquest and the early gold prospectors, to the great post-World War II migration and its contemporary immigrants—have been arriving for generations in pursuit of opportunities, a pristine environment, and a better quality of life. Difficulties and growing pains not withstanding, this great blending of peoples continues to be a testimony to the Golden State and its open arms.

NOTES

1. Carey McWilliams, *California: The Great Exception* (Westport, NY: Greenwood Press, 1971), p. 24.
2. Christopher Isherwood, as quoted in Leonard Michaels, David Reid, Raquel Scheer, eds., *West of the West: Imagining California* (Berkeley: University of California Press, 1989), p. 310.
3. Quoted in Sucheng Chan and Spencer C. Olin, *Major Problems in California History* (New York: Houghton Mifflin Co., 1997), p. 30.
4. Philip L. Fradkin, *The Seven States of California: A Human and Natural History* (New York: Holt and Co., 1995), p. 3.
5. James N. Gregory, "The Shaping of California History," in Sucheng Chan and Spencer C. Olin, *Major Problems in California History* (New York: Houghton Mifflin Co., 1997), p. 18.
6. David Lavender, *California: Land of New Beginnings* (Lincoln, NE: University of Nebraska Press, 1972), p. 69.
7. The State Railroad Museum in Sacramento's Old Town is a superb testament to the contribution Chinese Americans made to California's emerging importance as a political and economic power.
8. The Southern Pacific Railroad was acquired by the Central Pacific to provide regional rail links with the state, and eventually became the namesake of the entire corporate identity.
9. Ward McAfee, *California's Railroad Era: 1850–1911* (San Marino, CA: Golden West Books, 1973), p. 123.
10. By the 1850s the Huntingtons were constructing in Los Angeles a vast inter-urban streetcar system known as the Pacific Electric Company and constructed some 1,200 miles of tract for their streetcars which would feed the new main railroad depot built as Central Station.
11. See H. Eric Schockman, "Is Los Angeles Governable?" in Michael J. Dear, H. Eric Schockman, and Greg Hise, eds., *Rethinking Los Angeles* (Thousand Oaks, CA: Sage Publications, 1996), pp. 57–75.

CHAPTER 3

Political Culture and Politics in Postwar California

What thoughts I have of you tonight, Walt Whitman, for I walked down the side-streets under the trees with a headache self-conscious looking at the full moon.

In my hungry fatigue, and shopping for images, I went into the neon fruit super-market, dreaming of your enumerations!

What peaches and what penumbras! Whole families shopping at night! Aisles full of husbands! Wives in the avocados, babies in the tomatoes!—and you, García Lorca, what were you doing down by the watermelons?

I saw you, Walt Whitman, childless, lonely old grubber, poking among the meats in the refrigerator and eyeing the grocery boys.

I heard you asking questions of each: Who killed the pork chops? What price bananas? Are you my Angel?

I wandered in and out of the brilliant stacks of cans following you, and followed in my imagination by the store detective.

We strode down the open corridors together in our solitary fancy tasting artichokes, possessing every frozen delicacy, and never passing the cashier.

Where are we going, Walt Whitman? The doors close in an hour. Which way does your beard point tonight?

(I touch your book and dream of our odyssey in the supermarket and feel absurd.)

Will we walk all night through solitary streets? The trees add shade to shade, lights out in the houses, we'll be lonely.

Will we stroll dreaming of the lost America of love past blue automobiles in dri-veways, home in our silent cottage?

Ah, dear father, graybeard, lonely old courage-teacher, what America did you have when Charon quit poling his ferry and you got out on a smoking bank and stood watching the boat disappear on the black waters of Lethe?

—Allen Ginsberg, "A Supermarket in California,"
from *Reality Sandwiches*. Reprinted by permission.

The term *political culture* describes the shared beliefs and values that people hold re-garding the relationship between government and citizens and between individuals in public life. Researchers have sought to explain how political culture accounts for variations in the behavior of individuals and institutions, as well as the public policies of states and nations. American political culture emphasizes the values of classical liberalism, including individualism, freedom, equality, democracy, and capitalism. But these values often collide, as in the tax revolt of the 1970s. Debates over public spending often mask conflict over more fundamental values.

Contemporary ideologies such as liberalism and conservatism represent popular belief systems that emphasize competing values within the same political culture.[1] They offer a prescription for the appropriate role of government in society. Liberals tend to place more of an emphasis on equality, tolerance, and aid to the disadvantaged, for example, while conservatives tend to emphasize order, economic growth, and preserving what they perceive as "traditional values." Even when accounting for variations in the variables that explain voting patterns such as race, income, education and religion, Californians are more likely to hold liberal views on social issues than residents of other states, while at the same time being more likely to identify with the Republican party.[2]

Individualism is a central tenet of California's political culture. Since statehood California history was written by an eclectic cast that includes frontier explorers and exploiters, opportunity-seeking migrants, and progressive reformers with a strong belief in the active, virtuous citizen of the polis. This unique history produced a political culture that encourages policy innovation by politicians, mistrust of large traditional organizations such as political parties and big business, and a strong belief in direct democracy. The political successes—and failures—of state government between the 1940s and 1990s reflect California's iconoclastic, and often conflicted, political culture.

THE POSTWAR ERA

After World War II, California's political culture was transformed as the parties adapted to changing conditions. Rapid growth and change upset the balance of state politics, invigorating the Democratic party and ending the dominance by moderate Republicans such as Earl Warren and Goodwin Knight. In the late 1950s, California's post-Progressive, nonpartisan politics gave way to the more competitive, ideologically charged politics of two-party rivalry.

California experienced unprecedented growth in the postwar period. The promise of prosperity attracted migrants from all over the country and the world. Here they found warmer climes, inexpensive housing, and well-paying jobs in a booming economy, particularly in the Cold War defense and aerospace industries. By 1962, California had become the most populous state in the nation. During this period, increasing ideological polarization of the parties upset the equilibrium in state politics that had built a consensus on several bipartisan issues, including government efficiency, weak parties, citizen participation, and popular New Deal social programs. Bipartisan support was instrumental to the success of Republican Governors Warren and Knight, since Democrats held a substantial voter registration edge from the time of the Great Depression.

The Republican party had dominated state government for most of the century, from the Progressive Era until 1957. During this time, Republicans had the winning edge in all but one election for governor. They also controlled both houses of the legislature, except for a brief period in the 1930s when Democrats controlled the assembly.

One factor that impeded the Democrats' success was the reform mechanism left over from the Progressives known as cross-filing. Cross-filing was based on the logic that voters of California should have the right to elect the most qualified individual for an office and not be swayed by the candidate's party label. A single ballot was distributed in California primaries, allowing the cross-filing of candidates from one party to seek the nomination of another party. Under this confusing system, Democrats could run as Republicans and vice versa, and nominations were consequently won on the basis of a candidate's ability to spend on his or her campaign. This sometimes had odd results. In 1952, for example, Republican Senator William Knowland was the nominee of both the Republican and Democratic parties.[3]

Although registration numbers favored the Democrats, party loyalty was weak. It was a common strategy for Republican candidates to appeal to Democratic voters. The system of cross-filing was modified by a 1952 statewide initiative, requiring candidates to list their party affiliation on the ballot, although a sunset provision ended cross-filing altogether in 1959.[4]

Republican Governor Earl Warren was elected in 1942, carried into office by his commitments to restoring the nonpartisan spirit of the Progressive tradition and reforming state government. Warren was less conservative than his Republican predecessors, bringing to Sacramento what seemed like a Democratic agenda (although it could be called a "nonpartisan" agenda), including such statutory priorities as unemployment insurance, better pensions, and increased health insurance coverage. Thus, Warren had established himself as a moderate-to-liberal executive even before he was tapped by President Eisenhower to the Supreme Court. As Chief Justice, Warren was criticized by some conservatives for controversial decisions in cases ranging from school desegregation to school prayer to the rights of the accused.

Eisenhower's appointment of Warren more than midway through his third term as governor left the incumbent lieutenant governor, Republican Goodwin Knight, to assume the governorship. Knight governed as a moderate, supporting legislation popular with labor and other Democratic constituencies, while keeping much of Warren's agenda alive. He successfully preserved his predecessor's bipartisan electoral base, winning election in 1954 in his own right. With increasing party polarization, however, Democrats turned out in force to elect Democratic state attorney general Edmund G. "Pat" Brown to the governor's office.[5]

THE PAT BROWN LEGACY

The 1958 election was a turning point in California's political history. Pat Brown's victory and Democratic majorities in the legislature began an era of Democratic dominance of state politics. The professionalization of the state legislature bolstered the party by bringing in candidates with working- and middle-class backgrounds, who would never have run as candidates in a part-time, or "amateur," legislature that favored wealthy candidates and those with outside sources of income. The effect of this reform was to help Democrats attract better candidates and retain good legislators by making politics a practical career alternative.

Yet, this era was marked by an ideological struggle between two competing strains of liberalism. Long excluded from governing, California's liberals now saw an opportunity to fulfill the promises of the New Deal, which they felt had been compromised by a generation of Republican leadership. However, conditions had changed since the 1930s, and there was little agreement on exactly how the New Deal should be applied in the more prosperous—and populous—California of the 1950s and 1960s.

The intraparty tension over competing visions of the proper role of government was personified by the political rivalry between Brown and the assembly's powerful speaker, Jesse M. Unruh. Brown represented the traditional view of liberalism in California: the need for an activist government to invest in the state's future through large-scale capital projects and social programs. Unruh, on the other hand, was a pragmatist concerned with the future of the Democratic party in a post-New Deal world. Brown's ideology was an "emotive," or "soft" liberalism, strongly committed to advancing the agenda of the New Deal, while Unruh represented more of a "rational," or "hard" liberalism designed to sustain the party's majority by adapting the New Deal agenda to contend with changing realities.[6]

PAT BROWN'S "SOFT" LIBERALISM

Pat Brown may best be remembered as the "master builder" of modern California. He pushed for a large bond measure funding the construction of the State Water Project to bring Northern California water to the aqueducts of the Central Valley and to the cities and suburbs of Southern California. The measure passed by a slim margin. The Brown administration wrote the "Master Plan for Higher Education," expanding college admissions to all qualified children of California residents, as well as expanding the physical infrastructure of the entire system by building more accessible regional campuses for the University of California and the California State University systems. As the process of suburbanization took hold, Brown oversaw the transfer of federal transportation dollars to the state, aiding in the construction of hundreds of new miles of freeways and the funding of public transit. Brown signed the Unruh Civil Rights Act, a state version of the 1964 U.S. Civil Rights Act, preventing discrimination in public accommodations, employment, and housing. He also stood firm, at great political peril, against the 1964 repeal of the Rumford Fair Housing Act, which prevented racial discrimination in the sale of homes. The ballot measure passed overwhelmingly, only to be declared unconstitutional by the courts.

JESSE UNRUH'S "HARD" LIBERALISM

Unruh stood for a new liberalism, less interventionist and less generous than many of his fellow Democrats wanted. He recognized that it was becoming increasingly problematic for Democrats to adhere to an ideology that vilified big business and greedy capitalists in an age when workers enjoyed unprecedented economic opportunities and a rising standard of living. It was also problematic because of the numerous partnerships that had developed between government and business during the Cold War. Furthermore, he understood that the depression era logic of appealing to the interests of the disadvantaged and minorities could no longer guarantee enough votes to win elections in a large state. So many people had benefited from postwar prosperity that the old Democratic strategy seemed like a recipe for failure.

A World War II veteran and son of a sharecropper, Unruh was elected from an assembly district representing Inglewood and southcentral Los Angeles and ascended quickly to the leadership. After becoming speaker in 1961, Unruh became known as the "Boss" and the "Big Daddy" of California politics because of his strict control of the assembly and his use of the institution as a vehicle for his own legislative agenda. His strategy was to manage the state's panoply of programs as efficiently as possible, while continuing to champion the working poor. Thus, Democrats could claim for themselves the banner of "good government," which had been the property of the Republicans ever since the Progressive era.

In contrast to the expansive policy proposals of the past, Unruh's Democrats advanced a much more limited, incremental policy agenda. Even as he shepherded Brown's legislative agenda through the assembly to build aqueducts and universities, Unruh himself favored a more modest role for government. Through progressive civil rights and consumer protection legislation, Unruh sought to make life easier for "the common man."[7]

Unruh's brand of liberalism created tension among the party faithful. In particular, Unruh's approach was at odds with the volunteers of the California Democratic Council (CDC). The CDC was a political club founded by Alan Cranston to overcome the confusion of cross-filing by endorsing candidates, providing Democratic voters with information and direction prior to election day. The CDC favored stronger bonds between organized labor and the party, as well as an activist role for government, including an expanded welfare state and détente with the Soviet Union. While Brown was content to enlist their support, Unruh sought to curtail the influence of CDC volunteers in state Democratic politics, fearing that their presence might jeopardize the party's appeal to the mainstream.[8]

Pat Brown lost his bid for a third term in 1966. Though Brown had defeated former Vice President Richard Nixon to be re-elected in 1962, he lost four years later to a Hollywood actor named Ronald Reagan by more than a million votes. At the time, the state and nation were undergoing profound social and economic changes. The Democratic party was wounded politically by civil unrest, including opposition to the war in Vietnam and racial strife in urban enclaves such as the Watts neighborhood of Los Angeles and San Francisco's Hunter's Point. While the election was in some part a referendum on the social turmoil of the late 1960s, the voters were losing their taste for the government activism that Brown symbolized.[9] Two years later, the Democrats lost their majority in both houses of the legislature. After more difficult lessons at the polls, the hard liberalism of Jesse

Unruh would come to be embraced as the dominant ideology of the party. This conversion took place both in California and nationally, as Democratic leaders from Dianne Feinstein to Bill Clinton took up the cause of "good government," calling for fiscal conservatism while advancing modest legislative agendas designed to make life easier for the average working person. Unruh himself would play little part in the party's changing ideology. He served the remainder of his political career as California's state treasurer after losing his own bid for governor in 1970—to the incumbent Ronald Reagan.

CONSERVATISM MEETS POPULISM: THE REAGAN REVOLUTION

Part of Reagan's appeal was that of an outsider unsullied by Sacramento politics, much like his early predecessor, Hiram Johnson. An effective manipulator of symbols, Reagan emulated the cowboy heroes of his western films, riding into Sacramento for a showdown with big-spending Democrats in the legislature. With the Republican success in the 1968 election, driven in part by Californian Richard Nixon's successful bid for the presidency, Reagan was able to partner with a Republican-controlled legislature. But that Republican majority was short-lived.

Reagan's style of conservatism was as different from the Progressive and Eisenhower era Republicans as Unruh's liberalism was from the New Deal Democrats. Like his Republican predecessors, Reagan supported conservative causes such as low taxes, deregulation, anticommunism, and self-reliance over government aid. He also tapped a reservoir of frustration by railing against government itself, criticizing lawmakers and the bureaucrats in public service as contributing to the problems they purported to solve. He gave voice to popular frustration with the state's rapidly-expanding welfare system, striking a moral tone in his attacks on welfare recipients. Reagan's mean-spirited attack on AFDC recipients as financially irresponsible and sexually promiscuous "welfare queens" polarized the discourse. The "welfare queen" stereotype reinforced a populist view that welfare recipients were not like you and me and were undeserving of government largess. After his loss to Reagan, former Speaker Unruh predicted that conservative politicians would have an easy time dividing the white working class in future elections.[10]

Reagan had some success in trimming the state budget by forcing counties to pick up services, passing on the demands of the growing population through unfunded mandates.[11] By the end of his two terms as governor, however, California's taxes and the state budget had increased dramatically. Even if he lost those battles, Reagan eventually won the war. His fusion of conservatism and populism became the dominant ideology of the right wing in state and national politics. After leaving office in 1974, Reagan mounted a strong primary challenge to President Gerald Ford. Later, Reagan's populist-conservative message resonated nationally, helping him win two terms as president.

THE POLITICS OF DIVIDED GOVERNMENT

The election of Reagan as governor in a year when Democrats retained their majority in the legislature began what seems to have become a permanent fixture of contemporary California politics—divided government. When no single party controls the apparatus of state government, either during a particular legislative term or over the long haul, internal divisions make policy innovation extremely difficult. Control of California's executive and legislative branches of government has often been divided. Except for the periods of unified Republican government (1969–1971) and unified Democratic government (1975–1983), California has lived with divided government since 1967, with a Republican governor and a Democratic majority in at least one chamber of the legislature. The election of Democratic Governor Gray Davis and Democratic gains in the legislature in 1998 brought the first single-party majority in state politics in 30 years.

California is not unique in this respect. Since the 1950s, divided government has become an increasingly common outcome of state and national elections.[12] Divided government disappeared temporarily in California after 1974, a banner election year for Democrats. The Watergate scandal had not only brought down the Nixon administration, but Republican candidates nationwide were wounded politically in the fallout. When Governor Reagan decided not to seek a third term, Lieutenant Governor Ed Rienecke hoped to succeed him, but was indicted (and later acquitted) for perjury in a scandal of his own over campaign finance. Amid a powerful anti-Republican tide, the Republican nominee, State Controller Houston Flournoy, lost by just 180,000 votes to Edmund G. (Jerry) Brown, Jr.

THE JERRY BROWN YEARS

The son of former Governor Pat Brown, Jerry Brown represented a new generation of Democratic leaders. His philosophy of government was more akin to the hard liberalism of Jesse Unruh than the soft liberalism of his father. Unlike Democrats of an earlier era, Brown rejected traditional big-government approaches to public problems, although he shared their commitment to the values of fairness and equality. Brown's campaign for governor received a boost by a wave of popular support for campaign finance reform in the aftermath of Watergate. As secretary of state, he drafted the political reform initiative Proposition 9, which appeared on the 1974 primary ballot. The successful linkage of his candidacy to the creation of his own self-designed "citizen's initiative" captured the popular sentiments of the time and would come to be a model for many subsequent candidates and other ambitious politicians in California.

Brown, who had studied for many years as a Jesuit seminarian, thought in global and environmental terms and connected well with those traditionally marginalized from the political process. He understood the plight of the United Farm Workers and helped move the legislature in establishing the Agricultural Labor Relations Board as a state arbitrator between the rights of field laborers and the production goals of agribusiness. He opened the door to executive appointments for women and people of color on state boards, commissions, and the judiciary. He worked hard for the expansion of education, the health and safety concerns of all workers, and for the environmental movement. But his efforts to balance his policy agenda often put him at odds with his traditional allies. In the name of environmental protection, Brown cut the state transportation budget for highway construction, diverting funds instead into mass transit development, and even bicycle paths. And, though a strong proponent of higher education, Brown earned the ire of state university professors by suggesting that their intellectual satisfaction with their work constituted a type of "psychic income," making an actual salary increase less necessary than for other state employees.

TAXPAYER REVOLT

The 1970s saw an extended period of high inflation, economic stagnation, and high unemployment in California and around the nation. Ironically, as the state's fiscal health deteriorated, the tax system continued to reap large surpluses. Property taxes soared during the mid-1970s, as average property values in the state increased at an annual rate of 12 percent. As consumer prices and salaries increased, so too did revenues from sales and income taxes. By 1978, the state budget had accumulated a $6 billion surplus. Property tax reformers Howard Jarvis and Paul Gann read this popular frustration and successfully petitioned to have Proposition 13 placed on the June 1978 primary ballot. The initiative cut property taxes by 60 percent and limited future taxes to 1 percent of assessed real estate value. While Governor Brown backed a more moderate proposal, which failed at the ballot box, Proposition 13 passed by a two-to-one margin.

Proposition 13 represented a contest over political culture as much as it was an effort to provide taxpayer relief. Under the surface of the tax revolt were deep-seated attitudes about the proper role of government in society. As Table 3.1 (on page 32) suggests, the strongest support for Proposition 13 came from white, middle-aged, fully employed male homeowners. Minorities and the poor were less likely to support the initiative, even though they were the most likely to suffer the effects. Supporters were more likely to believe that there was a problem with government waste, and this view was strongly related to a desire to cut welfare and other public assistance programs for the poor. At the same time, supporters were against cutting fire and police protection, education, mass transit, and mental health services. This paradox suggests that the support for the tax revolt was motivated, in part, to restrict government activism in specific unpopular policy areas. This observation led researchers David Sears and Jack Citrin to term the movement a "revolt of the haves."[13] Proposition 13 led directly to the reduced capacity of California's local governments to provide services to its burgeoning population.[14]

Brown's two terms in office stand as proof that political paralysis and tension can be a problem even when the governor and both houses of the legislature are of the same party. One of his strengths during his first term was connecting directly with the voters and bypassing the established rules and leadership of the legislative

TABLE 3.1   SUPPORT FOR PROPOSITION 13,
BY DEMOGRAPHIC GROUP, MAY 1978

GROUP	% IN FAVOR	GROUP	% IN FAVOR
INCOME		*AGE*	
Less than $10,000	52	18–24	49
$11,000–$20,000	59	25–34	56
$21,000–$30,000	67	35–49	62
More than $30,000	69	50–64	71
		65+	69
EDUCATION			
Less than high school	74	*SEX*	
High school	68	Male	66
Some college	64	Female	59
College grad	69		
Beyond college	49	*ETHNICITY*	
		White	66
RESIDENCE		Hispanic	60
Bay Area	64	Black	18
Other Northern California	59		
Other Southern California	58		
LA & Orange Counties	66		
Homeowners	69		
Renters	46		

Source: May 1978 California Poll, reprinted in Sears and Citrin, 1982. Entries are the percent of respondents from each demographic group expressing support for Proposition 13.

establishment. By his second term this became a liability, as his relationship with his Democratic colleagues soured. His opposition to Proposition 13 and his administration's philosophy of imposing an "era of limits" added to this tenuous relationship. His campaigns for the presidency in 1976 and 1980 left them feeling abandoned. Brown made some noteworthy achievements, yet he could have done more if he had worked to cultivate the support of his own party in the legislature, rather than grandstanding alone for policy change. His popularity waning, Brown was defeated by San Diego Mayor Pete Wilson in a 1982 bid for a U.S. Senate seat, which was being vacated by Republican S. I. Hayakawa. Brown remained active in politics, including a third unsuccessful run for the Democratic presidential nomination. He was elected Mayor of Oakland in 1998.

THE 1980s: RETURN TO DIVIDED GOVERNMENT

Attorney General George Deukmejian ran a strong law-and-order campaign and squeaked into the governorship in 1982, defeating Los Angeles Mayor Tom Bradley by less than 100,000 votes out of approximately 7.8 million cast. In a surprising rematch four years later, Democrats again fielded Tom Bradley against the incumbent Deukmejian. This time, Deukmejian won a smashing landslide over Bradley by more than 1.7 million votes. It was in many ways a battle of ideological extremes: a liberal African-American big-city mayor against a conservative, law-and-order, veteran of the Sacramento "beltway." The governor was helped by a high turnout of conservative voters, drawn to the ballot box to defeat a gun control initiative. With Proposition 62, an enhancement of Proposition 13's property tax reform, also appearing on the ballot, the gun lobby and the tax reform lobby were given a strong incentive to mobilize conservative voters.

A former attorney, Deukmejian had a style that was rather bland compared to his charismatic predecessors, Reagan and Brown. But he possessed important managerial skills necessary for the chief executive of the nation's largest state. At times his leadership style could be partisan, as when he battled for the creation of a redistricting commission (Proposition 39) to oversee the state reapportionment process then controlled by the Democratic legislature. On the issue of the judiciary he was uncompromising. He successfully campaigned for the recall of California Supreme Court Justices Rose Bird, Cruz Reynoso, and Joseph Grodin (all appointed by Jerry Brown) for their reluctance to enforce the death penalty. With their removal by the voters, he was given a windfall opportunity to name three new justices who reflected his own judicial philosophy. Yet, Deukmejian at times found common ground with Democrats and the legislative leadership. He signed legislation for a bold experiment to mandate new welfare-to-work rules by establishing the GAIN (Greater Avenues for Independence) workforce program. An American of Armenian heritage and personally sensitive to issues of human rights, Deukmejian also pushed for a $5 million state allocation for the Los Angeles-based Museum of Tolerance to educate future generations about ethnic diversity and genocide.

CALIFORNIA POLITICS IN THE 1990s

The mood of the electorate in 1990 was one of dissatisfaction, if not rage. California's economy was sliding into recession, and several state legislators were implicated in scandals such as "Shrimpgate."[15] The most visible response by voters was the passage of Proposition 140. Proposition 140 created a constitutional amendment to limit legislator's terms of office, end pension benefits for future legislators, and cut legislator's personal office budgets by 40 percent.[16] Proposition 140 was an unambiguous expression of the public's displeasure with the legislature, both for the ethical breaches of individual members, and for their collective inability to get things done. Term limits as an instrument for enacting better public policy and getting "new blood" into the system will be discussed in detail in Chapter 6.

Republicans nominated U.S. Senator Pete Wilson to replace the retiring George Deukmejian. Wilson went on to defeat the Democratic candidate, former San Francisco Mayor Dianne Feinstein, by 3 percentage points (49 to 46 percent) after she survived a bruising primary battle with Attorney General John Van de Kamp. Initially,

Wilson's election as governor in 1990 was marked by some Democratic lawmakers with a sigh of relief and as the end to gridlock partisan politics in Sacramento. Wilson was known in his party as a "traditional moderate," a pragmatic middle-of-the-roader, pro-business and pro-choice. Early in his first term as governor, Wilson demonstrated his willingness to work with Democrats. For example, faced with unrelenting budget crises he agreed to a round of new taxes. Wilson also supported policies protecting the rights of gays and lesbians. He supported legislation that prohibited discrimination by private sector employers, and he continued an executive order, first issued by Jerry Brown, to protect state government workers from discrimination based on sexual orientation.

But by 1994, with his public approval plummeting, Wilson had moved from the center to the right and adopted a more confrontational style. He frequently clashed with the Democratic state legislature. He battled over reapportionment, threatening to veto any plan that he found unacceptable.[17] He also pushed controversial initiatives on hot-button issues including crime (e.g., Three Strikes Proposition 220), illegal immigration (Proposition 187), and affirmative action (Proposition 229).[18] Wilson won re-election by a wide margin over the Democratic challenger, State Treasurer Kathleen Brown, which helped him build support for his candidacy for the Republican presidential nomination.

Although much of Wilson's tenure in office was marred by a recessionary fiscal crisis, a booming economy in his second term freed up resources to repair the state's infrastructure. When the state received an unprecedented $4.4 billion windfall, Wilson called for more spending on education, public works, and social programs.[19] Wilson directed new state dollars to education to reduce class size (see Chapter 11) as well as to augment the state's child care budget in anticipation of lifting poor, single, working women out of welfare by providing support for their children while they are at work.

POLITICAL CULTURE AND POLITICS
IN POSTWAR CALIFORNIA

Political culture in California is a contested terrain. The policy approaches emerging over the past 50 years are as much about defining the cultural nature of politics as they are about mitigating specific problems. Democrats from Pat Brown to Gray Davis have sought to build statewide consensus on traditional liberal values such as public education, infrastructure investment, civil rights, and broad social safety nets. There are different approaches—from the New Deal approaches of Brown to the cautious approaches of Unruh and Davis—but Democrats continue to see an important role for government in meeting the state's challenges. Republicans from Reagan to Wilson have worked to reduce the scope of governmental regulation in the lives of Californians, arguing consistently that most problems are better resolved in the private sector.

SUMMARY

This chapter has argued that California politics is as much a contest over values as a vehicle to solve problems. As the state experienced phenomenal growth and change, the centrist, nonideological politics of postwar California gave way to competitive, highly partisan politics by the 1960s. Then, for several years, Republicans were largely on the sidelines as Democrats battled over two competing visions of liberalism. The emotive liberalism of Pat Brown envisioned an active government to preserve and advance the New Deal agenda in a new age, while the bureaucratic liberalism of Jesse Unruh envisioned a limited government, one with more modest goals, which would still protect the interests of the disadvantaged. Before this debate was settled in favor of Unruh's vision, a new generation of California Republicans emerged with a drastically different prescription for the role of government. By infusing conservatism with populism, politicians such as Ronald Reagan promoted an appealing new style of conservatism, more "anti-government" than the old "good government" philosophy of previous Republicans. This anti-government sentiment was felt in the passage of Proposition 13, which severely curtailed activism by local governments. The tension between these competing strains of political ideology redefined the boundaries of the state's political culture. And yet, the contest remains unfinished. It is likely that Californians will continue to use the apparatus of state government to push specific visions of political culture. And, as the state's demographic makeup continues to shift, this contest is likely to become even more passionate.

NOTES

1. See Herbert McClosky and John Zaller, *The American Ethos* (Cambridge, MA: Harvard University Press, 1984).
2. Robert S. Erikson, John P. McIver, and Gerald C. Wright, Jr., "State Political Culture and Public Opinion," *American Political Science Review* 81 (1987): 797–813.
3. For more on the problems associated with cross-filing, see James R. Mills, *A Disorderly House* (Berkeley, CA: Heyday Books), pp. 204–205.
4. Cross-filing re-emerged in 1998 in the form of the blanket primary, after voters approved Proposition 198.
5. Republican U.S. Senator William Knowland decided he wanted to win his party's gubernatorial primary, rather than defer to Knight, the incumbent, who had expressed interest in running for re-election. Hoping to avoid a political bloodbath, a "big switch" deal was brokered by another native-son Californian, Vice President Richard Nixon. Knight would simply run for the Senate seat, and Knowland would run for the governorship. The switch failed, and neither Republican won election, handing the statehouse to Brown.
6. Garrin Burbank, "The Ambitions of Liberalism: Jesse Unruh and the Shape of Postwar Democratic Politics in California," *Southern California Quarterly* 21 (1997): 487–502.
7. James Mills, *A Disorderly House: The Brown-Unruh Years in Sacramento* (Berkeley, CA: Heyday Books, 1987).
8. Ibid.

9. Of course, other factors contributed to Brown's loss. These included a falling-out with the party's left wing over his handling of antiwar protests on college campuses, the refusal of the CDC and organized labor to endorse him, and a primary challenge by Los Angeles Mayor Sam Yorty, which weakened him politically.

10. Burbank, "The Ambitions of Liberalism."

11. Before the passage of Proposition 13, the counties still had the capacity to absorb some of these additional expenses.

12. For an analysis of this phenomena at both the national and state levels, see Morris Fiorina, *Divided Government* (New York: MacMillan, 1992).

13. David O. Sears and Jack Citrin, *Tax Revolt: Something for Nothing in California* (Cambridge, MA: Harvard University Press, 1982).

14. Chapter 5 discusses Proposition 13 in detail.

15. Shrimpgate was an FBI sting operation that created a fictitious shrimp-packing company willing to trade money for member's votes. Several Sacramento lawmakers and lobbyists were snared. In its aftermath, the public became much more pessimistic about the state's campaign finance system and about state politics in general. See Steve Scott, "The Legacy of the Capitol Sting," *California Government and Politics Annual 1995–1996* (Sacramento, CA: California Journal Press, 1995), pp. 35–38.

16. See Chapter 6 for a complete discussion of Proposition 140.

17. A. G. Block, "The Reapportionment Failure," *California Journal* 22, no. 11 (November 1991): 503–505.

18. See Chapter 6 for a full discussion on these initiatives.

19. Dan Morain, "Upbeat Wilson Sees More School Spending," *Los Angeles Times*, 15 May 1998, A1.

CHAPTER 4

People, Diversity, and Culture

Together, we have created what Gloria Anzaldua celebrated as a "borderland"— a place where "two or more cultures edge each other, where people of different races occupy the same territory." How can all of us meet on communal ground? "The struggle," Anzaldua responded, "is inner: Chicano, *indio*, American Indian, *mojado*, *mexicano*, immigrant Latino, Anglo in power, working-class Anglo, black, Asian—our psyches resemble the bordertowns and are populated by the same people.... Awareness of our situation must come before inner changes, which in turn must come before changes in society."

Such awareness, in turn, must come from a "revisioned" history. What Gloria Steinem termed "revolution from within" must ultimately be grounded in "unlearning" much of what we have been told about America's past and substituting a more inclusive and accurate history of all peoples of America. "To finally recognize our own invisibility," declared Mitsuye Yamada, "is to finally be on the path toward visibility." To become visible is to see ourselves and each other in a different mirror of history....

By viewing ourselves in a mirror which reflects reality, we can see our past as undistorted and no longer have to peer into our future as through a glass darkly. The face of our cultural future can be found on the western edge of the continent. "California, and especially Los Angeles, a gateway to both Asia and Latin America," Carlos Fuentes observed, "poses the universal question of the coming century: How do we get along with each other?" Asked whether California, especially with its multiethnic society, represented the America of the twenty-first century, Alice Walker replied: "If that's not the future reality of the United States, there won't be any United States, because that's who we are."

—Ronald Takaki, from *A Different Mirror: A History of Multicultural America*
(Boston, MA: Little, Brown and Company, 1993).

THE MULTICULTURAL STATE

California is neither a melting pot nor a salad bowl. From the first civilizations among native American communities, through the period of Spanish conquest and the cultural imperialism of the missions, to the period of Mexican settlement, and ultimately the mass white migration of the 1870s and 1880s, California has evolved into an often uneasy jigsaw of competing interests. California's complex network of urban, suburban, and rural areas make up what is now the nation's most diverse population, representing hundreds of distinct cultures and communities. Ethnicity is arguably the most salient cleavage in American politics. Yet, a striking trend in California's demography is the rate at which the "majority," non-Hispanic whites, are becoming a minority. In 1940 whites comprised 89.5 percent of California's population; Latinos, 6 percent; Asians, 1.9 percent; African Americans, 1.8 percent; and Native Americans, 0.2 percent. By 1995, whites made up only 52.8 percent, while Latinos grew to 31 percent of the state population, Asians and Pacific Islanders collectively to 9.3 percent, African Americans to 5.9 percent, and Native Americans, 0.7 percent.[1] As Table 4.1 suggests, California is far more diverse than the nation as a whole.

But these numbers tell only part of the story. Births among California's communities give us a glimpse of the state's evolving ethnic character. Latinos represent 44.8 percent of new babies born in the state; whites, 36.9 percent; African Americans, 7.5 percent; Filipinos, 2.6 percent; Chinese, 1.9 percent; Vietnamese, 1.3 percent; Koreans, 0.7 percent; Asian Indians, 0.6 percent; Japanese, 0.5 percent; Native Americans, 0.5 percent; Pacific Islanders, 0.5 percent; and Cambodians, 0.4 percent.[2] California's population represents more than 30 distinct ancestries, as Table 4.2 illustrates.[3] At the same time, immigration brings in over 200,000 people a year into the state, increasingly from Latin American countries, Asia, and Eastern Europe. By 2040, California's population is expected to be 50 percent Latino, 32 percent white, 12 percent Asian, and 6 percent African American.[4]

California's diversity reaches well beyond ethnic differences. Geography is playing an increasingly important role in cultural definition. In 1990, 92.6 percent of Californians lived in urban areas, up from 80.7 percent in 1950, 52.3 percent in 1900, 20.7 percent in 1860, and only 7.4 percent in 1850.[5] California has been the most urbanized state in the nation since 1980. This urbanization, however, is split among classically urban cities—such as San Francisco, Oakland, Sacramento, Los Angeles, and San Diego—and growing suburban areas—such as Sonoma, Fresno, Orange, Riverside, and Ventura Counties. The residents of suburban areas remain suspicious of urban cores, while residents of urban areas see suburban growth as the abandonment of cities by the upper middle class. Add to this the rural Californians in the San Joaquin Valley and northern portion of the state, and geography comes into focus as a second dimension of California's cultural mosaic.

TABLE 4.1   DEMOGRAPHIC CHARACTERISTICS
OF THE UNITED STATES, AND OF CALIFORNIA, 1990

	POPULATION	WHITE	BLACK	LATINO	ASIAN	AMERICAN INDIAN
United States	248,710,000	80.3%	12.1%	9.0%	2.9%	0.7%
California	29,668,000	69.9	7.4	25.8	9.8	0.8

Source: *The 1992 Information Please Almanac* (Boston: Houghton Mifflin, 1991) and California Department of Finance, State Census Data Center, *Current Population Survey* (March 1994).

TABLE 4.2 CALIFORNIA POPULATION BY NATIONAL ANCESTRY, 1990

ANCESTRY	POPULATION	% OF STATE POPULATION
Mexican	6,070,637	21.4
German	3,676,049	12.9
English	2,370,828	8.3
Irish	1,951,628	6.9
Italian	1,079,022	3.8
Filipino	731,685	2.6
Chinese	704,805	2.5
French	580,485	2.0
Scotch-Irish	399,870	1.4
Scottish	393,809	1.4
Polish	378,077	1.3
Swedish	370,470	1.3
Salvadoran	338,769	1.2
Dutch	335,739	1.2
Russian	327,675	1.2
Japanese	312,989	1.1
Vietnamese	280,233	1.0
Portuguese	275,492	1.0
Norwegian	263,646	0.9
Korean	259,941	0.9
Danish	163,964	0.6
Asian Indian	159,973	0.6
Guatemalan	159,177	0.6
French Canadian	132,643	0.5
Puerto Rican	131,998	0.5
Arab	123,933	0.4
Welsh	119,081	0.4
Pacific Islander	110,599	0.4
Hungarian	104,722	0.4
Greek	102,178	0.4

Source: U.S. Bureau of the Census, *1990 U.S. Census.* All groups over 100,000.

Urbanites are concerned with rebuilding aging city infrastructure, as well as improving social and economic conditions, including minimizing crime, improving urban schools, bringing jobs back into urban cores, and improving public transit. Suburbanites are fundamentally concerned with keeping urban problems out of their neighborhoods, though increasingly the suburbs are facing similar challenges. Rural residents are concerned with maintaining their rural economies, be that agriculture or timber products, and with battling encroaching urbanization. The interaction of these three Californias creates a heady mix of politics that is exacerbated by the racial undercurrent: Since urban cores are increasingly African American, Latino, and Asian, and suburban and rural areas are generally white, racial tensions accent the claims of competing geographic interests.

Income represents a third dimension of California's diversity. As Table 4.3 demonstrates, uneven income distribution across the state and across ethnic lines adds further tension to California's cultural mosaic. While the median household income statewide is $40,706, median incomes across counties vary markedly. For example, Marin County, just across the Golden Gate from San Francisco, enjoys a median household income of $60,689, the highest in the state. In the farming areas of Imperial County, the median household income is $19,872. The median household income in California's urban counties are far lower than in the largely suburban counties, while the rural counties are lower yet. For example, Los Angeles County (the state's most urban) has a median household income of $36,541, while neighboring Ventura County (largely suburban) has a median household income of $44,764. At the same time, the rural counties in the northernmost portion of the state are significantly lower: Trinity County has a median household income of $27,933; Siskiyou County of $28,499; Modoc County of $29,570.[6] Looking at income across ethnic lines reveals that while 10 percent of white families live below the poverty line, 17 percent of Asian families live below the poverty line, 29 percent of black families, and 32 percent of Latino families live in poverty.[7] Personal economic security has become a contentious issue throughout the state.

Beyond the three dimensions discussed, there are several communities of interest that face unique problems and present distinct pressures on politics and policy. The issues reflected in these communities include religion, gender equality, sexual identity, age, and employee rights. Religion continues to play a major role in California. Urban Jews and Catholics, for example, continue to vote overwhelmingly democratic. In several areas the religious right has targeted local school boards in an effort to influence curricula. Gender politics has remained a dominant influence throughout the state as organizations such as NOW (National Organization of Women) and CARAL (California Abortion Rights Action League) fight for women's issues, from equal rights to abortion rights. Gays and lesbians have organized to pursue equal rights and to combat homophobia and hate crimes. Much of the passion in the fight over gays in the military and the current battle over same-sex marriages originated in California's powerful gay communities in Los Angeles and the Bay Area.

In the past 20 years age has emerged as a defining characteristic in identifying communities of interest. Seniors have organized in interest groups such as AARP (The American Association of Retired Persons) to balance the strong influence of the baby boomer generation. Boomers (those born in the boom of births following World War II between 1945 and 1964) are now the generation in power in most economic, political, and social institutions. And, like all previous generations who have attained positions of influence, boomers have pursued political and economic agendas that maximize their generational interests.

Unlike previous generations, however, boomers have developed extraordinarily high levels of power. This is a result of two phenomenon. First, having come of age

TABLE 4.3   MEDIAN FAMILY INCOME AND POPULATION BY COUNTY, 1990

COUNTY	MEDIAN INCOME	RANK	POPULATION
Alameda	$49,625	5	1,362,900
Alpine	34,444	33	1,230
Amador	34,655	31	33,850
Butte	30,516	46	204,300
Calaveras	34,015	35	38,700
Colusa	21,251	57	18,000
Contra Costa	55,888	2	883,400
Del Norte	31,056	43	29,250
El Dorado	43,376	11	148,600
Fresno	32,602	40	764,800
Glenn	25,648	56	27,100
Humboldt	34,468	32	128,900
Imperial	19,872	58	141,500
Inyo	35,441	28	18,900
Kern	35,915	27	627,700
Kings	29,999	47	116,300
Lake	27,848	52	57,500
Lassen	36,050	26	29,800
Los Angeles	36,541	23	9,244,600
Madera	30,861	44	109,500
Marin	60,689	1	245,500
Mariposa	31,244	42	16,550
Mendicino	30,751	45	86,200
Merced	29,123	49	202,800
Modoc	29,570	48	10,700
Mono	36,578	22	11,250
Monterey	32,754	38	371,000
Napa	41,342	13	120,600
Nevada	35,206	29	89,500
Orange	46,730	7	2,641,400
Placer	44,157	9	210,000
Plumas	33,239	36	21,500
Riverside	36,082	25	1,393,500
Sacramento	43,502	10	1,149,200
San Benito	36,106	24	43,050
San Bernadino	39,039	17	1,618,200
San Diego	39,115	16	2,720,900
San Francisco	37,196	20	759,300
San Joaquin	38,120	18	530,700
San Luis Obispo	37,009	21	236,000
San Mateo	52,981	4	695,100

TABLE 4.3 (CONT.)

COUNTY	MEDIAN INCOME	RANK	POPULATION
Santa Barbara	37,740	19	396,900
Santa Clara	54,672	3	1,607,700
Santa Cruz	39,376	15	242,600
Shasta	33,137	37	166,100
Sierra	34,416	34	3,360
Siskiyou	28,499	50	46,500
Solano	47,457	6	377,600
Sonoma	43,279	12	432,200
Stanislaus	34,929	30	420,000
Sutter	32,170	41	74,900
Tehama	27,314	54	55,700
Trinity	27,933	51	13,950
Tulare	27,274	55	355,200
Tuolumne	32,744	39	53,300
Ventura	44,764	8	720,500
Yolo	40,211	14	153,700
Yuba	27,484	53	64,100
State Median	**$40,706**		**Total: 32,344,000**

Source: California Franchise Tax Board, 1995; California Department of Finance, Population Research Unit, *California Statistical Abstract Report 95 E-1, 95 E-2.*

during a period of unprecedented economic growth, boomers have attained unprecedented wealth. Second, the sheer number of boomers relative to the general population have given them a distorted sense of self-importance. Partly in response to the boomer generation and partly in response to the issues that have always affected older citizens, seniors have become uniquely politicized and efficiently organized. AARP, for example, has emerged as one of the strongest interest groups in the state and nationwide, providing a counterbalancing interest to the boomers.

The most recent generation of Americans to come of age is only now beginning to develop a cohesive political identity. The so-called Generation X can expect to earn less than their parents while facing significantly higher costs for housing and durable goods. In short, this postboomer generation will absorb most of the costs while enjoying few of the benefits of America's postwar economic boom and the stifling debt-based growth of the 1980s. As a generation, Xers are understandably cynical. Simultaneously, they are uniquely prepared for the political and economic shifts expected over the next 25 years. Unlike their predecessors, Xers anticipate a shifting political and economic environment and are developing the skills necessary to cope. Xers are generally more concerned with deficit spending and the growing national debt than either boomers or seniors and are generally less committed to any single political party. Only now beginning to flex their political muscle, Xers will likely become important players in policymaking over the next decade.

There are, of course, a variety of other communities of interest that exist within California. Organized labor continues to be a major influence in policy debates. And, while union representation continues to drop in the private sector, public sector unions such as SEIU (Service Employees International Union) are gaining membership and influence. As well, environmentalists as a community are gaining influence, presenting challenges to traditional power centers in timber, agriculture, and industry throughout the state. These communities of interest are increasingly adding demands to the policy discourse. In response to this ever increasing diversity in ethnic, social, and economic interests, the state has developed a unique equilibrium-based politics with an ever shifting center of balance.

CULTURE AS POLITICS

Each of the communities discussed contribute to California's complex political environment. The multitude of political and demographic subcultures in California has led to an amazingly fluid, and often conflicted, political culture. California is not merely heterogeneous, it is full of crosscutting schisms and overlapping memberships in communities of interest. Each of these communities share some common experience and values, giving rise to unique political subcultures.

Culture can be understood as a set of experiences and symbols that frame community cognitions. Language, history, rituals, and values all give focus to the way one sees the world. Political culture, therefore, can be understood as the set of experiences and symbols that focus political cognitions. California's diverse population represents a complex web of political subcultures, giving the state more a mosaic of cultural influences and political pressures rather than a single culture. The result of these competing influences is an extremely passionate pluralistic process. Ultimately, though, it is California's diversity that may give the state its greatest strength.

MONTEREY PARK: A CASE STUDY IN DIVERSITY

Ten miles east of downtown Los Angeles, drivers on the freeway will notice a sign welcoming them to "Monterey Park, All-American City." This middle-class suburb made national news in the 1980s as it struggled to maintain a sense of identity after years of change and growth. After World War II, it was a mostly white bedroom community where Laura Scudder used home recipes to begin her peanut butter and potato chip business. By 1990, the city had a population of 61,000 and was home to a thriving retail center. A significant factor in this transformation was a change in demographics due to a rapid influx of Asian residents. Asians comprised only 3 percent of the city's population in 1960. This group was mostly of Japanese heritage and native-born. In 1990, 56 percent of the population was Asian, due mainly to migration by ethnic Chinese from downtown Los Angeles, mainland China, Taiwan, Hong Kong, Vietnam, and other Southeast Asian nations. Of the Chinese immigrants living in Monterey Park, more than 65 percent arrived in the 1980s. During that decade, more than 30 times as many U.S.-bound immigrants from Taiwan reported Monterey Park as their destination than San Francisco.[8]

Monterey Park became known as "Little Taipei," replacing downtown Los Angeles' Chinatown as the center of Chinese cultural activity in Southern California. Surrounded by the predominantly Latino neighborhoods in the San Gabriel Valley, Monterey Park also saw its Latino population grow from 12 percent to 31 percent during this time. At the same time, non-Hispanic whites became a minority compared to the newcomers, dwindling from 85 percent of the population to just 12 percent. The Chinese did not fit the traditional pattern of immigration. Earlier waves of immigrants to the San Gabriel Valley—from Japan, Mexico, and Central America—had arrived gradually and had initially occupied the bottom rung of the economic ladder in the community. The Chinese community arrived rapidly in large numbers and reflected significant economic diversity.[9]

Ethnic tensions increased during the 1980s as white residents began to perceive the rapid growth and changing character of the neighborhood as a threat. The city council, representing an "old guard" of established whites, passed an ordinance making English the city's "official" language and requiring English wording on all business signs. The council rescinded the law after public outcry. Nonetheless, a coalition of progressive Asian and Latino activists waged a campaign in 1987 to recall the three city council members who were behind the English ordinance. The recall failed, although the council members were voted out in subsequent elections.

The confluence of the issues of ethnic diversity and development allowed many residents to support nativist candidates and positions in the name of "slow-growth," without appearing to be racist. Whites could oppose ethnic candidates as the agents of development interests. Thus, electoral politics were essentially deadlocked between multicultural, progrowth forces and nativist antigrowth forces. Even though the majority of the city's residents were Asian, with whites comprising a small minority, this impasse kept the old guard in control of city hall. In 1988, a breakthrough occurred when a Chinese-American slow-growth advocate, Judy Chu, won election to the city council in a contest where ballots were printed in Chinese, English, Japanese, Spanish, and Vietnamese.[10]

The election of Chu was the watershed event in the city's transformation from a stronghold of nativism to a model of multiculturalism. Chu successfully forged a multiethnic coalition by appealing to Asians, Latinos, and whites who wanted to control growth, yet were dissatisfied with the nativist sentiments of local white politicians. Asian Americans had been elected to city government previously, but only with heavy support of white voters. The effect of the English-only controversy and the recall drive was to politicize the immigrant and minority communities in Monterey Park, which led to large-scale ethnic voting in local elections. Even in San Francisco, a city with a significant Asian population, no Asian was elected to city office before Supervisor Mabel Teng in 1994.

FEAR AND LOATHING IN CALIFORNIA'S CHANGING POPULATION

Political leaders have accepted and even embraced California's multicultural character as part of the political landscape. At the same time, many voters have been less tolerant, even fearful, of California's changing population. In recent years, the voting public has often used the direct democracy provision of the state constitution to roll back opportunities for non-whites. Examples include Proposition 63 (1986), Proposition 187 (1994), and the anti-affirmative action "California Civil Rights Initiative" (1996). This has been possible because the impressive numeric strength of California's minority communities has not yet translated into proportional political clout. In 1998, there were no African-American state legislators representing districts outside the Los Angeles metropolitan area. Many Latinos and Asian Americans, the two largest minority groups in the state, are ineligible to vote either because they are not yet citizens or because they are too young. For example, Latinos constitute one-fourth of the state's population, but only one out of thirteen voters is Latino.[11] Consequently, Latinos are severely underrepresented at the state and local levels of government.

PROPOSITION 63

In 1986, the same year Monterey Park passed and rescinded its "official English" law, a similar proposal appeared in the form of an initiative on the state ballot. Proposition 63 was designed to "protect" the English language through an amendment to the state constitution declaring English the common language of the state. It directed the legislature to make no law that diminishes the role of the language and granted citizens standing to bring suit against the state to enforce the law.[12] Despite opposition from state political leaders, including Governor Deukmejian, California voters passed Proposition 63 by nearly a three-to-one vote. Statewide, 73 percent voted for the initiative. The vote margin was more narrow in Monterey Park, where only 53 percent voted "yes" on the initiative. Two years later, voters in Florida, Colorado, and Arizona passed similar initiatives. It is no coincidence that the four states with the highest proportion of non-English speaking minorities were the first to consider "official English" initiatives on their ballots.

PROPOSITION 187

In seeking to stop undocumented immigration into the state, Proposition 187 requires that "all persons employed in the providing of (public) services shall diligently protect public funds from misuse" by excluding anyone who has not been "*verified*" to be in the country legally. Further, the law states that

> If any public entity in this state to whom a person has applied for public social services determines *or reasonably suspects*, based upon the information provided to it, that the person is an alien in the United States in violation of federal law, the following procedures shall be followed by the public entity: (1) The entity shall not

provide the person with benefits or services. (2) The entity shall, in writing, notify the person of his or her apparent illegal immigration status, and that the person
must either obtain legal status or leave the United States. (3) The entity shall also
notify the State Director of Social Services, the Attorney General of California,
and the U.S. Immigration and Naturalization Service of the *apparent* illegal status,
and shall provide any additional information that may be requested by any other
public entity.[13] (*Emphases added.*)

The policy reflects the growing frustration within the state and represents an exag-
gerated response. Proposition 187 has remained controversial because it evolved
against the backdrop of Latino immigration and because it precludes due process.
For example, according to the law, a child can be denied medical attention in a
county facility based on a clerk's *suspicion* that the child is undocumented. With constant media messages focusing on Latino immigrants, the practical implication is defacto suspicion, and potential exclusion, of Latinos generally. Ultimately, California's
courts struck down Proposition 187.

CALIFORNIA CIVIL RIGHTS INITIATIVE

CCRI sought to dismantle the state's longstanding commitment to affirmative action. The law states the following:

> The state shall not discriminate against, or grant preferential treatment to, any in-
> dividual or group on the basis of race, sex, color, ethnicity, or national origin in the
> operation of public employment, public education, or public contracting.[14]

The initiative has stirred controversy because it targets equity programs that are
largely responsible for giving traditionally underrepresented communities (women,
blacks, Latinos, Asians) access to education, business, and the professions. Critics
argued that CCRI is somewhat disingenuous, arguing that such discrimination is
already banned by federal civil rights laws and pointing out that the third clause of
the initiative presents an explicit attack on the protections against sexual discrimination ensured by Title X of federal Civil Rights law. The third clause of CCRI declares the following:

> Nothing in this section shall be interpreted as prohibiting bona fide qualifications
> based on sex which are reasonably necessary to the normal operation of public em-
> ployment, public education, or public contracting.[15]

What "bona fide qualifications" are "reasonably necessary" has not been defined.
Since public safety agencies (e.g., police and fire departments) have traditionally
used this line of argument to exclude women, this language has elicited protest.

"Official English," Proposition 187, and CCRI are all examples of policies that reflect the ethnic tensions within the state. Frustrated by the perception that ethnic minorities were getting more than their share, voters bypassed the legislature to enact new policies designed to hasten the assimilation of new immigrants, limit immigration, and restrict opportunity for certain groups. As with ballot initiatives in other policy areas, California's controversial responses to diversity have been adopted nationwide. The success of California's Proposition 63 ignited a national "English-only" movement as activists raced to qualify similar initiatives for their own state ballots. Several states now are watching how the courts interpret Proposition 187 to see what will ultimately be viable policy, and interest groups throughout the nation are introducing legislative proposals that mirror CCRI. As California goes, so goes the nation.

SUMMARY

California's social and cultural diversity reflects a dynamic tension that is organic to the state. The multiplicity of communities, cultures, and interests contributes to an engagingly pluralistic process of assessing public problems and determining public solutions. David Broder once commented in the *Washington Post* that California policy suffered from "Californocracy."[16] This, he argued, was a result of California's initiative and referendum process, which allows average citizens both to place measures on the statewide ballot and to approve or disapprove specific policies. This form of direct democracy encourages the legislature to pass difficult decisions on to the public—a public that is too often apathetic and uninformed. As an East Coast proponent of representative democracy, Broder misses the point. Californians demand input and participation—even if the result is often less than desirable. The *potential* to participate is more important to Californians than the outcome. This is pluralism—California style.

Such hyperpluralism plays against the backdrop of California's competing political cultures—ethnic, geographic, economic, and otherwise. California is the most diverse state in the nation. Whites are barely a majority in the state: Soon they will no longer be even a plurality of the population, as Latinos are expected to become the largest ethnic group by 2015. As one of the largest states, California often experiences geographically based political conflict among urban, suburban, and rural interests. Some of the most extreme examples of opulence and poverty in the nation are found in California's upscale suburbs and poor agricultural communities—highlighting the sharp economic differences California's households experience. And because the population is younger on average than in other states, there is also potential for sharp intergenerational conflict as the emerging minority-majority population reaches voting age and begins participating in higher rates. Designed by Progressive reformers to counteract the influence of special interests, the initiative process has become an instrument of the majority to try to slow the trend toward a multicultural society. Whether or not they prove to be effective tools to resist change, such referenda will continue to exacerbate social tensions.

NOTES

1. California Department of Finance, *Population Research Unit, Report 88 P-4, 93 P-1.*
2. California Department of Health Services, *Vital Statistics*, 1994.
3. U.S. Bureau of the Census, 1990 U.S. Census.
4. California Department of Health Services, 1994.
5. California Department of Finance, *Report 86, P-3*; California Department of Health Services, 1994.
6. California Franchise Tax Board, 1995.
7. California Department of Finance, State Census Data Center, *Current Population Survey*, March 1994.
8. Immigration and Naturalization Service statistics reported in Timothy P. Fong, *The First Suburban Chinatown: The Remaking of Monterey Park, California* (Philadelphia: Temple University Press, 1994).
9. John Horton argues that it was the absence of gross economic inequality that may be the reason Monterey Park was spared much of the turmoil of the 1992 Los Angeles riots. See John Horton, *The Politics of Diversity: Immigration, Resistance and Change in Monterey Park, California* (Philadelphia: Temple University Press, 1995).
10. For a detailed account of the recall and subsequent elections in Monterey Park, see Horton, 1995.
11. Leo Estrada, "Latinos in California's Future," *California Journal* (January 1995): 45–49.
12. Jack Citrin, "Language Politics and American Identity," *The Public Interest* 99 (spring 1990): 96–109.
13. Ballot Text of California's Proposition 187 (1994), now state law. Several elements of the law are under review by federal courts.
14. Ballot text of the California Civil Rights Initiative (1996), clause 1, lines 1–3.
15. Ballot text of the California Civil Rights Initiative (1996), clause 3, lines 5–7.
16. David Broder, "Californocracy in Action," *Washington Post*, 13 August 1997, A21.

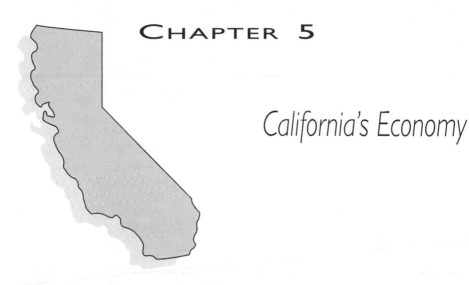

CHAPTER 5

California's Economy

Over the past century California has evolved from a sparsely populated frontier state to the most populous state in the nation. The state's size, strong economy, cultural influence, and its diversity have propelled the state into becoming a dominant player in national affairs. Based on GNP alone, California would rank as the eighth largest economy on the planet. California's manufacturing base has long been critical to the nation's military, and its lead in aerospace and high technology has positioned the state for continued growth throughout the twenty-first century. In addition, California's entertainment industries—film, music, and television—have served to export a cultural self-image that, while somewhat artificial, has served to foster the evolution of popular culture throughout the nation.

California's status as an economic powerhouse is due in part to its capacity to exploit its location, encouraging open economic borders, open markets, and an open labor pool. If California were a self-contained nation it would be one of the world's largest economies—ranking eighth behind such giants as Japan, Germany, and the United States itself as Table 5.1 (on page 50) illustrates. The state's attractiveness as a global production center is linked not only to a highly developed, culturally diverse internal labor and consumer market but also to the state's position as a springboard to the Pacific Rim and Latin American external markets. Its improved competitiveness is linked to the state's focus on investment, its role as a gateway for diffusing technology, and its bolstering of the export and import markets.

THE POLITICS OF NAFTA

The desire of building a "free-trade" zone in California took an even deeper hold in January 1994 with the implementation of the North American Free Trade Agreement (NAFTA). The treaty was produced by the efforts of the Clinton White House and the vast majority of Republicans and a good proportion of Democrats in both houses of Congress. NAFTA was to create a single quasi-common market of 360 million

TABLE 5.1   COMPARATIVE GROSS DOMESTIC PRODUCT

1996	GDP (IN BILLIONS)
United States	$7,418.7
Japan	4,595.2
Germany	2,341.6
France	1,538.8
Italy	1,213.7
United Kingdom	1,153.4
California	**962.7**
Canada	592.3
Spain	582.2
Korea	484.6

Source: Organisation for Economic Cooperation and Development, July 1999. Data are broadly consistent with those in the latest issue of the annual OECD national accounts publication. However, where revised data are available from countries' submissions, they have been used in compiling this table; U.S. Department of Commerce, Bureau of Economic Analysis, 1999. <http://www.bea.doc.gov>.

people linking Canada, Mexico, and the United States. It was designed to remove all tariffs and allow for the free exchange of goods, services, and investments among the partners. California's political leadership was strongly divided over the issue, crossing traditional partisan lines.[1] At the time, both Democratic Senator Alan Cranston and Republican Senator John F. Seymour supported the development of NAFTA. Seymour voted in favor of "fast-track" authorization of the treaty, yet publicly tempered his recorded vote by his expressed concerns for the treaty's impact on the particularly powerful agricultural sector. Other California delegation members with strong ties to agricultural contributors and constituencies acted similarly. Two "moderate" Democrats from the Central Valley—Representative Gary A. Condit and Richard H. Lehman—vacillated back and forth, ultimately opposing NAFTA since high tariffs and protective legislation have historically given California's export market of agricultural goods a competitive advantage. As another moderate Democrat, Representative Robert Matsui (a supporter of NAFTA), pointed out

> ... an agreement would affect nearly every segment of the state's economy. Admittedly, some industries would suffer, but others would gain. The onus is on each senator and representative to determine whether the potential gains from a Mexican/North American free-trade agreement would outweigh the short-term losses that are certain to occur. Balancing competing interests is never easy when the final determination may cause injury to even one industry or individual.[2]

The boosters of NAFTA had a difficult battle within the U.S. Congress. Organized labor, mobilized by congressional districts, was the chief opposition to the treaty. Labor claimed that NAFTA was no more than a sell-out of American jobs. Labor felt that the lure of non-union low-wage labor pools in Mexico would suck American jobs south. The fears labor mobilized were grounded in the realities of the downsizing, de-industrialization, and globalization of the economies of the 1980s and 1990s. Fighting alongside organized labor was a segment of the environmental movement that feared

American and Canadian entrepreneurs would shift the most polluting segment of their industries to Mexico, in search of softer environmental laws. Mexico's environmental protection agency, the SEDUE, had only 300 inspectors at the time to cover the entire country's regulatory enforcement. Defenders of NAFTA are quick to point out that the budget for SEDUE grew from $5 million in 1989 to $39 million in 1991, indicating a political will to keep Mexico from becoming more inundated with industrial pollution.[3] Yet SEDUE's recent per capita environmental budget is 48 cents, compared to the EPA's $24.40.[4]

The General Accounting Office (GAO) found that a substantial number of American firms were already moving their most polluting factories south of the border to escape U.S. environmental laws. The GAO study focused on wood manufacturers in the Los Angeles area from the period of 1988–1990. The report found that 83 percent of the factories were relocated to take advantage of the lower Mexican wages (77 cents an hour, compared with $8.92 an hour in Los Angeles). Furthermore, 78 percent of manufacturers leaving the Los Angeles basin blamed tough air pollution standards imposed by the South Coast Air Quality Management District.[5]

While the majority of the export trade has gone from the "West to the East," the aspiration of NAFTA is to develop an increased "north-south" trading axis. California could serve as a natural land bridge, linking Mexico with the rest of the United States and Canada. As it currently stands, Canada buys over $3 billion worth of California goods and services each year and is the top foreign investor in the state. Estimates show that elimination of Canadian tariffs alone would increase U.S. exports to that country by up to $1 billion each year. California would be positioned to compete for a good share of that $1 billion growth.[6]

It may be many years before the costs and benefits of NAFTA are fully assessed, but California is one of the states that expects to gain the most from the trade agreement. As Table 5.2 (on page 52) shows, the state's economic recovery has been driven largely by its international export sector. California generates 15 percent of U.S. trade with other countries, providing billions of dollars in revenues and more than a million jobs for the state. Yet, the trade sector of California's economy is only part of the bigger economic picture. Of California's 2.1 million manufacturing jobs, only 12.4 percent are export-related.

CALIFORNIA AND THE U.S. ECONOMY

California leads the nation in several sectors of the national economy. It remains a leader in the computer, film and animation, multimedia, biotechnology, semiconductor, and aerospace industries and has been incubating a new manufacturing base in the apparel and furniture-making industries. Over the past several years it has further diversified its economy, making it more resistant to fluctuations in the global market. The growing service industry accounts for approximately one-third of the state's workforce (see Table 5.3 on pages 53–54). The rapid growth in this sector, with its low to moderate wage scale, has raised some concerns about how the economy will make the adjustment from one dominated by a shrinking manufacturing sector, which traditionally employed moderate- to high-wage workers.

TABLE 5.2 VALUE OF EXPORTS AND IMPORTS THROUGH CALIFORNIA PORTS, BY ALL MODES OF TRANSPORTATION, 1988 TO 1996 (IN MILLIONS)

CUSTOMS DISTRICT	1988	1989	1990	1991	1992	1993	1994	1995	1996	% CHANGE '95 TO '96
EXPORTS[a]										
California	$53,567.7	$63,048.7	$68,551.8	$73,860.3	$81,139.0	$82,173.5	$95,614.6	$116,778.4	$124,120.0	6.29
San Francisco[c]	19,079.9	21,441.0	23,117.2	23,892.9	27,188.4	29,391.6	34,195.1	43,691.4	47,723.5	9.23
Los Angeles[d]	31,962.5	38,596.5	42,069.0	46,050.5	49,399.6	48,279.8	55,834.7	67,004.3	68,923.2	2.86
San Diego[e]	2,525.3	3,011.2	3,365.5	3,916.9	4,550.9	4,502.1	5,584.9	6,082.7	7,473.3	22.86
IMPORTS[b]										
California	$86,600.5	$94,080.0	$97,121.5	$100,744.1	$111,547.6	$125,348.4	$144,002.0	$165,221.6	$169,980.7	2.88
San Francisco[c]	25,062.0	27,259.3	28,141.0	29,308.0	33,386.3	38,910.4	46,307.8	59,113.9	57,803.6	-2.22
Los Angeles[d]	58,082.1	62,773.8	64,591.6	66,651.0	72,580.9	80,169.8	90,239.4	97,177.4	101,184.8	4.12
San Diego[e]	3,456.4	4,046.9	4,388.9	4,785.1	5,580.4	6,268.2	7,454.8	8,930.3	10,992.3	23.09

[a] f.a.s. Value Basis
[b] Custom Value Basis
[c] Customs district extends from Northern California border south to Monterey Bay, and east to Salt Lake City.
[d] Customs district extends from south of Monterey Bay to Carpinteria and east to Las Vegas.
[e] Customs district extends from San Diego east to Phoenix.

Sources: U.S. Department of Commerce, Bureau of the Census, *Highlights of U.S. Export and Import Trade* (FT 990) (December 1984–1988) and U.S. Exports and Imports of Merchandise on CD-ROM (1989 forward), Department of Finance, Financial and Economic Research Unit.

TABLE 5.3   WAGE AND SALARY WORKERS IN NONAGRICULTURAL ESTABLISHMENTS BY MAJOR INDUSTRY CALIFORNIA, 1939 TO 1997 (IN THOUSANDS)

YEAR	TOTAL	MINING	CONSTRUCTION[a]	MANUFACTURING	TRANSPORTATION AND UTILITIES	WHOLESALE TRADE	RETAIL TRADE	FINANCE, INSURANCE, REAL ESTATE	SERVICES	GOV'T[b]
1939	1,812.2	40.0	78.8	384.4	185.1	—504.7—		93.9	274.7	250.3
1940	1,931.8	40.0	92.1	440.2	190.3	—524.2—		98.3	280.4	266.3
1941	2,264.9	40.1	138.5	593.6	213.0	—572.1—		102.4	297.4	307.8
1942	2,689.6	33.8	155.5	876.0	233.8	—588.1—		97.2	321.3	384.1
1943	3,083.6	29.4	140.3	1,165.5	250.8	160.2	435.9	94.9	341.5	465.0
1944	3,116.4	29.9	135.9	1,109.7	268.0	156.3	457.7	93.2	355.2	510.6
1945	2,961.3	30.6	139.0	860.8	279.5	167.6	486.7	97.8	365.7	533.7
1946	2,972.6	33.5	177.7	706.7	295.5	189.2	547.9	116.9	405.0	500.2
1947	3,080.0	34.2	209.0	721.8	312.6	203.5	571.2	125.8	418.9	483.0
1948	3,162.8	35.6	232.7	734.2	317.9	213.3	577.2	132.3	418.7	500.9
1949	3,088.1	34.4	204.4	701.5	306.0	207.7	559.5	134.2	415.6	524.6
1950	3,209.4	32.3	235.0	759.7	307.1	211.7	571.5	142.1	416.8	533.3
1951	3,518.3	35.0	250.9	892.5	327.1	221.8	599.1	150.3	441.7	599.9
1952	3,737.8	35.9	250.6	994.6	336.3	226.6	626.0	157.9	469.0	640.9
1953	3,890.7	37.3	261.5	1,060.8	346.6	234.3	646.8	166.7	480.4	646.4
1954	3,866.1	36.1	255.0	1,048.6	336.5	235.7	641.5	170.4	487.8	654.5
1955	4,082.9	36.8	284.0	1,121.1	347.4	244.4	671.2	180.4	516.5	681.2
1956	4,352.3	37.0	302.3	1,218.0	364.9	259.9	703.2	193.2	549.2	724.6
1957	4,525.2	36.5	287.5	1,283.8	372.8	272.5	714.4	203.7	593.1	760.9
1958	4,498.6	33.4	286.7	1,217.4	353.7	268.8	704.2	212.6	623.2	798.6
1959	4,774.8	32.4	308.4	1,312.6	354.8	282.5	748.3	226.2	677.2	832.4
1960	4,896.0	30.6	294.8	1,317.2	356.9	292.2	775.4	243.2	711.7	874.0
1961	4,996.1	30.3	294.4	1,318.0	351.2	296.3	784.3	253.0	748.3	920.3
1962	5,217.7	30.2	307.7	1,382.5	357.0	303.3	818.1	265.4	790.7	962.8
1963	5,412.3	29.6	329.0	1,394.3	360.3	311.9	857.1	281.0	847.5	1,001.6
1964	5,606.5	31.0	340.4	1,389.4	371.0	320.0	904.5	296.7	910.0	1,043.5
1965	5,800.3	31.7	323.7	1,411.2	387.1	330.5	939.2	306.7	964.8	1,105.4
1966	6,145.2	32.3	305.6	1,531.3	410.3	345.4	983.9	310.6	1,029.1	1,196.7
1967	6,367.6	31.9	275.2	1,594.0	428.7	352.7	1,006.0	319.3	1,085.5	1,274.3
1968	6,642.1	32.5	290.7	1,639.7	440.7	361.8	1,056.3	337.8	1,146.8	1,335.8
1969	6,931.5	32.6	310.6	1,661.3	460.7	377.0	1,116.0	358.4	1,223.2	1,391.7
1970	6,946.2	31.4	303.0	1,558.0	459.1	—1,529.3—		374.5	1,266.2	1,424.7
1971	6,917.0	30.4	301.5	1,473.2	452.6	—1,545.2—		386.8	1,281.0	1,446.3
1972	7,209.9	29.2	312.4	1,542.7	454.1	409.6	1,199.0	409.3	1,361.0	1,492.7
1973	7,621.9	30.5	333.4	1,660.7	467.0	441.6	1,261.9	431.6	1,470.6	1,524.8
1974	7,834.3	32.7	317.8	1,701.3	470.7	460.6	1,291.4	444.8	1,529.1	1,586.0
1975	7,847.2	33.9	285.9	1,593.7	458.1	465.9	1,320.4	446.4	1,572.4	1,670.6
1976	8,154.2	34.7	301.3	1,659.8	463.9	485.3	1,390.2	468.7	1,654.6	1,695.6
1977	8,599.7	35.6	350.4	1,737.8	476.5	507.5	1,474.9	505.4	1,770.9	1,740.7
1978	9,199.8	37.1	401.9	1,884.6	506.4	534.3	1,591.7	553.2	1,937.4	1,753.1
1979	9,664.6	39.3	448.7	2,012.7	534.7	564.1	1,659.7	595.9	2,074.6	1,735.0

TABLE 5.3 (CONT.)

YEAR	TOTAL	MINING	CONSTRUCTION[a]	MANUFACTURING	TRANSPORTATION AND UTILITIES	WHOLESALE TRADE	RETAIL TRADE	FINANCE, INSURANCE, REAL ESTATE	SERVICES	GOV'T[b]
1980	9,848.8	43.5	428.3	2,018.2	546.3	583.7	1,683.2	623.1	2,158.8	1,763.9
1981	9,985.3	49.2	407.6	2,032.3	554.8	590.6	1,710.9	642.9	2,240.5	1,756.4
1982	9,810.3	50.4	349.0	1,957.7	542.8	582.1	1,693.1	642.4	2,257.7	1,735.2
1983	9,917.8	47.7	366.9	1,927.0	531.9	600.7	1,731.1	653.8	2,334.4	1,724.3
1984	10,390.0	47.6	407.4	2,004.1	540.0	634.6	1,838.5	677.8	2,492.7	1,747.4
1985	10,769.8	47.8	435.8	2,024.2	553.5	660.4	1,914.7	697.3	2,643.3	1,792.8
1986	11,085.5	40.7	450.0	2,039.1	568.4	672.3	1,982.5	728.6	2,765.1	1,838.8
1987	11,472.6	37.3	487.2	2,060.1	583.2	688.0	2,067.9	755.1	2,910.2	1,883.7
1988	11,911.5	37.7	529.2	2,096.7	588.4	733.5	2,154.1	773.0	3,064.8	1,934.1
1989	12,238.5	37.3	560.0	2,107.0	598.2	758.2	2,193.9	789.0	3,196.2	1,998.7
1990	12,499.9	37.7	561.8	2,068.8	612.2	768.9	2,223.8	808.8	3,343.1	2,074.8
1991	12,359.0	37.0	514.0	1,970.9	613.3	741.7	2,180.5	799.4	3,411.7	2,090.6
1992	12,153.5	35.4	471.7	1,890.5	607.4	713.5	2,121.4	791.9	3,426.3	2,095.6
1993	12,045.3	34.9	445.7	1,805.1	610.6	686.7	2,125.2	794.2	3,462.4	2,080.6
1994	12,159.5	31.9	464.3	1,777.3	619.0	701.6	2,143.5	770.6	3,558.2	2,093.2
1995	12,422.2	30.0	485.4	1,794.2	630.2	724.5	2,190.6	731.9	3,728.5	2,107.0
1996	12,743.4	29.2	505.9	1,851.8	641.8	744.0	2,230.0	736.7	3,890.7	2,113.3
1997	13,167.1	29.4	554.3	1,913.8	662.5	774.9	2,282.5	755.7	4,050.5	2,143.6

[a]Includes employees of construction contractors and operative builders; does not include force-account and government construction workers.

[b]Includes all civilian employees of federal, state, and local governments regardless of the activity in which the employees are engaged.

Note: There may be breaks in series between 1971–1972 and 1987–1988 due to changes in Standard Industrial Classification. Does not include employers, own-account workers, unpaid family workers, domestic servants, and agricultural workers.

Source: Employment Development Department, Labor Market Information Division, Information Services Group (916) 262-2345 <http://www.calmis.cahwnet.gov>.

California's economy thrived for many years in part because of Cold War defense policies. Federal largesse had subsidized the Golden State in the form of military bases, defense contracts, and other defense-related industries that created high-paying jobs. With the end of the Cold War, however, California was targeted for more base closures than any other state. After two earlier rounds of base closings in 1989 and 1991, a devastating third round in 1993 shut down eight major military installations statewide. Because six of these facilities were located in the San Francisco Bay area, the region lost more than 30,000 jobs as a direct result of the shutdowns.[7] In Southern California, major base closings in the early 1990s included the San Diego Naval Training Center, the El Toro Marine Air Station, and the Long Beach Naval Hospital and Shipyard. Thousands of indirectly related service jobs were expected to evaporate due to the closures.

The defense cuts jolted California's economy beyond base closings. The reduction in federal defense contracts meant heavy losses in aerospace and high-tech civilian jobs. In Los Angeles County alone, employment in these two sectors dropped by more than half between 1988 and 1995.[8] During this period, nearly every defense contractor in the state downsized. Many of those laid off were middle-aged, working to support families, and highly paid—aerospace workers made an average salary of $18 per hour.[9] These workers have largely been unable to find work at the same level of skill and pay. But, devastating as they were, federal budget cuts were not the only shock to the flagging economy of the early 1990s.

The Golden State had lost much of its luster by the early 1990s, as national economic growth slowed, post-Cold War defense cuts, and a series of natural and social disasters plunged the region deeper into recession. The recession of 1991–1994 was preceded by a prolonged drought and the deadly 1989 Loma Pricta Earthquake. The Los Angeles riots of 1992, which were precipitated by the acquittal of the four Los Angeles police officers who beat Rodney King, resulted in 55 deaths, more than 1,000 injuries, and cost the state approximately $1 billion.[10] Floods, fires, and the 1994 Northridge Earthquake put further stress on the state's infrastructure.

BUDGET CRISIS POLITICS

The recession, federal budget cuts, and natural disasters exacerbated an ongoing fiscal crisis in California. Accelerated out-migration and a shrinking tax base was the final straw. The migration from California reached an all-time high in 1992, with 580,000 people moving away from the state.[11] The ongoing recession and reduced tax base brought an unprecedented crash on tax revenues, causing California's worst fiscal crisis since the depression. By July 1992, the state was out of funds, causing the state controller to issue IOU warrants. Many banks honored the warrants for only the first month. Both Democrats and Republicans used the fiscal crisis as a vehicle to push their favored agendas. Democrats, who at the time controlled both the senate and the assembly, pushed for a tax increase to protect the state's social safety net. Governor Wilson and his Republican colleagues in the legislature sought deep spending cuts. The deadlock persisted for 63 days, as the state limped along without a budget. Ultimately, a $57.4 billion budget was passed. While the governor received most of his demands, the legislators minimized the damage to their favored programs.

The struggle to balance the budget occurred against the backdrop of a sluggish economy, the taxing and spending restrictions of Proposition 13, and the abolition of such revenue sources as the state inheritance tax and business inventory tax. Thus, from fiscal years 1991–1992 through 1994–1995, the total budget shortfall was $38 billion, which was met by revenue increases of $10.4 billion and expenditure reductions of $27.6 billion. The state's population grew 10 percent during those four years. Purchasing power for persons receiving state subsistence during those years fell by 10 percent. Californians on disability took a 20 percent cut in their monthly state disbursements. University of California students paid 134 percent higher tuition fees;

California State University students paid 103 percent higher fees to help balance the budget. The 1994–1995 state budget in real dollars was 17 percent less than the 1990–1991 budget.

The cumulative impacts of the recession and budget crisis of the 1990s were most visible at the county level. The Tax Revolt of the 1970s restricted the ability of the counties to raise new revenues to meet the growing demands for services by their own residents, as well as the services required by the state. For more than a decade after Proposition 13 went into effect in 1978, the counties managed to avoid the full impact of its taxing and spending limitations. The same year as the measure's passage, a sympathetic legislature in Sacramento provided relief to local governments in the form of AB 8. This approach succeeded until the 1990s, when the state began experiencing a perennial budget crisis of its own. Governor Wilson and the legislature compensated by passing a series of temporary half-cent sales tax increases. This forced a shift in the way local government was financed, from property taxes to sales taxes. Anticipating some of the unintended consequences of this shift, Democratic State Senator Mike Thomson of Napa once dubbed the 1993 budget the "Factory Outlet Act of 1993."[12]

Because Proposition 13 reduced property tax revenues by as much as 60 percent, several California counties were in financial distress by the early 1990s. Rural counties were hurt the most because of their dependence on property taxes and the lack of alternative revenue sources. Butte County avoided becoming the first county in the nation to file for bankruptcy thanks to three consecutive state bailouts.[13] Rural counties from Siskiyou in the North to Imperial in the Southeast found themselves strapped for cash, unable to raise the necessary revenue to meet their expenses. These fiscal crises were not limited to rural counties, however. In 1995, Los Angeles County was teetering on the edge of insolvency when President Clinton came to its aid with a federal bailout.

THE CRISIS HITS SUBURBIA: MUNICIPAL BANKRUPTCY IN ORANGE COUNTY

In stark contrast to Los Angeles County with its urban problems and Northern California with its budgetary woes, suburban Orange County was perhaps the one place most insulated from these fiscal pressures. Orange County is known as the home of Disneyland, aerospace and high-tech industries, good school districts, and a stronghold of conservative politics. Just days after the 1994 election ushered in a Republican Congress on a platform of fiscal restraint, the county reluctantly announced that it had lost more than $1.6 billion in risky investments. When its lender banks began to seize Orange County securities as collateral, the county filed for Chapter 9 bankruptcy.[14]

The pages and airwaves of the national news media were filled with explanations of mismanagement by Orange County Treasurer Bob Citron. Citron borrowed twice as much money as he had on deposit, nearly tripling the size of the county's investment pool, to purchase high-risk, high-yield securities. When the Federal Reserve raised interest rates in 1994, however, the value of these investments crashed.

When the county filed for protection from its creditors in December, the Orange County fiasco became the largest municipal bankruptcy in U.S. history. The county was in real danger of defaulting on a $1 billion debt, a sum far greater than the total debt of all 362 municipal bankruptcies since 1937.[15]

Even though Citron received the lion's share of the blame for the disaster, the conditions that made it possible were in place well before the people of Orange County elected him to office. Three factors made the fiscal crisis possible: political fragmentation, voter distrust, and state austerity.[16] Political fragmentation (that is, the capacity of multiple government entities to pursue competing goals simultaneously) is a common characteristic of the growing suburbs. There is a lack of accountability as political power is diffused between a large number of small cities and county supervisors, who tend to focus on their own districts. In Orange County, this arrangement left Citron to act as a relatively autonomous figure, without much oversight.

A second factor, voter distrust, has been especially intense in suburbs such as Orange County. Voters have become more likely to view government as costly, inefficient, and they have begun to demand increasingly high levels of service with low taxes. Middle-class suburbs have tended to elect government officials who share the same small-government, anti-tax views. Ever since the Tax Revolt of the 1970s, elected officials have been reluctant to make the case for tax increases. The refusal of a majority of the county's voters to approve a modest tax increase after the bankruptcy was interpreted as an expression of their lack of confidence in government to use the money wisely. In 1996, even after the effects of the bankruptcy were publicized, the county's voters overwhelmingly voted for Proposition 218, reaffirming and extending the limitations of Proposition 13. Affluent suburbanites want their cake.

The third factor leading to the crisis was the state's fiscal austerity. The state revenue shortfalls of the early 1990s reduced the aid coming in from Sacramento. The state reduced the local governments' share of property tax revenues, increasing pressure on the county treasurer to make up for the lost income with investments. Furthermore, the state's dire fiscal condition also precluded the possibility of a bailout.

The bankruptcy lasted 18 months, but its effects will be felt for a long time to come. The county was forced to lay off nearly 600 employees and slash some administrative budgets by as much as 30 percent.[17] Public health and services for the poor sustained the deepest cuts. Despite the threat of deep cuts to their school budgets and other public services, Orange County voters shocked observers elsewhere in the nation by defeating Measure R, a half-cent sales tax increase designed to bail the county out. With neither the state, the federal government, nor the voters willing to come to their aid, county leaders adopted a strategy of "suing their way out" of the predicament. Twenty-seven lawsuits were filed against Wall Street brokers that had advised Citron in his risky investments. By 1998, settlements of many of these cases helped the county recover $639 million, about 39 percent of the $1.6 billion lost.[18]

SUMMARY

Californians have lived for many years under the myth that the state's economy was "recession-proof." It must have appeared to many people that the economic infrastructure laid down after World War II, with its unrealistic reliance on federal dollars and the defense establishment, would continue forever. That perception changed with the crisis of the early 1990s. The recession was costly in terms of ruptured human lives, jobs, and prestige. Declining confidence in government had prompted voters to pass such measures as Proposition 13, restricting the discretionary power of elected leaders to such an extent that they were unable to cope with the fiscal crisis effectively. The costs of the downturn were passed first from the national to the state levels, and ultimately to the local level. The counties continue to cope with the twin pressures of reduced revenues and a high demand for services. And, as county governments are forced to make hard choices, it is often those constituencies who are least able to fight for their fair share who are most severely impacted.

NOTES

1. See H. Eric Schockman and Zagros Madjd-Sadjadi, "After NAFTA," *California Policy Choices* 9 (Sacramento, CA: University of Southern California, School of Public Administration, 1994), pp. 95–113.
2. Robert T. Matsui, "California's Prosperity Is at Stake," *Los Angeles Times*, 22 May 1991, B13.
3. Bruce Stokes, "Greens Talk Trade," *National Journal* (April 13, 1991): 862–866.
4. Juanita Darling, et al., "Can Mexico Clean Up Its Act?" *Los Angeles Times*, 17 November 1991, A1.
5. John Dillin, "Mexico's Pollution Threatens Free Trade," *Christian Science Monitor* (May 13, 1991): 1.
6. Yvonne D'Angela, *California, Canada and Free Trade: A Guidebook for California Business* (Sacramento, CA: California World Trade Commission. December, 1989).
7. Mary Beth Barber, "When Johnny Comes Marching Home," *California Journal* 25 (January 1994): 19–25.
8. Steve Scott, "The Morphing Economy," *California Journal* 28 (July 1997): 14–20.
9. Mary Beth Barber, "Can You Make a Buck When Peace Breaks Out?" *California Journal* 25 (January 1994): 27–28.
10. Cost estimate from Rebuild L.A., quoted in "Rebuilding South Central," *California Journal* 28 (July 1997): 20.
11. Lou Cannon, "The Abiding Dream," *California Journal* 26 (January 1995): 7–10.
12. Mary Beth Barber, "Local Government Hits the Wall," *California Journal* 24 (August 1993): 13–15.
13. A. J. Block and Claudia Buck, eds., *California Political Almanac* (Sacramento, CA: State Net Services & Publications, 1999), p. 80.
14. Mark Baldassare, *When Government Fails: The Orange County Bankruptcy* (Berkeley: University of California Press, 1998).
15. Ibid.
16. Ibid.
17. E. Scott Reckard and Michael Wagner, "Broker to Settle with O.C. for $439 Million," *Los Angeles Times*, 3 June 1998, A1.
18. Ibid.

CHAPTER 6

California's
Constitution and
Constitutional Officers

My son asked me what I hoped to accomplish as governor. I told him, essentially, to make life more comfortable for people, as far as government can. I think that embraces everything from developing the water resources vital to California's growth, to getting a man to work and back fifteen minutes earlier if it can be done through a state highway program.

—Edmund G. "Pat" Brown, Sr., Governor of California, 1959–1967, quoted in *California Journal*, January 1990, p. 8.

This chapter examines the state constitution and the executive bureaucracy it designed. California's plural executive is discussed, as are the multiple and independent responsibilities of its constitutional officers. The state constitution outlines the structure of government, establishing the rules of the policy process, which government officials must apply and interpret.

Like the U.S. Constitution, the state constitution codifies the rights of the state's people: Article I—the Declaration of Rights—addresses concrete issues as well as high principles, much like an elaborate version of the U.S. Constitution's Bill of Rights. Unlike the U.S. Constitution, the California constitution explicitly addresses several questions of institutional design, going into great detail about the size and function of specific public agencies. This attention to detail makes California's cumbersome constitution one of the longest of any state or nation. It was adopted in 1879 and has grown significantly in length, thanks to nearly 500 amendments.

Though it is possible to overhaul the state constitution through a constitutional convention, the delicate balance of power in the state makes such an event extremely unlikely.[1] It is more common to change the constitution either by constitutional amendment or through a constitutional revision commission. Most constitutional amendments are initiated through the legislative process. A constitutional measure must be approved by a two-thirds vote in both houses of the state legislature. It is then placed on the next statewide ballot and becomes constitutional law if approved by a majority vote of the electorate. Citizens may also bring about a constitutional amendment in the form of an initiative, bypassing the state legislature altogether. This process is described in the section on direct democracy.[2]

THE CONSTITUTIONAL OFFICERS

In order to govern the nation's largest state, California has developed an elaborate executive branch and an expansive bureaucracy. Some of this growth can be attributed to new offices created through reform efforts. Because California's constitution is easier to amend than that of other states, it has been relatively easy to pass initiatives creating new constitutional offices.[3] California's executive branch is populated with eight elected offices. In addition to the governor, voters choose candidates for seven other constitutional offices, including the Lieutenant Governor, Attorney General, Controller, Secretary of State, State Treasurer, Superintendent of Public Instruction, and Insurance Commissioner. These officers each serve four-year terms, with a Proposition 140 limit of two terms in any one office.

THE GOVERNOR

California's governor must share, and in some cases bow to, the constitutional authority of seven other statewide independent elected "chief executives." In this way California has a "plural executive" rather than a strong governorship. California's governor has remarkably few cabinet and commission appointments, compared to other states, largely because most of these high administrative positions are nested within the protective civil service realm and are insulated from being politicized. Despite this, the governor is the focal point of state politics. Since California has the largest economy, population, and the most electoral votes of any state, its governors are often significant figures on the national political scene. Ambitious governors such as Ronald Reagan, Jerry Brown, and Pete Wilson used the office to launch presidential campaigns. Other governors, such as Pat Brown and George Deukmejian, were considered as potential running mates by their parties. Earl Warren left the governor's office to serve as Chief Justice of the U.S. Supreme Court. Every governor since World War II has been re-elected at least once. Mastery of the office entails the effective use of three kinds of authority: explicit powers, independent powers, and informal powers.

Explicit Powers The governor is expected to be the electorate's leader and a check on the power wielded by the other branches of government. Explicit powers—those constitutional powers explicitly delegated to the governor—provide the basic tools governors use to fulfill these responsibilities. One such tool is the "line-item" veto. This permits the governor to remove, or "blue-pencil," single line-item appropriations and initiatives from legislation without vetoing the entire bill. The governor may employ a full veto of any legislative bill, with vetoes subject to override by two-thirds vote of both the assembly and the senate. In practice, only about 8 percent of all laws are vetoed, and overrides are extremely rare. Normally the governor's office gets involved well before the final passage of a bill, thereby reducing the probability of a veto at the end of the process. The governor has 12 days to sign a bill into law or to use the veto, thereby sending it back to the legislature. If the governor does nothing, the bill becomes law without his or her signature.

Other explicit powers of the governorship include acting as the head of state and as the commander-in-chief of the California National Guard. The California National Guard is activated at the discretion of the governor, typically in response to natural disasters and emergencies and in large-scale civil disturbances.[4] The governor also has the authority to call a special session of the legislature to address issues of critical importance should they occur while the legislature is out of session. Further, under the exercise of "executive clemency" the governor may unilaterally grant reprieves (postponement of sentences), pardons (a full release from custody), or commutations (reductions of sentences) to convicts within state jurisdiction. Executive clemency, however, is "checked" by the will of the majority on the supreme court when it comes to those convicts with past felon records whom the governor wishes to pardon or commutate.

Explicit powers of the governorship may also be shared with other branches of government. For example, the governor has the prime responsibility to watch over the "fiscal ship of state," submitting to the legislature a state budget spending plan on or before January 10th of each year. The legislature has until June 15th to alter, modify, or confirm the state budget, though this deadline is rarely met in practice. Another significant power that governors must share is that of naming appointees to prominent positions in state government and to part-time "citizen-panels" spanning over 300 state boards, commissions, and councils. Of these gubernatorial appointees, 600–700 require confirmation by a majority of the state senate. Judicial appointees, usually experienced lawyers who share a similar judicial philosophy as the governor, must be approved by the Commission on Judicial Appointments.

Independent Powers   The governor's independent powers are most visible in his obligatory role to enforce state law through a sprawling 200,000-person administrative bureaucracy consisting of over 60 departments, most of which are grouped within six mega-agencies: Business; Transportation and Housing; Resources; Health and Welfare; State and Consumer Services; Trade and Commerce; Youth and Adult Corrections; and Environmental Protection. The executive heads of these agencies are appointed by the governor (subject to senate confirmation) and play a key strategic role in determining how legislative policy should be implemented.

There is wide policy discretion that cabinet officials may choose to follow as implementation orders from the governor filter down through the respective bureaucracy.

The ultimate "will" of the sitting governor through these independent entities are felt throughout the governance of the state. Thus, for example, Governor Jerry Brown's appointment of Adriana Gianturco to head the State Department of Transportation (CALTRANS) irritated the highway lobby and the legislature because she articulated a more pro-environmental, mass-transit administrative vision, much like Brown's "small-is-better" orientation. In much the same manner, the senate's veto against the confirmation of Victor Veysey as Governor George "Duke" Deukmejian's head of the Department of Industrial Relations was in large part due to Veysey's noted "pro-business bias" and fear by a Democratically controlled senate that worker safety, among other issues, might get short shrift. The governor's independent powers are also reflected in various "independent" boards and commissions that cover a range of issues impacting a wide arena of state policy—from education policy to ethics to agricultural relations. Among the most important of these are the following:

- The five-person Public Utilities Commission, appointed by the governor for six-year terms, which regulates public and private utilities ranging from gas, water, electricity, and telephone service.
- The Fair Political Practices Commission. The FPPC was created by voters in June 1974 to police ethical reforms of the State's Political Reform Act covering in part campaign disclosures, lobbying activities, and legislators' election spending.
- The Board of Governors of the California Community Colleges. Oversees 71 locally controlled community college districts. The 16-member board is appointed for four-year terms by the governor.
- The University of California Regents, which governs the nine campuses of U.C. The Board of Regents consists of 18 members appointed by the governor for 12-year terms, 7 ex-officio members, and 1 U.C. student representative, who serve a one-year term.
- The Trustees of California State University, which governs the 23 campuses of California State University. There are 24 voting trustees, including 16 trustees appointed by the governor, who serve eight-year terms; an alumni trustee, a faculty trustee, and a student trustee, each of whom serve two-year terms; and five ex-officio members, including the Governor, Lieutenant Governor, Speaker of the Assembly, State Superintendent of Public Instruction, and the Chancellor.

The affirmative action debate launched by Governor Pete Wilson and some of his appointed regents is demonstrative of the governor's capacity to use independent powers to shape public policy discourse and direction.[5]

Informal Powers   Perhaps the most intangible asset, given the legacy of anti-governor feelings that date back as far as the colonial period, are the informal powers the governor wields. California governors have found that the informal powers associated with the office afford them a wide range of influence and control beyond the formal powers. For instance, the governor is the symbolic head of his or her party and, with allies in the state legislature, can move legislation through the process consistent with the prevailing ideology that defines the party. The governor traditionally plays a critical role during elections in helping to raise campaign funds to assist the party faithful and in shaping the party platform. In this role, some governors have come up against strong intra-party rivalries. Jerry Brown, a Progressive, clashed with the more "moderate" segment of the Democratic party. Moderates felt that Brown's "new spirit" campaign—based in part on his opposition to nuclear power, empathy for farm workers, and pro-consumerism—would alienate the middle-class and corporate supporters of the party. Pete Wilson was tested in holding off conservative challenges to keep the California Republican party from adopting a "pro-life" platform. The need to balance personal conviction with party politics remains the greatest challenge a governor can face.

The most significant of the governor's informal powers is the ability to use the "bully pulpit" of the office to move policy in a particular direction. Governors have immediate access to the state and national media and have used this leverage to manipulate public opinion. This power, however, is a double-edged sword: Governors also serve as lightning rods for frustrations in the state. Lackluster economic conditions, riots, even natural disasters are often laid at the feet of governors, reflected in poor job ratings and popularity polls. In Spring 1981, for example, Jerry Brown's perceived mishandling of the medfly crisis in the rich Central Valley region cost him dearly in votes and in earning nicknames like "Lord of the Flies."

The combination of explicit, independent, and informal powers enhances and limits gubernatorial authority in California. Gubernatorial style varies from governor to governor, with some more successful than others. Ronald Reagan leveraged his folksy style from the governor's office to the White House. Jerry Brown worked his progressive platform to the national race, but fell short. Still, he has reinvented himself as the mayor of Oakland, one of California's oldest and most significant cities.[6] Pete Wilson, an extremely successful governor, fell flat in each of his two unsuccessful attempts at national office. To paraphrase presidential scholar Richard Nuestadt, a governor's most important power may be his or her power to persuade.[7]

THE LIEUTENANT GOVERNOR

Like the vice president on the national level, the lieutenant governor is next in line for succession should the chief executive become incapacitated, but the actual powers of the office are few. Eight states have no such constitutional office. The lieutenant governor casts tie-breaking votes in the state senate, as the vice president must do in the U.S. Senate. The state constitution places the lieutenant governor as an ex-officio member of several powerful state boards and commissions, including the state Lands Commission, the California State University Board of Trustees, the Regents of the University of California, and chair of the California Economic Development Commission.

Unlike the vice president, however, the lieutenant governor is able to exercise executive power by sitting in as the acting governor when the governor travels outside state boundaries. Candidates for governor and lieutenant governor do not run together on the same ticket in California, as they do in many other states. And since the lieutenant governor is independently elected, winners are frequently from different parties. This can hamstring a governor with presidential aspirations. Republican Lieutenant Governor Mike Curb was a thorn in Democrat Jerry Brown's side during Brown's fundraising and campaign trips for his 1980 primary challenge to President Carter. During his short-lived run for the White House, Republican Pete Wilson had to contend with the prospect of then-Lieutenant Governor Gray Davis, a democrat, taking charge. In this sense, the election of two democrats in 1998, Gray Davis as Governor and Cruz Bustamante as Lieutenant Governor, was unusual.

THE ATTORNEY GENERAL

The attorney general is the head of the Department of Justice and the state's chief law enforcement official. Under Article V, Section 13 of the Constitution of the State of California, the attorney general must ensure that all state laws are "uniformly and adequately enforced." As chief legal advisor, the attorney general represents the state in lawsuits, offers "legal opinions" to the legislature on pending bills, and prepares titles and summaries for circulated propositions. In rare cases, the attorney general may step in as a district attorney in any of California's 58 counties if it becomes necessary for the state to enforce a legal mandate. Democrat Bill Lockyer promises to be much more of an activist than his recent predecessors in the attorney general's office. A former president pro tem of the state senate with close ties to the Davis administration, Lockyer has pledged to work as an advocate on consumer, environmental, and health issues.[8]

In government, it is often said that "A.G." stands not for attorney general, but for "aspiring governor." California is no exception. Pat Brown and George Deukmejian both held the office of attorney general before they were elected governor. Other attorneys general who tried unsuccessfully to make the move to the top spot include Republicans Evelle Younger and Dan Lungren, as well as Democrat John Van de Kamp.

THE CONTROLLER

The controller is the state's chief fiscal officer and the overseer of government finance. In that role, the controller chairs the Franchise Tax Board (which collects state income tax), is a member of the Board of Equalization (which collects state sales tax), and is a member of the state Lands Commission. The controller oversees the state payroll and has wide latitude in making sure state expenditures meet state law requirements. This once sleepy outpost of the executive branch has recently been turned around as an electoral staging area for other offices. Democrat Gray Davis used the office as a stepping stone on his way to the governorship, much as Alan Cranston moved from controller to the U.S. Senate in 1974. Controller Kathleen Connell has become a rising star in the Democratic party by conducting audits of the state government to identify potential savings.

THE SECRETARY OF STATE

The secretary of state is the chief election officer and the state's guardian of documents and records. The office grants charters to corporations, incorporates non-profit organizations, maintains the state archives, and is the keeper of the Great Seal of the State of California, which is affixed to all documents requiring the governor's signature. Much of the responsibility of the secretary of state's office revolves around its duties as chief elections officer. Not only does the secretary of state verify qualified voters' signatures on petitions for ballot measures, but he or she oversees all state election laws throughout the counties of California. From the printing of ballot arguments to the actual counting and centralization of election results, this office holds a prominent place within the plural executive. Former state Assemblyman Bill Jones won election as secretary of state in 1994 and is currently the highest-ranking Republican in the executive branch of the state government.

THE STATE TREASURER

The treasurer is the state's investment banker and the official in charge of maintaining the state's high credit rating. With an annual portfolio of more than $3 billion in state bonds, the treasurer is a major force on Wall Street, although he or she remains relatively obscure to the citizens of California. The treasurer prepares the selling and redemption of state bonds (mainly to finance large infrastructure projects such as dams, roads, and bridges) and also oversees the investment of securities and stock investments of public employee pension funds. Essentially, what the controller collects, the treasurer invests. Jesse Unruh raised the profile of the office during his 13 years as state treasurer, a tenure of service that ended with his death from cancer in 1987. In recent years, the job has been used as a staging area to campaign for higher office. Democrat Phil Angelides was elected to the post in 1998, after Republican incumbent Matt Fong chose to run for the U.S. Senate.

THE SUPERINTENDENT OF PUBLIC INSTRUCTION

The superintendent of public instruction heads up the State Department of Education. In this role the superintendent is both an independently elected official and an administrator who implements the policies of the ten-member appointed board of education. Although most decisions about education rest at the local level, the State Department of Education is often involved in such areas as teacher credentialing, text approval, curriculum adoption, and state fiscal assistance to local school districts. The superintendent sits ex-officio on the Board of Regents of the University of California, the California State University Board of Trustees, and on the Board of Governors of the Community College System.

While technically nonpartisan, the superintendent's office is at times swept up in politics. California public schools languished during the 1980s as a bitter political feud between Republican Governor George Deukmejian and Democratic leaning Superintendent Bill Honig prevented the two offices from cooperating on education policy. In 1994, former Assembly Education Committee Chair Delaine Eastin, a liberal Democrat, became superintendent. In the election, Eastin defeated Maureen DiMarco, a protégé of Republican Governor Pete Wilson. Over the next four years, Wilson seized the initiative on education policy and worked with his own appointed Secretary of Education and the legislature to increase funding and push for reduced class size in primary grades. Finding herself shut out of the process, Eastin used the office mainly as a bully pulpit. Under the Gray Davis administration, former State Senator Gary K. Hart, Davis' Secretary of Education, promised a closer relationship between the administration and the superintendent's office. Hart did deliver on his promises and helped steer several key educational bills through the legislature in Davis' first 100 days in office. Hart has left the administration but left his mark definitely on the fate of education in this state.

THE INSURANCE COMMISSIONER

Created with the 1988 passage of Proposition 103, voters added this statewide constitutional office to oversee the operations, rate setting, and regulatory functioning of the state Department of Insurance. Prior to the passage of Proposition 103, the commissioner was appointed by the governor. Consumer advocates had for years complained that there was "too cozy" a relationship between the insurance companies doing business in the state and the commissioner, who usually came from the insurance industry. Two years following the passage of Proposition 103, Democrat John Garamendi ran as a pro-consumer advocate and became the state's first elected insurance commissioner. He was succeeded in the commissioner's office by Republican Chuck Quackenbush, whose campaign was supported in large part by heavy contributions from the insurance industry. Quackenbush has since resigned amid accusations of financial misappropriations.

THE BOARD OF EQUALIZATION

In addition to these eight constitutional officers, California voters elect the five members of the state Board of Equalization. The state controller has a seat on the board, and the others are elected from four districts, each consisting of roughly one-fourth of the state's population. Two of the districts—one in coastal Northern California and the other in Los Angeles County—have a majority of Democratic voters. The other two are majority-Republican: one consisting of the Central Coast, Central Valley, and Sierra Nevada region, and the other consisting of Orange, San Diego, Riverside, and Imperial Counties. Despite the low political profile of this board, members wield a great amount of power in collecting state and local sales taxes as well as use taxes and excise taxes from the sale of gasoline, beverages, alcohol, and cigarettes. Another important function is to review and harmonize the tax assessments of California's 58 counties.

THE BUREAUCRACY

Working under the direction of the executive officers are the civil servants who do the work of government, from the clerks processing driver's licenses to CALTRANS crews repairing freeways to the officers of the California Highway Patrol. This is the "face" of California government embodied in the dedicated public employees comprising the state's civil service. By the beginning of Gray Davis' tenure as governor, the number of state employees had grown to 277,903. Figure 6.1 outlines the various agencies within the executive bureaucracy. Most of these positions have civil service protection, a reform designed to limit political patronage. In order to ensure that an incoming administration can be effective, agency heads and members of boards are exempt from this rule and serve at the will of the governor. The number of exempt positions has long been a point of contention between elected officials and agency staff. In his two terms as governor, Pete Wilson more than doubled the number of exempt positions, from 550 when he took office to 1,351 in 1996.[9]

Today's civil servants are addressing broad institutional pressures designed to make the system more efficient and less costly for taxpayers. Included in the agenda for change are issues ranging from privatization of key state industries to affirmative action to the right for collective bargaining. The state's public servants walk a delicate line between what we normally term as being "political" and being "technical." Civil servants hold an enormous amount of power since they are the ones who must actually implement the rules and dictates made by elected officials. Civil servants are foremost professionally minded individuals operating within a prevailing partisan environment. Ideally, they are neither Republican nor Democrat but neutral when serving in their official capacities, using their technical expertise to achieve the goals set by legal statute. In practice, however, there is some "wiggle-room" to mold a certain policy: In a particular fashion and depending upon which party controls the executive branch, we sometimes see a partisan-tinged outcome (yet still within the mandate of the law). In California, we see less of this behind-the-scenes manipulation than in other high-patronage states. Through competitive civil service examinations, the ethical constraints of a public administration career, and a workforce that is almost entirely covered by civil service's merit system protections, state employees are not beholden to elected officials to gain or keep their positions.[10] While the old dicta that "politicians come and go, but the bureaucrats last forever" rings somewhat true: California's civil service system has served Californians well since created in 1934. Explicit political pressure or favoritism is rare within the bureaucracy.

In 1977 state employees won the constitutional right to enter into collective-bargaining agreements to set wages, benefits, and working conditions. The Public Employment Relations Board was created to oversee collective bargaining and prevent unfair labor practices. State workers are mostly represented by the powerful California State Employees Association (CSEA), a major player in state politics and a major contributor to Governor Davis' campaign. As the state employee's political arm, CSEA has battled over such issues as closed-agency shops (meaning union dues can be collected from nonunion members) and the dismantling of state employment programs around affirmative action with the 1996 passage of Proposition 209.

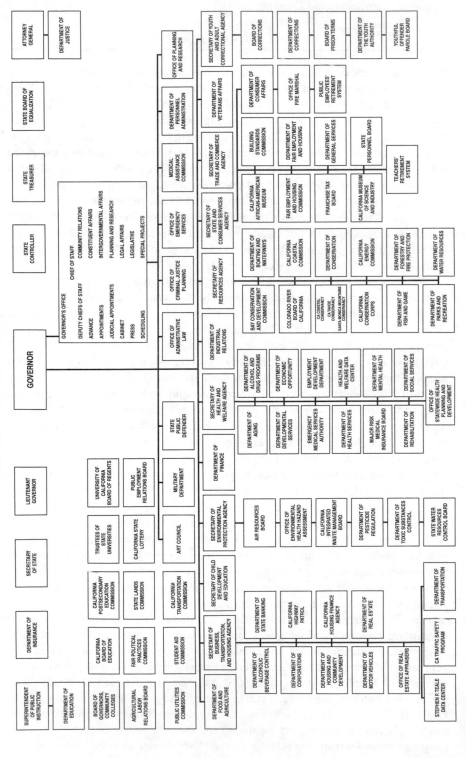

FIGURE 6.1 THE EXECUTIVE BUREAUCRACY

SUMMARY

In summary we can see that California's plural executive, with its vast bureaucracy, is functionally responsible for implementing programs and enforcing laws. And while the executive agencies play a major role in rulemaking[11] only the legislature or initiative process can create laws. This separation of powers is important in allowing for democratic oversight, as the following chapter suggests.

NOTES

1. Since the second constitution was adopted in 1878, the voters have called for a constitutional convention only once—in the 1930s—and the state legislature refused.
2. A third way to change the state constitution is for the legislature to set up a constitutional revision commission comprised of citizen appointees. These blue-ribbon commissions mainly "tinker-at-the edges," rather than systematically overhaul the document. Once the commission's recommendations are finalized, they are submitted back to the legislature for a two-thirds approval vote before they are sent on to the voters. Some modernizing efforts, such as the Sumner Commission (headed by Judge Bruce Sumner) in the 1960s–1970s made it to the voters and were approved. Another Constitution Revision Commission issued several recommendations in 1995 to overhaul state government, including a unicameral legislature, having the governor and lieutenant governor run for office together as a single ticket, reducing the number of elected constitutional offices to simplify the state ballot, and switching from an annual budget to a two-year budget. Unfortunately, the voters may never have an opportunity to consider these proposals because the legislature never took action on them. See Dan Bernstein, "Constitutional Reform Proposal Stuck in Limbo," *Sacramento Bee*, 1996, A4.
3. See Roger Noll, "Executive Organization: Responsiveness vs. Expertise and Flexibility," in *Constitutional Reform in California*, Bruce Cain and Roger Noll, eds. (Berkeley, CA: Institute for Governmental Studies, 1995).
4. The Guard was called out, for example, during the Northridge Earthquake in 1994, as well as in the civil unrest in Berkeley during the 1960s and in Los Angeles during 1965 and 1992.
5. Kit Lively, "A Jolt from Sacramento," *The Chronicle of Higher Education* (June 9, 1995): 25.
6. Though often in the shadow of San Francisco, Oakland has been a major force in the state's race relations and economic development since the nineteenth century.
7. Richard Neustadt, *Presidential Power* (New York: John Wiley and Sons, Inc., 1980).
8. Dan Morain, "Lockyer Prepares to Move into Leading Role," *Los Angeles Times*, 5 November 1998, S5.
9. A. J. Block and Claudia Buck, eds. *California Political Almanac* (Sacramento, CA: State Net Services & Publications, 1999), p. 80.
10. Ninety-eight percent of the state's civil servants are protected.
11. Rulemaking refers to an agency's responsibility to develop day-to-day rules for implementing state law. Statutes are written in a necessarily broad way, requiring agency interpretation during implementation.

CHAPTER 7

Lawmakers:
The Legislature
and Direct Democracy

This chapter explores the lawmakers, including both the state legislature and the unique elements of California's direct democracy: the initiative process, the referendum, and the recall. While most people think of the state legislature as the state's lawmakers, many of California's most significant laws have emerged through the initiative process—Proposition 13 and Proposition 209 are two examples. Still, the legislative authority of our elected representatives continues to provide the foundation and framework of California's democratic system.

THE LEGISLATURE

The state legislature is comprised of two bodies—the assembly and the senate. This bicameral arrangement is typical of every state in the union except Nebraska. The 80 members of the assembly are elected for two-year terms, and the 40 members of the senate are elected for four-year terms. Under Proposition 140, assembly members may serve a maximum of three terms (six years) and senators are limited to a maximum of two terms (eight years). Half of the senate and the entire assembly are elected in November of every even-numbered year.

The size and representation of each assembly and senate district is extremely important in the balance of democratization. Between 1923 and 1965 California's legislature was fashioned much like the congressional model: Representation in the assembly was based on population (like the House of Representatives) and the senate on counties (like geographic area in the U.S. Senate). The result was that rural central and northern counties dominated the legislature. For example, under the "federal plan" adopted in 1926, 21 senators from small northern and central counties represented less than 10 percent of the population; Los Angeles County, at the time with 35 percent of the state's population, had only one senator. The U.S. Supreme Court decision of *Reynolds v. Sims* (1964), and the subsequent decisions mandating "one-person-one-vote" in legislative districting, had a profound effect on the California Legislature.[1] California's 1966 elections ushered in a younger, better-educated, urban-based, more diverse cast of legislators, breaking the northern and central state's rural veto power over southern urban interests.

Legislative mapping is critical in defining power relations in the legislature. Every ten years, following the national census, the legislature must reapportion itself, drawing new district boundaries to equalize the shifting demographic changes. The intense political competition in California has made redistricting a hardball sport, pushing more mundane legislative business aside during reapportionment battles.[2] Typically, the majority party in the legislature will manipulate the district boundaries to increase its number of "safe" (non-competitive) seats.[3] The legislature adjusts all 120 districts in the state and realigns California's 52 congressional districts, so the stakes are quite high. The results are an abstract art, with some districts having very unusual patterns—one senate district ran from a section of the California coast clear across the mountains and deserts to the Arizona border. More importantly, the process gives an unfair advantage to the majority party in open-seat races. So gridlocked and distasteful have the last few reapportionment battles in California been that the state Supreme Court has been drawn into the fray. Following the 1991 redistricting plan the Court appointed three retired judges ("special masters") to draw up a more "objective" plan for the state to adopt. The year 2001 promises to be just as bad.

THE STATE OF THE LEGISLATURE

In November 1966 California voters overwhelmingly approved Proposition 1A, which sought to "professionalize" the part-time legislature.[4] Staff consultants were added, as were specialized adjunct offices including the senate and assembly offices of Research, Legislative Counsel, the Audit General, and the Legislative Analyst office. The California legislature was *the* model for other states to emulate. It was efficient, orderly, modern, and, most essentially, corruption-free. In the early 1970s it was rated by most experts of state governance as the nation's best state legislature. By the 1990s, however, California's legislature had lost much of its luster. Corruption, ideological and institutional gridlock, and budgetary politicking have given momentum to government reform efforts, though the results have been underwhelming.[5] While legislators collect annual paychecks of $99,000, plus generous expense accounts, the multibillion dollar state budget languishes each year past its constitutional deadlines. While partisan gridlock continues to dominate both houses, special interests have been amassing warchests to circulate confusing, often self-serving, propositions onto the California ballot through the initiative process. Reforming the legislature has proven to be a massive undertaking. Many argue that campaign finance reform heads the list of necessary changes. To be competitive in a typical state legislative race, a candidate must raise between $500,000 and $750,000. Proposition 112 cut down on potential payola scenarios by outlawing the practice of giving large honoraria to legislators. Proposition 140 term limits have not led to reduced campaign costs. Institutional reform will continue to be a major issue through the next decade.

THE HUMAN SIDE OF THE LEGISLATURE

The composition of the legislature's membership does not mirror the state's diversity. Asian legislators are grossly underrepresented given their proportion in the general public, as are Latino legislators (although Latinos are the fastest growing group of legislators, reflecting the statewide increase in Latino politicization). About one-quarter of the legislators are female—although women comprise over half of the state's population. African-American legislators comprise around 8 percent of the total legislature—about equal to their percentage in the overall public. There are currently three open lesbians who serve in both houses. White male legislators make up around 75 percent of the California legislature. The predominant occupation of most who enter the legislature are attorneys, followed by businesspeople. Critics argue that the lack of diversity represented by sitting legislators is a problem, especially when scarce resources are carved up. Others argue that representative democracy was never meant to be a pure looking-glass at ourselves. Indeed, it is the political parties who need to create an inclusive "big-tent" perspective, reflecting the concerns of all constituencies, if the legislature is to be successful.

The work of the legislature goes beyond the introduction and voting on individual pieces of legislation. Beyond pure lawmaking, legislators do the following: They provide constituent services, act as monitors to oversee and check executive agencies, function as budget negotiators during annual appropriations time in setting the state's budget, and, for those who sit in the state senate, they have responsibilities in confirming or rejecting hundreds of gubernatorial appointments to state boards, agencies, and commissions. Little of this could be accomplished without the professional assistance of personal member and institutional legislative staff. Personal staff helps the member in a number of ways: They are his or her "eyes and ears" in the district—helping constituents and looking after state issues as they impact the district; capitol personal staff help draft speeches, prepare and analyze bills for the member, and work with other party caucus staff to coordinate joint efforts. Institutional staff assist the entire membership of the legislative branch. For example, the legislative analyst office prepares an analysis of the governor's annual budget as well as assessing the fiscal implications of other legislative proposals and ballot measures. The legislative counsel office drafts the actual pieces of legislation introduced by every member of the legislature and offers legal opinions to members on state matters. Finally, the audit general office conducts both management and fiscal audits on behalf of the oversight function the legislature constitutionally possesses.

LEGISLATIVE ORGANIZATION AND PROCEDURES

The assembly and senate each have unique internal rules regarding their leadership structure, committee formation, and constitutional responsibilities. The senate serves under the state constitution as a confirming or ratifying body for gubernatorial appointments. And while the "power of the purse" is a joint legislative responsibility, the annual state budget bill traditionally starts in the assembly, which is closer to the electorate. A member of either house may introduce a bill, and a majority—21 votes in the

senate and 41 in the assembly—is needed for passage. A two-thirds majority is needed for "urgency" measures, constitutional amendments, and to pass the state budget.
As in the U.S. Congress, most legislative work gets done in standing or select committees. Assembly members generally serve on at least three committees, while senators, due to their smaller numbers, serve on four or five committees.

As on the federal level, leadership differs in each house. The lieutenant governor
is technically the senate's presiding officer, yet he or she is rarely present and only votes
to break a tie. The presiding officer of the senate is the president pro tempore, who also
sits as ex-officio chair of the powerful Senate Rules Committee. The Rules Committee assigns all senators to their respective committees and assigns all bills to committee.[6] The pro tempore is third in line of succession should the governor or lieutenant
governor be unable to administer their offices or are absent from the state.

The speaker of the assembly has long been regarded as the second most important office in the state.[7] Other than the governor, no one commands more centralized
power, visibility, and control over legislation as the office once dubbed the "Imperial Speakership." At one time, such speakers as Jesse Unruh and Willie Brown enjoyed the power to preside over the chamber and dominate all assembly floor action,
the power to select all chairs and vice chairs of the assembly's committees, and the
power to distribute all resources of the chamber—including such "perks" as prime
capitol office space, additional staff, and larger district budgets for sympathetic allies.
The speaker can also influence the nomination of other majority leadership positions—including the speaker pro tempore, majority floor leader, and caucus chair.
Successful speakers have maintained party discipline by centralizing campaign contributions from influential special interests who wish to curry favor with the majority party. During assembly elections, the speaker has traditionally used his or her
campaign war chest and consultants on behalf of his or her party faithful in order to
win or retain legislative seats. Once a member was elected—aided in large part by the
speaker's generosity—the member was expected to be loyal to the speaker's leadership and agenda. While many of the absolute powers of the Imperial Speakership
have been eroded or chipped away through the passage of term limits and restrictions
on the transfer of campaign funds, the speaker still retains a central role in California's
legislature and governance.[8] In the post-Willie Brown era, future speakers will have
to quickly advance their agendas and seek new governing coalitions (perhaps with
independents and moderates) to cement their leadership.[9]

THE LEGISLATIVE PROCESS

There are three types of legislation. A *bill* is simply a proposed statute that, if passed,
becomes a codified law. A *constitutional amendment* is a change to the state constitution, requiring a two-thirds vote of each house to be placed in front of the voters
in the next election. *Resolutions* are legislative expressions or opinions. They may
vary from an expression honoring a single constituent to a demand that another tier
of government do something or take a particular action. Resolutions have no legal
force, only that of moral suasion. They are normally passed on a voice vote and are

not subject to a gubernatorial veto. All legislation is signified by a set of initials, denoting its type and origin, as well as a unique identification number. For example, the number of a bill originating in the assembly is designated with an "AB," while a bill that originates in the senate begins with an "SB." The 3,000 bills introduced each year in the legislature come from every sector of California. While they must be carried and authored by a member of either chamber, the ideas for bills may come from the suggestions of average constituents or from any of the other actors in California politics, such as the governor, the judiciary, state constitutional officers, lobbyists and special interests, media, local and county governments, or from bureaucrats.

Figure 7.1 outlines the life cycle of a bill. When a bill is submitted, the member asks legislative counsel to do a legal "mock-up" of the bill and then delivers a signed copy to the "hopper" of the clerk of the assembly or the secretary of the senate. Its title is read, given a number, and printed. The state constitution requires that each bill receive three readings. After its first reading, the Rules Committee assigns it to a specific committee. After listening to testimony on both sides, the committee can act in several ways: It can pass it on by a majority vote; it can pass it with certain amendments; it can reconsider the bill at some future time; it can refer the bill to another committee; or it can effectively kill the measure by holding it in committee or sending it for interim study. Bills that have significant fiscal implications must not only be heard in a "policy committee," but also in a "fiscal committee," such as Assembly Ways and Means. If the bill is approved by the committee(s) it is sent back to the floor of its originating chamber to be read a second time and is scheduled for floor debate. Bills are read for the third time, debated, and followed up with an electronically recorded roll-call vote in the assembly or a voice vote in the senate. Only by unanimous vote of the entire chamber can a vote be switched, and only if the change does not recast the outcome.

If the bill passes one chamber, it is sent on to the other and the process is replicated. If amendments are added in the second house, it must go back to the house of origin for a vote on the changes. If the changes are approved, the bill goes immediately to the governor for signature or veto. If changes are not approved the bill goes to a conference committee composed of three senators and three members of the assembly. The conference committee may kill the measure if there is no agreement or amend it still further and issue a conference report, which is then sent back to both houses for approval. If both approve, the measure goes to the governor. If one house rejects the report, additional conference committees may be formed to try to iron out differences.

DIRECT DEMOCRACY: INITIATIVES, REFERENDA, AND RECALLS

Another important aspect of California's political structure are the mechanisms of direct democracy. Because of their belief in the corrupting influence of big business over politics, reformers in the Progressive era were convinced that an active and attentive electorate should check their elected representatives through direct ballot

FIGURE 7.1 THE LIFE CYCLE OF LEGISLATION

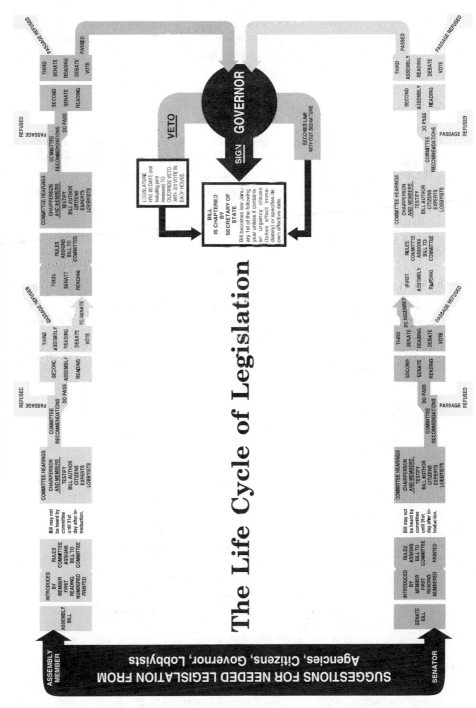

The Life Cycle of Legislation

75

measures. By 1911 the Progressives succeeded in adding three instruments to the state constitution, empowering Californians to make policy themselves—and even to reverse the actions of government—while preserving the framework of representative democracy.

THE INITIATIVE

The initiative is a tool that citizens may use to amend the state constitution or establish a state statute. To place a constitutional amendment on the ballot, petitioners must gather the signatures of 8 percent of registered voters (based on the number of voters in the last gubernatorial election). For a simple statute, only 5 percent is needed. In real numbers, this means that in the 150 days permitted to circulate a petition, one needs to collect over 690,000 valid signatures for a constitutional change and over 430,000 valid signatures for a statutory initiative. This is no easy task for grassroots activists. It has become relatively easy, however, for well-financed interests to place initiatives on California's ballot. The business of proposing initiatives, circulating petitions, and campaigning for the measures has become a major industry in California.

The use of paid signature-gatherers to qualify ballot proposals increased dramatically in the 1960s and 1970s. An attempt to restrict spending on ballot initiatives in 1974 was struck down by the California Supreme Court after the U.S. Supreme Court ruled that most campaign spending limits were unconstitutional on the grounds that they violate free speech.[10] It has become common for political consulting firms to initiate ballot measure drives simply to generate business. It is not unusual for a single company to gather the signatures, raise money, and produce ads in favor of an initiative that it initiated in the first place. In the 1980s, a Georgia manufacturer of lottery tickets, working with the firm of Butcher-Forde, spent $2.3 million to qualify and campaign for Proposition 37, which resulted in the California state lottery.[11] In 1992, all seven of the initiatives that appeared on the general election ballot were qualified with the help of just two firms: Kimball Petition Management, based in Los Angeles, and American Petition Consultants, based in Sacramento.[12] Ironically, the initiative process, which originated in a reform movement meant to limit the influence of special interests, has empowered those interests at the expense of representative democracy. Table 7.1 reveals the broad range of subject matter and the increasing frequency of proposed initiatives and statewide referenda in the decades since 1912.

Of the 23 states that allow statewide initiatives, only 17 allow constitutional amendments through this process, and California places the fewest restrictions on the content of these initiatives.[13] The only check to the citizen initiative constitutional amendment is final judicial review by the courts. For example, in 1964 the U.S. Supreme Court ruled unconstitutional Proposition 14, which was intended to repeal the Rumford Fair Housing Act, which prevented racial discrimination in the sale of homes. The constitutional amendment passed with over two-thirds of the statewide vote, yet was ruled null and void.[14] A similar fate may be awaiting the review of two recent constitutional amendments: Proposition 187 (see Chapter 13) and Proposition 209, also known as the "California Civil Rights Initiative" (see Chapter 14).

TABLE 7.1   INITIATIVES AND REFERENDA BY SUBJECT, BY DECADE:
NUMBER ON BALLOT (NUMBER APPROVED)

DECADE	BOND ACTS*	ELECTIONS	TAXATION	ECONOMIC REGULATION	EDUCATION	HEALTH	MORALS	ENVIRONMENT	CIVIL RIGHTS & LIBERTIES
1912–1919	2 (1)	6 (0)	6 (1)	5 (2)	1 (1)	2 (0)	10 (2)	0	0
1920–1929	1 (1)	5 (2)	8 (1)	12 (2)	3 (1)	7 (3)	6 (2)	1 (1)	0
1930–1939	1 (0)	2 (1)	7 (0)	11 (4)	3 (0)	3 (0)	8 (3)	7 (1)	0
1940–1949	0	0	3 (1)	3 (0)	3 (2)	1 (0)	3 (0)	1 (0)	1 (0)
1950–1959	0	1 (0)	4 (1)	1 (0)	3 (2)	0	1 (0)	1 (0)	
1960–1969	0	0	1 (0)	1 (1)	0	0	1 (0)	0	2 (1)
1970–1979	1 (1)	1 (1)	5 (3)	1 (0)	3 (1)	1 (0)	4 (0)	4 (2)	4 (2)
1980–1989	1 (1)	4 (3)	11 (5)	8 (3)	2 (2)	10 (5)	0	7 (4)	8 (4)
1990–1996	19 (7)	8 (5)	21 (8)	18 (5)	7 (4)	7 (1)	3 (1)	13 (4)	14 (13)
Total	**25 (11)**	**27 (12)**	**66 (20)**	**60 (17)**	**25 (13)**	**31 (9)**	**36 (8)**	**34 (12)**	**29 (20)**

*General category. Bond acts are broken down into specific categories, such as education.

THE REFERENDUM

There are two types of referenda. The first is the "protest" referendum, giving voters the power to cancel a piece of legislation approved by the legislature and the governor before it actually goes into effect. Typical legislation (except for urgency measures) have a time delay of 90 days after passage before the law is enacted. A petition of at least 5 percent of the votes cast for all candidates for governor in last gubernatorial election can suspend this legislation until the next statewide election, giving the voters an opportunity to register their preferences. The referendum has rarely been used at the state level because of the difficulties of gathering so many signatures within a 90-day window. In one recent exception, voters overwhelmingly approved Proposition 163, overturning the state "snack tax" in 1992.[15]

Referenda have been more common at the local level to halt unpopular municipal acts. The second type of referendum, which is used more frequently, follows the state constitutional requirements that all legislatively based efforts to sell state bonds, as well as all legislatively sponsored constitutional amendments, be put before the voters. Thus, it is by legislative action rather than by petition that this type of referendum appears on the ballot. If the legislature wants to amend a proposal previously passed through the initiative process, such action must first pass both houses of the legislature and then appear on the ballot for popular vote.

THE RECALL

The recall election was designed as a mechanism to remove corrupt politicians from office. In order to mount a recall, petitioners must gather signatures of 12–20 percent of those who voted in the last election. If this effort is successful, a special election is held to decide whether to remove the official before the end of his or her term. A recall is not the same as impeachment, which is available to the legislature if it seeks to remove a sitting official for malfeasance. Because there are no specified grounds needed to remove an official, recalls have been increasingly used to punish politicians for taking unpopular policy positions. In some recent examples, former Assembly Speaker Doris Allen, a Republican, was recalled for being too cozy with assembly Democrats. The gun lobby unsuccessfully tried to recall Senate Pro Tem David Roberti over his support of an assault weapon ban. These types of recalls against state representatives have escalated, not because of concern over corruption as the Progressives had envisioned, but purely for revenge by highly mobilized interest groups.[16]

SUMMARY

California's political institutions are in need of repair. Blue-ribbon panels have issued numerous proposals to reform the system, ranging from a unicameral legislature to reducing the number of constitutional offices. Proponents of reform argue that these reforms would reduce the fragmentation of power, cut legislative gridlock, strengthen the governorship, and simplify the ballot. However, the state's elected officials have not embraced these ideas.

Direct democracy, an innovative reform of the Progressive era, has become problematic in the setting of modern-day California. Frustrated voters have preferred to use the initiative process to lash out at the system through term limits and other initiatives, which undermine the effectiveness and discretionary power of elected representatives by heaping new amendments onto the constitution. Term limits may only serve to enhance the power of the bureaucracy, as legislative and constitutional "short-timers" lacking experience in government are forced to rely on agency expertise. At the same time, special interests have learned to effectively exploit the initiative process by running big-budget campaigns and inducing policy changes at the ballot box, effectively bypassing the opportunity for meaningful debate within a democratically elected legislature.

Columnist David Broder expressed this sentiment when he commented that California policy suffered from "Californocracy."[17] By allowing non-elected citizens to place measures on the statewide ballot and to approve or disapprove specific policies, he argued, representative democracy suffers. The legislature is too often encouraged to pass difficult decisions on to the public— a public that is too often apathetic and uninformed. On the other hand, there is a valid reason for the endurance of direct democracy. Californians demand input and participation, even if the result is often less than desirable. A process that grants citizens the *potential* to participate is perhaps more important to Californians than the outcome.

Notes

1. See *Baker v. Carr*, 369 U.S. 186 (1962); *Wesberry v. Sanders*, 376 U.S. 1 (1964); *Reynolds v. Sims*, 377 U.S. 533 (1964); *Mahan v. Howell*, 410 U.S. 315 (1973); *City of Mobile v. Bolden*, 446 U.S. 55 (1980).
2. See A. G. Block, "The Reapportionment Failure," *California Journal* (November 1991): 503–505.
3. This is often referred to as gerrymandering.
4. Proposition 1A was a product of legendary Assembly Speaker Jesse Unruh.
5. Between 1986 and 1994, for example, Shrimpgate, an FBI sting centered on the shrimp market, netted several legislators, staff, and lobbyists in extortion, racketeering, and conspiracy charges.
6. Much of the power of the Rules Committee is in their power to "kill" a bill simply by sending it to an unsympathetic committee.
7. Dan Morain, "Assessment of Brown's Speakership Is a Mixed Bag," *Los Angeles Times*, 8 June 1995, 1.
8. As demonstrated in Propositions 68 and 73.
9. John Borland, "Fade from Brown," *California Journal* (April 1996): 8–13.
10. See *Hardie v. Eu*, 18 Cal. 3rd 371 (1976); *Buckley v. Valejo*, 424 U.S. 1 (1976).
11. For a discussion of the unintended consequences of direct democracy, see Peter Schrag, *Paradise Lost: California's Experience, America's Future* (New York: The New Press, 1997), pp. 188–256.
12. Charlene Wear Simmons, "California's Statewide Initiative Process" (Sacramento, CA: California Research Bureau, 1997).

13. Some critics have called the state constitution "hyper-amendable." For example, 27 constitutional amendments appeared on the ballot in the form of initiatives between 1980 and 1994, 10 of which were approved by the voters. See Bruce Cain, Sara Ferejohn, Margarita Najar, and Mary Walther, "Constitutional Change: Is It Too Easy to Amend our State Constitution?" in *Constitutional Reform in California*, Bruce Cain and Roger Noll, eds. (Berkeley, CA: Institute of Governmental Studies, 1995).
14. See discussion in Raphael J. Sonenshein, *Politics in Black and White* (Princeton, NJ: Princeton University Press, 1993), pp. 68–73.
15. Amy Chance, "Welfare Measure Loses: Snack Tax Repeal Wins," *Sacramento Bee*, 4 November 1994, A1.
16. Eric Bailey and Dan Morian, "Capitol Game: Revenge of a Spurned Politician," *Los Angeles Times*, 7 June, 1995, A1. Also A. G. Block, "A Twisted Tale of Revenge," *California Journal* (January 1996): 34–41.
17. David S. Broder, "Californocracy in Action," *Washington Post*, 13 August 1997, A21.

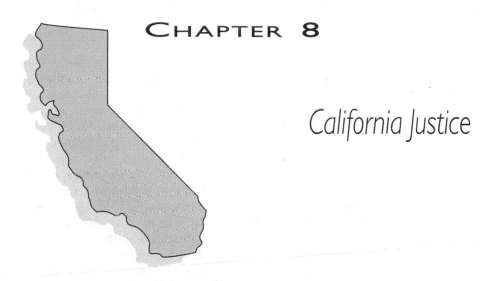

CHAPTER 8

California Justice

We're here ... to carry out the will of the people. If the people and the State want three strikes, then we say that's fine, but they have to realize that we need ... resources.... What worries me is when people begin to feel (that) they don't have access to the courts, that they have to go to [private alternatives]. If you're rich, fine; if not, tough, go to the streets.

—Los Angeles Superior Court Judge Gary Klausner

The judiciary is often held up as insulated from the daily machinations of politics. In reality, the judiciary and the entire justice system are political institutions, and judicial outputs (e.g., legal decisions, court resource allocation, police oversight) are political variables that render a specific judicial philosophy. Politics permeates the justice system from every corner: Governors select like-minded jurists to sit on the benches of California courts; the legislature sets and approves court budgets, prison construction and judicial laws; California's multiple law enforcement chiefs—from the attorney general to each county's district attorney—are elected officials responding to political pressures from their respective constituencies; judges must face the electorate in judicial elections and are subject to recall, sometimes falling prey to public opinion and special interests. Judicial outputs therefore are politically-tinged but have a great amount of power in molding public policy and the political process.

From the 1940s through the 1960s California's system of justice was held up as a model for other state judiciaries. It won praise for its independence and judicial decision making. Under the guidance of forceful leadership, demonstrated by chief justices such as Donald Wright, Roger Traynor, and Phil Gibson, the California Supreme Court often influenced the path that the U.S. Supreme Court would follow. The California Court became a national leader because it pioneered the "independent-state-grounds" doctrine to provide expanded individual rights beyond those mandated under the U.S. Constitution. Justice Stanley Mosk (an Edmund G. "Pat" Brown appointee) argued that while the U.S. Supreme Court sets the constitutional rulings for the nation, those constitutional grounds should be regarded as the basic floor, or minimum, not the ceiling. Thus individual states are always free to provide more expanded constitutional guarantees than the more restrictive ones interpreted from the U.S Constitution.

This doctrine has, at times, encouraged the California Supreme Court to follow a more liberal interpretation. For example, the court expanded the Ninth Amendment's "zone of privacy" to guarantee women in California greater reproductive rights. Critics of the doctrine argue that this is inappropriate judicial rulemaking fostered by judicial-activism, preventing a proper separation of powers, and producing inconsistent rulings across the mosaic of states as each is left to provide its own interpretation on what is constitutional and to what degree. With the conservative turn of the California Supreme Court by the mid-1980s, this doctrine has fallen from being in vogue, deferring more often than not to the U.S. Supreme Court for judicial direction. It is left to be seen if the Gray Davis future judicial appointments to the State Supreme Court will take the court back in the opposite direction. Chances are these new jurists will be centralists (as is Davis' style and tendency)—conservative on questions of criminal law; more liberal on civil liberties, labor, and environmental issues. An interesting perspective that may indeed lead California's judiciary back to the model for the nation.[1]

THE COURTS

The state and local courts are the backbone of the nation's justice system. Nine out of every ten court cases in the United States are conducted in state courts. Each year state court systems throughout the United States process approximately 80 million civil, criminal, and traffic cases.[2] It is also on the state judicial level that most citizens interact with the state—either in the form of settling conflicts or in the manifest of state law, ranging from wills and probate to contracts and torts to marriage, divorce, and adoption. The structure of California's judicial system is outlined in Article VI of the state constitution. The courts can be divided into two distinct levels: trial courts and appellate courts. Trial courts are the initial points of access to the judiciary. Trial courts have original jurisdiction because the cases originate there. Municipal courts, justice courts, and superior courts make up this lower level. Appellate courts are designed to hear appeals from the lower courts and have no original jurisdiction. The appellate level includes the Court of Appeals and the California Supreme Court. In addition to the courts, four important institutions assist the judiciary. They include the Commission on Judicial Appointments, the Commission on Judicial Performance, the Judicial Council, and the Commission on Judicial Nominees Evaluation.

MUNICIPAL COURTS

Municipal courts have jurisdiction in both civil and criminal law cases. These courts hear misdemeanor criminal cases, civil lawsuits involving less than $25,000, small-claims actions, and preliminary hearings on some felony charges. Felony trials are held in superior court. Municipal court judges are elected in nonpartisan races for six-year

FIGURE 8.1   CALIFORNIA COURT SYSTEM

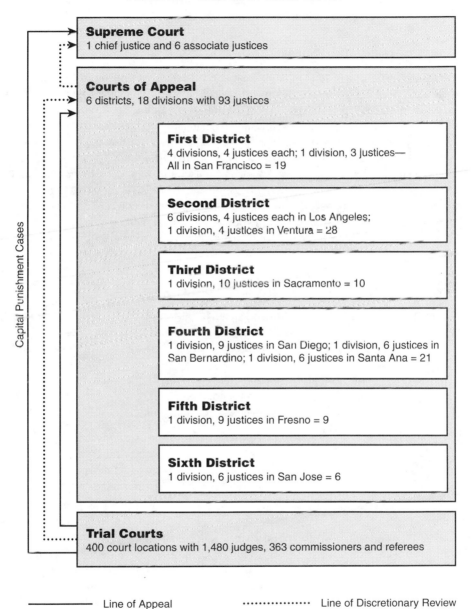

Supreme Court
1 chief justice and 6 associate justices

Courts of Appeal
6 districts, 18 divisions with 93 justices

First District
4 divisions, 4 justices each; 1 division, 3 justices—
All in San Francisco = 19

Second District
6 divisions, 4 justices each in Los Angeles;
1 division, 4 justices in Ventura = 28

Third District
1 division, 10 justices in Sacramento = 10

Fourth District
1 division, 9 justices in San Diego; 1 division, 6 justices in
San Bernardino; 1 division, 6 justices in Santa Ana = 21

Fifth District
1 division, 9 justices in Fresno = 9

Sixth District
1 division, 6 justices in San Jose = 6

Trial Courts
400 court locations with 1,480 judges, 363 commissioners and referees

Capital Punishment Cases

————— Line of Appeal   ·············· Line of Discretionary Review

Note: Death penalty cases are automatically appealed
from the Superior Court directly to the Supreme Court.

Source: Judicial Council of California/Administrative Office of the Courts.

terms. With over 600 judges throughout the state, municipal courts process over 90 percent of the state's judicial business.[3]

SUPERIOR COURTS

The state constitution requires that at least one superior court reside in each county of the state. Superior courts hear felony criminal cases and civil matters over $25,000.[4] Superior courts may also act as courts of appeal for municipal court renderings. Due in large part to the rise of juvenile crime and the mandatory "Three Strikes You're Out" initiative, criminal felonies (crimes that carry a penalty of one year or more) have been jamming the court caseload in urban and suburban superior courts. The average time to hear a civil law case in Los Angeles County for example, is between five and seven years. Over 700 superior court judges are elected for six-year terms in nonpartisan races. If a vacancy occurs, the governor may appoint a replacement to sit on the bench until the next election. Given the power of judicial incumbency, these gubernatorial appointments are typically retained during the following election cycle, guaranteeing long-term employment as a jurist.

DISTRICT COURTS OF APPEAL

The state is divided into six court of appeals districts with over 88 jurists elected for 12-year terms. These courts serve as a screening mechanism to reduce the workload of the state supreme court. They usually grant appeals considering only "questions of law," not "questions of fact." There are no juries, no introductions of evidence, or interrogations of witnesses. In the appellate court, normally three jurists sit as a full panel, considering transcripts from the lower court and brief oral arguments. The court of appeals also has jurisdiction over decisions of quasi-judicial state boards. While most verdicts are upheld from the lower court, an appeal is still possible directly to the state supreme court.[5]

CALIFORNIA SUPREME COURT

The California Supreme Court is composed of one chief justice and six associate justices. As the highest court in the state, it has been an active participant in the major public policy debates from civil rights to the death penalty to the status of immigrants in the state. The court has broad discretionary authority to decide which civil and criminal cases it will hear, with cases involving capital punishment receiving proforma review. The state supreme court does have original jurisdiction to issue writs (or orders) over the following areas: (1) *habeas corpus* ("produce the body"), which requires that a state-detained person must be brought before a judge so that legal detention can be determined; (2) *prohibition*, which prevents a lower court from exercising jurisdiction over a certain case; and (3) *mandamus* (or mandate), which commands a public servant to perform a specific duty under their domain. An example of mandamus would be the state supreme court ordering a county district attorney to enforce provisions of the "Three Strikes" initiative.

In its role as the state's final court of appeals, the state supreme court considers approximately 150 of the 3,000–4,000 cases appealed. In the cases that are decided, written majority and minority opinions are rendered based on a legal analysis of state statutes and the state constitution. As a symbol of its separation from the political world, the supreme court makes its home not in Sacramento, but in foggy San Francisco. Supreme court judges are confirmed for 12-year terms in the same manner as district court judges.

The court must begin by first determining if it wants to review a lower court's decision based primarily on the constitutional grounds of the California constitution. In this first stage is largely how we come to define the "tone and character" of a particular sitting supreme court. A "judicial activist court" will lean in favor of pursuing broad policy and political debates, reaching if necessary into the lower courts to pull cases that best reflect a ripeness for judicial review. A less activist court, following what judicial scholars term a "court of judicial restraint," would tend to rule very narrowly on cases it accepts, shying away from overturning legislative decisions or inserting itself in the political battles around the controversial policy battles of the moment.

Starting with the court clerks who prepare and research a conference memorandum, the court at its weekly conference meeting decides which cases shall be reviewed or which decisions "shall be left standing" (meaning the decision rendered from the lower courts shall be final). The granting of a case to move forward requires four affirmative votes. One of the justices voting for review of a particular case will be assigned the task of preparing a calendar memorandum (closely resembling a draft legal opinion) for the rest of his judicial colleagues to review. At this stage there is some legal horse-trading back-and-forth as each individual jurist renders his or her own deletions/additions; approval/dissenting positions on the draft. When four or more jurists approve with the outline of resolving the case, the chief justice will then move forward in scheduling it for oral arguments.

Hearing oral arguments from attorneys from both sides of a case takes place for one week of every month, except July and August. The oral argument phase of determining a case is not an opportunity to re-try the matter at hand. Rather it is an opportunity for the court to inquire about the fine points of the law and for individual justices to reexamine their initial position on the pending case. After oral arguments, the justices will reconvene and if there is still a majority of the court (four or more members) in favor of resolution of the case, the chief justice will assign one of the members in the majority to draft the final legal decision. After the majority opinion is finished and circulated to all the seven justices, dissenting and concurring opinions may be issued as the court publicly hands down its legal rendering.

JUDICIAL SELECTION

Vacancies of judges on the district court of appeals and the supreme court are chosen in the following three-step method: (1) governor's nomination; (2) approval by the Commission on Judicial Appointments (in consultation with the Commission on Judicial

Nominees Evaluation. Both are discussed later in more detail); (3) in the first guber-natorial election after an appointment has been approved, a confirmation vote (good for a 12-year term) is held. There are no opposing candidates, only a voter's choice between "yes" and "no" with the question: "Shall _____ be elected to the office for the term prescribed by law?"

Judges on the municipal and superior courts are chosen by the voters in a non-partisan election for six-year terms. The only requirement for judges who serve at this level is that they must have practiced law for at least five years and be in good standing with the state bar. Since most voters know little about a jurist's temperament or judicial renderings, incumbency plays a major role. Over 95 percent of judges throughout California face no opposition and are automatically re-elected. While tra-ditional endorsements for judicial candidates may mean something (especially in the few contested judicial races), little campaign money is raised overall (especially in comparison to, say, state legislative races). Most of the money raised goes to "state mailings" and other direct voter contact.

In the end, the prevailing question on most citizens' minds in California is: Should we have an elected judiciary at all? Or should judges be "above electoral politics" and perhaps appointed for life terms? In which case is democracy better served? Is there a danger in compromising impartiality of the judiciary if unpopular legal deci-sions come back to haunt a judge during election cycles? Or should judges be ac-countable to the "will of the people" keeping judges (like every other public servant) responsive to the needs of the governed?

The balancing act between judicial accountability and judicial independence is a sensitive one. Throughout the decades of the 1960s and 1970s, the California Supreme Court was held in high esteem for its professional and progressive decisions that went head-on into the controversies of the day. From equalizing school funding formulas across the state regardless of local tax bases; to desegregating school districts by court-ordered busing; to intervening to broaden the legal rights of defendants in criminal cases; to ending the quota system in higher education by highlighting "reverse dis-crimination," yet affirming affirmative action as a lofty goal; to declaring the uncon-stitutionality of the death penalty (later restored by legislative mandate)—the California Supreme Court was in the eye of the hurricane practicing what some would call "ju-dicial activism"—an active partner in shaping major public policy debates.

By 1986 an unprecedented event occurred: Supreme Court Chief Justice Rose Bird and two associate justices, Cruz Reynoso and Joseph Grodin, were voted out of office by the voters. Rose Bird especially became a lightning rod of the voters' frus-tration—losing by a landslide of 32 points, the first time this has happened in Cali-fornia's 52 years under its judicial-retention election process.

The defeat of three liberal judges gave Governor George Deukmejian the rare opportunity to stack (or "pack") the court with conservative "judicial restraint" ap-pointees. Governor Pete Wilson followed in this path as well. Thus, under the "Mal-colm Lucas and Ronald George court era" we have witnessed a 180-degree turn in the tendencies of the court. For example, in the area of criminal law, the post-Bird courts have rarely turned down a lower-court-ordered death penalty decision, except in some unusual cases where gross trial errors were made. As the court now enters its next era with Governor Gray Davis nominees for judgeships coming forth, we will again probably see a shift (although not as drastic) in the court's direction.

THE JUDICIAL BUREAUCRACY

There are four institutions that assist the courts in California and are themselves key actors in the judicial system. The state Judicial Council is a 21-member board that oversees the overall administration of the court system. The Judicial Council consists of 15 judges from all tiers of the court system, plus four lawyers from the state bar and two members of the state legislature. The chief justice chairs the council. The purpose of the council is to improve the efficiency and workload of the courts, keep records, organize various seminars for trial and appellate court judges, conduct research on the court system, periodically brief the legislature on the "state of the courts," and propose judicial reforms.

One recent blue-ribbon report issued by the Judicial Council is worth noting. California has used the traditional standard jury system. *Grand juries* (19–23 citizens depending on the county) investigate public officials and agencies and can return indictments. *Trial juries* usually consist of 12 registered voters in civil and misdemeanor cases; fewer than 12 may be used if both parties agree.

The Judicial Council has put forth a reform proposal to transform California's jury system by allowing non-unanimous verdicts (11–1 vote) in felony convictions except in the cases of death penalty or life in prison; encouraging jurors to confer during trial; and punishing jurors who shirk their civic responsibility.[6] All eligible citizens of California are required to serve on a trial jury if summoned. Only a few individuals are automatically excused from serving: ex-felons, police officers, and some government employees. Trial juries are composed of citizens whose names are drawn from the state's voter rolls and vehicle registration lists. Being a juror is not glamorous—with limited court compensation and long delays in getting impaneled on a jury (some describe this as waiting in a "cattle-car" environment or indentured servitude approaching "state slavery"). Despite the hassles, jurors serve as critical participants in the democracy we all treasure via a judicial system we all recognize is a cherished commodity. The controversies surrounding the jury systems are set in historical record. Some, like Alexis de Tocqueville, saw jury service as "one of the most efficacious means for education of people which society can employ."[7] Others viewed the jury system with disdain for its capriciousness of lay citizens unfamiliar with the law.

A second panel is the Commission on Judicial Performance. Created in 1961, the commission is made up of 11 members, only 3 of whom are judges. This commission investigates complaints about judicial misconduct or malfeasance and can recommend the censure, recall, or removal of a judge ruled unfit to serve. The supreme court may discipline or remove a judge (or a court referee or court commissioner) upon recommendation of the Commission on Judicial Performance. The supreme court must remove any sitting judge found guilty of a felony or a crime involving "moral turpitude." Lastly, the commission can also recommend the censure, removal, or retirement of justices who are on the supreme court after the approval of a tribunal of seven court of appeals judges selected by lot.

In 1994, the legislature proposed a constitutional reform measure (Proposition 190) that opened up the commission to greater public scrutiny and review. Monitoring the professional ethics of more than 1,500 judges that sit on California's tribunals at all levels is no easy mandate. Having a "closed system" whereby judges would essentially monitor other judges just seemed outdated and fraught with the potential for accusations of cover-ups. Proposition 190, passed overwhelmingly by the voters, established new guidelines for the commission and a "sunshine strategy" to remove these past hearings from secrecy to open exposure. Furthermore, it rearranged the composition of the commission itself, tipping the scales to "citizen non-lawyers" as the controlling majority on the commission in charge of regulating judicial behavior and conduct.

The two remaining commissions rate judicial appointments. The Commission on Judicial Nominees Evaluation is a 25-member body of the California Bar Association and rates the judicial nominees of the governor. The governor is required by statute to submit nominees for judgeships to the commission to determine fitness for the position. Confidential recommendations are supposed to be returned to the governor regarding each name he submits. The rankings are quite simply: "exceptionally well-qualified," "well-qualified," or "not qualified." The commission thus acts as a "pre-screen" for evaluating gubernatorial appointees and can actually act as a check on the governor should a "not qualified" candidate be moved ahead—perhaps using the public stage to embarrass the governor when this jurist runs for judicial office on the ballot. The "checks and balances" historically provided by this commission, may itself be up for reinterpretation. Former Governor Pete Wilson for example, tossed aside the "unqualified" rating by the commission in his nominee to the supreme court, Janice Rogers Brown.[8] What normally would have been an embarrassment for Pete Wilson, turned out to be "political fodder" for him. Wilson took on the commission, arguing that the individual members were biased against Ms. Brown, who happened not only to be a politically conservative woman, but also an African American.

Finally, the Commission on Judicial Appointments must approve a governor's nominee to the court of appeals. A majority must vote in approving the nomination, normally with input from the Commission on Judicial Nominees Evaluation. Only once has the commission officially rejected a governor's nomination, but in the past the commission has also caused the governor to view "the political tea leaves on the table" causing him to remove his nominee from consideration based on the prevailing votes. Supporters of this commission process insist this body serves as a "de-politicized" reviewing mechanism against a governor's appointment of unqualified individuals to the appellate bench. They point to the highly politically charged process on the federal level where a president's judicial nominee must be confirmed by a majority of the U.S. Senate. Critics, however, are still dismayed that the commission may still block nominees—not so much based on their legal qualifications, but on their pronounced judicial philosophy. This was clearly evident during the Jerry Brown days when then Attorney General George Deukmejian threw his weight around to block several liberal (yet highly qualified) Brown judicial nominees. In another case described earlier, where Pete Wilson pushed ahead with his nomination of Supreme Court Judge Janice Rogers Brown despite her "unqualified" ratings, she was able to muster a unanimous vote of approval from this three-member commission. Proving once again, politics sometimes does override judicial standards.

Judicial policymaking is laden with political undertones. The criminal justice system is directly affected by what the courts, judges, and politicians decide to prioritize. California's prison system is one of the state's largest growth sectors—consuming almost 10 percent of the state's general fund revenues. This is not surprising, given the current "tough-on-crime" attitudes of the populace and the judicial system. Critics and supporters are still arguing over the end results of California's criminal policies: Has crime gone down because of stricter punishment, longer determined sentences, and capital punishment? Or are other less tangible issues, like a thriving economy, low unemployment rates, and a general aging of the population, driving the spiral downwards? However we cut the deck, Californians will continue to tinker with their judicial apparatus, which in turn will affect the criminal justice and civil law system.

NOTES

1. In fact, in many controversial areas (such as police searches, busing, and the death penalty), the voters of the state used the initiative process to overturn several unpopular judicial mandates.
2. Bureau of Justice Statistics, *State Court Caseload Statistics* (Washington, D.C.: U.S. Printing Office, 1983).
3. In 1994, all justice courts in California were converted to municipal courts. They were essentially holdovers from the days when jurists and juries were too far away from remote rural areas to obtain a judicial resolution. Once administered by "justices of the peace," mostly in rural counties, they functioned in the same jurisdictional arena as did the municipal court structure.
4. With the rise in civil litigation and the mandatory sentencing of the "Three Strikes" initiative, urban courts are severely overloaded. It currently takes between five and seven years to hear a civil lawsuit in Los Angeles County.
5. Judicial vacancies on the district courts of appeals and the supreme court are filled in the following method: First, the governor appoints a replacement, which must be approved by the Commission on Judicial Appointments. Then, in the first gubernatorial election after an appointment approval, a confirmation vote (good for a 12-year term) is held. There are no opposing candidates, and the voters may only vote "yes" or "no" for each judge.
6. Stephanie Wilson, "Major Reforms Proposed for California Juries," *Los Angeles Times*, 30 April 1996, A3.
7. Alexis de Tocqueville, *Democracy in America*, Phillip Bradley, ed. (New York: Vintage Books, 1945), p. 296
8. See Charles L. Linder, "Will Wilson Defy State Supreme Court History?" *Los Angeles Times*, 28 April 1996, 73.

CHAPTER 9

Intergovernmental Relations

The federalist model of American politics allows power to remain as close to the state as possible. The U.S. Constitution states that all powers not explicitly identified by the federal constitution, federal courts, or federal statute, reside with the state. In general, those issues that affect only the local jurisdiction are best left to the city, with those issues that affect a regional area left to the county, those that affect several counties left to the state, and those issues that affect two or more states left to the federal government. Beyond that, any issue that has constitutional implications can be regulated by the federal government. Clearly, with 50 states and some 83,000 local governments, intergovernmental relations are extremely important.[1] Within California, there are 58 counties, 414 municipalities, and 2,300 special districts.

Relations between levels of government have been both good and bad for California. The state has been the beneficiary of billions of federal dollars since World War II. This spending has delivered great defense and infrastructure projects to the state. California gets approximately $23 billion a year in federal largesse—in the form of programs for education, welfare, housing, or infrastructural assistance for mass transit and highway construction. However, with the end of the Cold War, the federal government has not hesitated to drastically reduce that cash flow. The brunt of the economic impact has been felt at the level of local governments, strapped for cash after years of state budget crises and unfunded mandates.

This chapter explores the different levels of California governments, as well as the way they interact with each other. To illustrate the intergovernmental relationships, the chapter concludes with a policy case study on welfare reform. While all policies require effective intergovernmental relationships, welfare reform impacted governments at all levels in an extremely deep way. And since welfare reform is, in many ways, a redistribution of service responsibilities and fiscal authority, the chapter concludes with an assessment of how different levels of government experience differential benefits.

CALIFORNIA IN NATIONAL POLITICS

California has figured prominently in national politics, in part because of the many Californians that have become national leaders. Governor Earl Warren went on to be Chief Justice of the U.S. Supreme Court from 1953 to 1969. Richard Nixon and Ronald Reagan used their California base to seek and win the presidency and appointed Californians to prominent White House posts. Nixon brought fellow Californians Casper Weinberger and David Packard. The Californians serving in the Reagan Administration included Ed Meese, William French Smith, Michael Deaver, James Watt, and George Schultz. Bill Clinton, who claimed to be a "special friend to California," brought out many highly visible native sons and daughters, including Secretary of State Warren Christopher and White House Chief of Staff Leon Panetta, Defense Secretary William Perry, Commerce Secretary Mickey Kantor, and economic advisor Laura D'Andrea Tyson.

No presidential campaign can afford to ignore California. California controls 54 electoral votes—the largest of any state—almost as many as the 15 smallest states combined. The state played a key role in the contest between Democrat Bill Clinton and Republican Bob Dole for the presidency in 1996. With the South becoming solidly Republican, California had become a critical state to Clinton's re-election prospects. Because California has one-fifth of all the electoral votes, Clinton could not have won re-election without carrying California. Is there any wonder why Bill Clinton has been a "special friend," based on this electoral scenario? As part of his re-election strategy, Clinton maintained a constant positive presence in California, made easier by a series of natural and other disasters, which helped the president look more presidential and sympathetic to the average Californian. Floods, earthquakes, fires, and even the 1992 Los Angeles riots kept Federal Emergency Management Agency (FEMA) dollars flowing into the state. In September 1995, Clinton promised and delivered $329 million to bail out the health system in Los Angeles County, keeping the county from going bankrupt. The state's influence in presidential elections will only increase because of the early-March primary, which promises to make California the decisive battleground of the nomination season.

CALIFORNIA'S CONGRESSIONAL DELEGATION

Beyond the White House, California has been something of a "sleeping giant" in Congress, with an unrealized potential to mobilize a voting block consisting of 12 percent of the House of Representatives. The consensus that had unified the California delegation in the 1940s and 1950s broke apart as early as the 1960s. For the last three decades, the delegation has been divided by ideological, geographic, and even ethnic differences. These divisions are somewhat understandable, given the complex and competing interests in a state as large and diverse as California. In the absence of a cohesive congressional delegation, an army of lobbyists has instead been employed by California's various interests. Thus, most major California cities have their own paid lobbyists in Washington, as does the state legislature, the University of California, and a myriad of private and public organizations.

When important state issues are at stake, however, California's house members have rallied and voted together. Rare examples of cooperation can be observed in votes on some critical issues, including funding for the space station, water restoration, the Bay Delta Accord, Medicaid reimbursement, intellectual-property protection, funding for the cleanup of military bases, and transportation projects such as the Alameda Corridor Project. One observer noted that if California's house delegation could only get its "bipartisan act together," then "with its 52 House seats [California] is uniquely positioned to control the game. Of course, other state delegations will be thinking the same thing. But none have the numbers that California does—almost half again as many as runner-ups New York and Texas."[2]

CALIFORNIA'S REPRESENTATIVES: BRINGING HOME THE BACON?

Between 1981 and 1985 the federal government spent nearly $25 billion more in California than it took back in federal taxes. California won between 18 percent and 22 percent of all federal procurement spending in the 1980s. But with the slowing of the defense boom, federal procurement spending peaked in 1986 at $187 billion. California's share of the federal procurement slipped from its high of nearly 22 percent in 1986 to under 15 percent today. As a result, California has been a "donor state" to the federal treasury over the past nine years. The state's taxpayers paid $10 billion more in federal taxes than they got back in federal services and spending. California's share of federal spending fell from a peak of 13 percent in 1984, to a stable 12 percent during the late 1980s and early 1990s, to a 15-year low of 11.4 percent in 1995.[3] In addition, California was hit harder than any other state by the first four military base closure rounds in 1988, 1991, 1993, and 1995.[4] During this period, 40 of California's military installations were either shut down or realigned. And, in its Quadrennial Defense Review (QDR), the Defense Department announced continued base closures. The California congressional delegation is attempting to protect the state's 34 remaining major installations.[5]

LOCAL GOVERNMENTS

Only Pennsylvania and Illinois have more sanctioned local government entities than does California. Because the constitution makes no explicit reference to local governments, they are "creatures of the states," created under state authority, and designed to enable the state to perform its functions throughout its territorial boundaries. It is through California's counties, cities, special districts, and regional agencies that residents come into contact with government authority: be it in public safety, education, rent control, air pollution, or land use.

COUNTIES

California's 58 counties are extremely diverse; they range from tiny Alpine County, with some 1,000 residents, to sprawling Los Angeles County, with its 11 million residents—larger than 42 states of the union. San Bernardino County is the largest in terms of area—covering over 20,000 square miles. San Francisco comprises one of the smallest areas—only 49 square miles. Nearly all California counties are administered by a five-member board of supervisors elected in nonpartisan races every four years. The lone exception is San Francisco, a combined city and county, which is governed by 11 board members and a mayor. Supervisors have legislative, executive, and quasi-judicial duties. In most cases, supervisors govern with the assistance of an appointed Chief Administrative Officer. Other county officials may be independently elected, including the Sheriff, the District Attorney, the Assessor, and the County Superintendent of Schools.

County governments were created as geographic subdivisions of state government in order to deliver administrative services. The county's role as an agent of the state has made it the major administrator of funds, which come from a combination of local taxes, the state, and the national government. Currently, more than half of county revenues come from the state, while 90 percent of their budget commitments are determined by state mandates.[6] On average, California counties spend approximately 26 percent of their annual budget on public safety, 13 percent on public health, and 40 percent on public assistance and welfare. Counties provide all-purpose services to unincorporated areas in their jurisdiction, as well as contracted services that smaller cities cannot provide. For example, the County of Los Angeles contracts with several cities to provide such services as policing, fire protection, ambulance services, jail facilities, tax assessment, and elections. Because the suburban city of Lakewood was the first municipality to contract with the county for these services, this model has become known as the "Lakewood Plan."

Cities

There are 414 cities in California. Cities may incorporate for a variety of reasons, including local pride, the retention of housing values, control of land-use and zoning decisions, or access to tax revenues. The two types of cities are *general law*, which derive their powers from statutes set by the state legislature, and *charter*, which have greater flexibility of home-rule because of locally crafted and implemented city charters. There are two basic forms of city government operating in California: the *council-manager* form and the *mayor-council* form. Most California cities use the council-manager form. Under the council-manager form of government, legislative authority rests with the city council, but the council appoints a city manager to administer city operations and administration. These governments may have an elected mayor, but the office is largely ceremonial. Because the city manager is a full-time professional executive who does not face the voters, the council-manager form is believed to be less political and less corruptible than the mayor-council form, though critics point to the fact that a city manager's job security depends upon pleasing a majority of city council members. In cities with the mayor-council form of government, voters elect a mayor, who wields executive power, as well as the city council, which is the legislative body of the city. In "strong" mayor systems, the executive branch has the power to set the budget, appoint city heads, veto legislation, and control policy debate. In systems with "weak" mayors, the balance of power favors the legislative branch. Thus, the city council has not only policy oversight, but administrative oversight in running city agencies. The mayor may be independently elected or may be one of the city council members who periodically rotate into the mayor's position. The major exception to these two basic forms of city government is the city-county of San Francisco, which is governed by an elected board of supervisors and an elected mayor.

As William Fulton points out in *The Reluctant Metropolis*, cities compete with one another to attract new sources of revenue.[7] In the post-Proposition 13 world, sales and business taxes are the primary sources of revenue for city governments to deliver the services city residents are increasingly demanding. Proposition 13 capped state property taxes, allowing an annual increase of only 1 percent, and reduced the cities share of property tax revenue. The impact on California's cities was immediate. In 1978, for example, just before Proposition 13 became law, the three major cities in Ventura County's Oxnard Plain collected $8 million in property tax and $10 million in sales tax. In 1979, after Proposition 13 became effective, the cities collected only $3.7 million in property tax and $12 million in sales tax.[8] It was clear where future revenues would be sought. To this end, local governments try, whenever possible, to attract affluent residents and to provide economic incentives for commercial or industrial growth—be it big-box retail, shopping malls, car dealerships, or light (non-polluting) industries.[9]

SPECIAL DISTRICTS

There are more than 2,300 special districts in California providing specialized services that no other local government provides within a defined area. Special districts include agencies that monitor, regulate, and tax for such services as water, street construction, pest control, flood control, public schools, community colleges, transportation, mosquito abatement, waste disposal, land reclamation, and air quality control. In the post-Proposition 13 era, they also serve as a mechanism to provide public services by sidestepping existing constitutional limits on taxation. Even though two-thirds of special districts are governed by elected boards of directors, most of these bodies are little-understood by the average citizen. Critics have argued that special districts are problematic because of their lack of overall coordination and planning, as well as the number of staff and personnel each employ at a direct cost to the taxpayer. Because of a popular belief that special districts are unaccountable and inefficient, state law has limited their growth since the 1960s.

REGIONAL GOVERNMENTS AND AGENCIES

Most regional "governments" in California exist to aid local governments in planning, coordination, and data generation. Municipalities join regional governments voluntarily, hence these agencies have little or no real power other than the "bully pulpit" to press for corrective policy changes that cross jurisdictional boundaries. Examples are the Southern California Association of Governments (SCAG) and the San Diego Association of Governments (SANDAG). There are also several regional agencies that deliver a specific service. For example, the Bay Area Rapid Transit District (BART) or the Los Angeles County Metropolitan Transit Authority (MTA) are agencies designed to deliver mass transit to regions that include more than a single county. The California Coastal Commission governs land-use in coastal areas. The Bay Area Air Pollution Control District and the South Coast Air Quality Management District (SCAQMD) are entrusted with considerable political power to regulate air pollution over vast regions (see Chapter 13). Regional governments and agencies serve the broader goals of multijurisdictional (regional) governance, through cooperative data collection, resource sharing, and state-mandated regulation implementation.

THE FUTURE OF STATE-LOCAL RELATIONS

In 1995, a blue-ribbon panel concluded that political power in California—with its myriad of government agencies—is fragmented, unaccountable, confusing, and in many areas, redundant. As part of its package of suggested reforms, the California Constitution Revision Commission sent to the state legislature a proposal suggesting a radical restructuring of local government. If placed on the ballot and approved by the voters, the plan would have authorized local "charter governments," allowing residents to combine existing agencies—including cities, counties, as well as school districts, water boards, sewer districts, and other types of agencies. It also would have redefined the relationship between the state and local governments by forcing the state to reconsider its unfunded mandates. The legislature has yet to act on this proposal, to the dismay of the financially strapped counties.

FEDERALISM TODAY: WELFARE REFORM AS A CASE STUDY

The United States is now engaged in a national experiment in the decentralization of social programs. These measures will significantly alter the major federal-state-county relationships pertaining to a myriad of social programs in all 50 states. In its simplest form, the experiment would unravel the fundamental principles that were shaped in the New Deal legislation of the 1930s and repeal major segments of the Great Society legislation of the 1960s.

Historically speaking, this "New Federalism" is the latest wave in a long succession of measures to shift more power and authority from the federal government to the states. Back in the 1970s, President Nixon proposed revenue sharing and simplifying government operations by transferring planning and management functions to state and local governments. The thrust of his new federalism policy was to consolidate grant programs in an effort to reduce the complexity of national programs into a manageable handful of block grants—and ultimately to save taxpayers money.[10] In the early 1980s, President Reagan won a major concession to realign the federal government's categorical grant program. His administration consolidated some 57 categorical grants into nine block grants.[11] The Nixon and Reagan block grant initiatives were designed to prune the federal bureaucracy, restrict paperwork, and enhance decision-making and control at the local level.

New Federalism has long been a contested terrain, however, because increasing state authority over programs allows states to fund some programs at a lower level and to terminate other support programs altogether. Republicans have favored reducing the federal role, while Democrats have argued for greater security and oversight in program delivery. President Clinton was able to bring about bipartisan support for one area of reform with the Personal Responsibility and Work Opportunity Reconciliation Act in 1996. This 500-page document was the cornerstone of Clinton's initiative to "end welfare as we know it." The proposal was not without controversy, however. One side of the debate contends that given sufficient discretion, the states can devise more innovative, cost-effective services, that are better able to reduce welfare dependency. On the other side of the debate are critics such as Peter Edelman, who resigned his post as the Assistant Secretary for Planning and Evaluation at the Department of Health and Human Services out of protest to the new welfare law. According to Edelman:

> [Welfare reform] does not promote work effectively and it will hurt millions of poor children by the time it's fully implemented. What's more it bars hundreds of thousands of legal immigrants from receiving disability and old-age assistance and food stamps, and reduced food-stamp assistance for millions of children in working families.... [Under block grants] there will be no federal definition of who is eligible and therefore no guarantee of assistance to anyone: each state can decide whom to exclude any way it wants, as long as it doesn't violate the constitution (not much of a limitation when one reads the Supreme Court decisions on this subject). And second, that each state will get a fixed sum of federal money each year even if a recession or a local calamity causes a state to run out of federal funds before the end of the year.[12]

The effects of welfare reform will be felt everywhere in the state. Welfare recipients are not concentrated in any one county or region. To assess the impacts in California, it is appropriate to review the major elements of the new law.

Title I: Block Grants for Temporary Assistance for Needy Families (TANF)

- Eliminates Aid to Families with Dependent Children (AFDC) and consolidates federal funding for AFDC and related programs (such as job training) into a TANF block grant.
- The state must implement the block grant by July 1, 1997, but can do so sooner upon submission of a revised state plan. The date is important because it triggers the beginning of the five-year time limit for assistance.
- Prohibits use of block grant funds for teen parents under age 18 unless they are (1) attending school and (2) living in an adult-supervised setting.
- Establishes five-year lifetime limit on family use of block grant funds. States may exempt up to 20 percent for hardship.
- Requires at least one adult in a family that has been receiving aid for more than two years to participate in "work activities," including employment, on-the-job and vocational training, and up to six weeks of job searching.
- Requires 75 percent of two-parent families to participate in work activities in fiscal year 1997–1998, increasing to 90 percent in 1999. Single parents must work 20 hours per week in 1997–1998, increasing to 30 hours in the year 2000, or 20 hours for families with a child under age six.
- Imposes penalties on states for noncompliance.

- States must place at least 25 percent of cash welfare recipients in jobs or work programs by 1997, and 50 percent by 2002.
- Federal funds cannot be used to provide cash benefits to adults who fail to find work within two years.
- Cash aid is reduced by 25 percent for recipients who do not cooperate with child-support enforcement agencies or in establishing paternity.
- States have the option to deny additional cash aid to welfare recipients who have additional children.
- States that have received federal waivers to conduct reform programs may continue to operate under those waivers.

In 1996, 2.7 million Californians were receiving public assistance through AFDC. Of these, 1.8 million were children. The state has already approved plans for a 4.9 percent cut in cash benefits, a figure that will be higher in rural counties.[13] The state has submitted a plan to the federal government outlining how it intends to use federal block grant money that replaces the AFDC program.

Title II: Supplemental Security Income (SSI)

- Eliminates benefits to children who are "relatively less disabled." Currently, children may be eligible if an impairment exists that precludes them from "age-appropriate" activities.
- Eliminates SSI payments to prison inmates incarcerated for more than 30 days.
- Children no longer qualify for SSI benefits unless they have a medically proven disability that causes "marked and severe functional limitations."
- Most elderly immigrants are denied SSI benefits unless they obtain citizenship or work in the United States for 10 years.

There are now 1,035,000 Californians receiving SSI benefits, and 87,000 of them are younger than 18. The Department of Social Services estimates that about 14,000 children would be subject to reevaluation of these SSI benefits.

Title IV: Restricting Benefits for Non-Citizens

- Legal immigrants already in the United States are ineligible for SSI and food stamps. States have the option to deny benefits under TANF and Medicaid. Legal immigrants arriving after enactment are ineligible for all federal benefits for five years.
- Exceptions include certain child nutrition and education programs, veterans and their dependents, refugees and asylum-seekers within the first five years of residency and persons who have worked for 40 quarters, or 10 years.
- Programs exempted include emergency medical services, non-cash disaster relief, treatment for communicable diseases, immunizations, and soup kitchens.
- States can continue to provide legal immigrants already living here with aid for families with children, as well as Medicaid (Medi-Cal in California).
- Illegal immigrants are denied virtually all federal assistance except short-term disaster relief and emergency medical care.

California leads the nation in the number of legal immigrants living in the state, and about two-thirds of the welfare funding cuts for California are in this section of the law. The state estimates that $5.9 billion in aid to non-citizens will be cut over the next six years, including $3.7 billion in SSI. As of December 1996, 322,000 legal immigrants were receiving SSI benefits in California. The State Department of Social Services estimates that about 173,000 of them will lose benefits. The SSI cuts will take effect following each recipient's annual SSI benefit review. Food stamp cuts for immigrants will affect about 270,000 recipients.[14] Over the next six years, California may lose more than $10 billion in federal aid, and nearly half of that will be from Los Angeles County.[15] Furthermore, almost 300,000 people could lose their food stamp eligibility; 200,000 families with children could lose benefits; under SSI, about 93,000 elderly and disabled people would become ineligible.

Sections III, VI, VII, and VIII affect child support enforcement, child care, child nutrition programs, food stamps, and commodity distribution. Food stamps will continue to operate as an entitlement program (the federal government guarantees that all eligible recipients will receive benefits), but the benefit formula and eligibility criteria will be tightened, producing significant savings for Washington and imposing new financial burdens on states that leave their current programs unchanged.

Titles III, VI, VII, and VIII: Child Care, Support and Nutrition, Food Stamps

- Individual food stamp allotments will be reduced across the board by 3 percent.
- The standard deduction applied to food stamp applications to determine eligibility will no longer rise with inflation.
- The deduction for housing costs will be frozen at $300 per month, beginning in 2001.
- Able-bodied adults with no dependents lose food stamps after three months (six months if laid off) unless they work 20 hours per week.

A total of 3.2 million Californians receive food stamps. When fully implemented, the average household benefit in California will be cut by 19 percent. The loss of entitlement status, funding reduction, and work requirements pose difficult challenges. Meeting the 50 percent and 90 percent working requirements will be hard because jobs may not be available, and although public sector jobs can be created, the cost would make such a solution unlikely.[16] Job training programs have a history of limited results and can be expected to produce only small increases in wage and employability. If the goals are not met, states face the financial penalty of a 5 percent cut in their block grant. Thus, the inherent question facing states is whether the costs of attaining the goals is less than or greater than the penalty. If the goals' cost is too high, states may opt for the penalty. Even if they do, however, that would not necessarily slow down the existing efforts within many states to change the terms of welfare, replacing an ongoing entitlement to those eligible with a reciprocal obligation involving public support in exchange for progress toward economic self-reliance.

Whether or not such self-reliance is achieved, the five-year lifetime limit means that the federal government would no longer be obligated to share the cost of public support of children and other members of families with adults who, though able-bodied, have long-term dependency needs. Many of these families would be transferred to General Assistance, the residual welfare program for those who do not fit into AFDC or other welfare categories. Since general assistance receives no federal funds, the cost burden would shift to state and local governments.[17] A shift from AFDC to block grants may thus create serious risks for the welfare population, the largest of which is the end of entitlements. Although general assistance provides a secondary safety net, its benefit levels are often considerably lower. Children, in particular, may be severely disadvantaged. Nor is there any requirement that states and localities fully fund general assistance. If they cannot or do not, it is not clear what resources will be available to needy families. Since counties are service providers of last-resort—for health care, housing, and general assistance—it is likely that services once provided for by the federal government will now fall to states and counties. This is particularly challenging for large urban counties like San Diego, Los Angeles, Alameda, San Francisco, and Sacramento.[18]

While the recent robust economy has filled California's state coffers with extra tax revenues, a major concern is how states will cope with an economic downturn, rise in poverty, or other factors leading to greater need for public assistance. The welfare reform law contains a "rainy day" fund that is intended to address this issue. Critics cite that this fund is insufficient to meet the likely need. California has been gaining population after the recession of the late 1980s–1990s. Coping with population growth alone will require a projected $700 million over the next five years. The law has only $100 million set aside.[19] So the New Federalism and election-year posturing may have handed the states a chain-saw rather than a scalpel to carve away at the defects of the welfare system. Whether California's experiment with welfare reform will succeed remains to be seen. One thing we know for certain—the federal government stands to gain the most, as about one-third of all the proposed projected savings from welfare reform will come from California alone.

SUMMARY

Ever since California was officially admitted to statehood in 1850 as the first noncontiguous American territory to become part of the Union, it has had to build its psychic and pragmatic bridges to protect its interests in Washington. The ongoing debate over where California stands in the federal system, and whether it can use its numeric clout to tip the balance of power in its favor, is really part of its historic legacy. This chapter has examined the complex structural and personal relationship the Golden State has developed over the years with the key centers of national power. In the federal system, states and their representatives must compete for their share of federal dollars without losing sight of the national agenda or the overall development of the United States.

NOTES

1. See Thomas Dye, *Politics in America* (Upper Saddle River, NJ: Prentice Hall, 1994), p. 106.
2. Tim Ransdell, "California's Prospects in Washington," *San Diego Union-Tribune*, 2 November 1996, 12.

3. U.S. Census Bureau figures, cited in Tim Ransdell, "No More Federal Largess for California," *San Diego Union Tribune*, 3 July 1996, E3.

4. Herbert Sample, "Downsizing California's Military-Industrial Complex," *California Journal* (September 1995): 39–42.

5. Faye Fiore, "State Delegation Braces for Base Closure Battle," *Los Angeles Times*, 23 May 1997, A1.

6. See Laureen Lazarovici, "Counties in Crisis," *California Journal* (November 1995): 32–34.

7. William Fulton, *The Reluctant Metropolis: The Politics of Urban Growth in Los Angeles* (Point Arena, CA: Solano Books, 1997).

8. Ibid., pp. 260–261.

9. Paul Kantor, *The Dependent City Revisited* (San Francisco, CA: Westview Press, 1995).

10. See Richard E. Thompson, *Revenue Sharing: A New Era in Federalism* (Washington, D.C.: Revenue Sharing Advisory Service, 1973).

11. George Peterson, et. al., *The Reagan Block Grants: What Have We Learned?* (Washington, D.C.: The Urban Institute Press, 1986).

12. Peter Edelman, "The Worst Thing Bill Clinton Has Done," *The Atlantic Monthly* (March 1997): 43–44.

13. See James S. Hosek and Robert Levine, eds., *The New Fiscal Federalism and the Social Safety Net* (Santa Monica, CA: RAND, 1996).

14. Fending off warnings that the National Governors' Association and the GOP leadership has no intention of tinkering with this provision, some moderate Republicans and most Democrats have joined the administration in pushing for legal immigrant waivers for elderly and disabled non-citizens already in this country before the measure's enactment. California has 40 percent of the nation's legal immigrant population.

15. According to estimates drawn by the Fair Share Network, based on data provided by the Los Angeles County Department of Public Social Services.

16. About 50 percent of these family heads are on AFDC, and of them about 15 percent are employed. Thus the work goal requires raising the percentage working from 15 percent to 50 percent. Among the 50 percent off AFDC, about 85 percent are employed. Robert Moffitt, "Incentive Effects of the U.S. Welfare System: A Review," *The Journal of Economic Literature* 30, no. 1 (March 1992): 11–14.

17. A proposal by the legislative analyst and endorsed by Attorney General Bill Lockyer would have the state take over general assistance from the counties. It could cost the state $300 million a year.

18. The preferred outcome of achieving self-reliance through employment—the goal of the new programs—raises further tough questions: Will additional education and training sufficiently increase skills and instill better work habits? Will child care and transportation be available? Will child care, Medicaid, and food stamps extend beyond welfare? Wisconsin, for instance, has determined that in its own welfare reform experiment, child care and Medicaid must be extended to all working poor, in part to maintain the incentive of welfare family heads to transition to work. Many other states have not yet developed an integrated perspective, leaving welfare recipients to wonder about interim support. Further, child care funding will be reduced under block grants, but AFDC work requirements will increase the demand for child care. This leads some to wonder whether the quality of child care will diminish—and with it, the positive effects of child care on child development. Funding for family protective services will also be reduced under block grants, raising the possibility that cases of child abuse and neglect will more often be handled by removing the children from families and placing them in foster care, which remains an entitlement.

19. Isabel Sawhill, *Welfare Reform: An Analysis of the Issues* (Washington, D.C.: The Urban Institute Press, 1995).

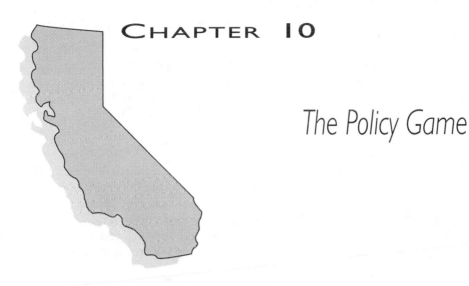

CHAPTER 10

The Policy Game

Public policy can be described as a public response to public problems. Governmental legislation, programs, and controls are all mechanisms that public bodies utilize in an effort to improve the public welfare. Public policy has been defined in different ways by different observers. Peters defines policy as "the sum of government activities ... (that have) an influence on the lives of citizens."[1] Lasswell pointed out that public policy determines "who gets what, when, and how."[2] Contemporary policy analysts might also include "why?" In a real world context, public policy can be understood as public responses to perceived public problems.[3] Policy actors are those individuals and groups, both formal and informal, who seek to influence the creation and implementation of these public responses.

Using the metaphor of game strategies, this chapter explores the function and influence of public policy in California. Beginning with an overview of the rules and strategies of the policy "game," the chapter moves on to explore how entrepreneurial policy "players" exploit the points of vulnerability in that process. In doing so, the chapter reviews the policy actors, including the institutional actors—the governor and executive bureaucracy, the state legislature, and the courts—and the noninstitutional actors—the media, parties, interest groups, and political consultants. Finally, the chapter explores California's budget as a case study of policymaking in the state.

RULES OF THE POLICY GAME

The public policy process has been described as a game by several observers. The game metaphor is not intended to trivialize the process, but rather to suggest that policy actors must utilize rational strategies to maximize their interests. Players will increase their chances of winning to the extent that they have knowledge of the policy bureaucracy (bureaucratic knowledge), access to individuals within the bureaucracy (network), citizen backing (size of constituency), money for political contributions, and resources to mount an effective public relations (media) campaign. But these resources are only one part of winning the policy game. It is also necessary to understand the rules and culture of the policy environment. The following discussion explores the context and environment of the policy game in California.

MAXIMIZING POLICY STRATEGIES

In *The Prince*[4] Machiavelli presents a blueprint for the effective development and maintenance of power. Machiavelli's notion of *virtu'*—controlling political destiny— is based on the successful manipulation of human circumstances. The virtuous prince is good, merciful, and honest, as long as expediency dictates, yet he must be prepared to be cruel and deceptive. Control is the primary consideration, both of one's populace and of one's neighboring states. Ultimately, *virtu'* requires successful strategies to maximize policy interests.

Murray Edelman[5] similarly argues that those who seek to maximize their policy interests will use deceit and symbolism to manipulate the policy discourse. No one person can possibly experience the entire world. Yet, everyone has an image or "picture" of the world. Burke suggests that however important that "sliver of reality each of us has experienced firsthand," the overall "picture" is a "construct of symbolic systems."[6] This construct is based on political cognitions that Edelman suggests are "ambivalent and highly susceptible to symbolic cues...."[7] Government, Edelman argues, influences behavior by shaping the cognitions of people in ambiguous situations. In this way, government, or policy elites, helps engineer beliefs about what is "fact" and what is "proper."

Maximizing policy strategies is critical for winning the policy game. Each player, regardless of his or her position in the policy environment, seeks to influence policy outcomes. The degree to which players utilize rational strategies, however creative, however slippery, will determine the degree to which policy success can be achieved. This is not to suggest that there are no ethical constraints on players; there are. Rather, the Machiavellian legacy in our political environment recognizes that strategy and cunning are acceptable and necessary components of the policy game.

Some suggest that democratic processes are dominated by the influence of economic elites—specifically, corporate elites. Domhoff argues that there is a social upper class that effectively operates as a ruling class by virtue of its dominance of economic resources. While there are other political resources—for example, expertise and bureaucratic knowledge—these other resources can and are purchased. Thus, as Domhoff[8] points out, financial power is often the basis of policy influence. If it is true that policy influence requires requisite political resources, inequality in resource distribution is tantamount to inequality in political representation. Maximizing policy strategy, therefore, includes maximizing the ability to raise funds.

POLICY ACTORS

The policy process is significantly more subtle than many realize. While the state constitution provides for a legislature that makes laws, an executive that enforces laws, and a judiciary that interprets laws, the policy process has evolved into a confusing web of state departments, agencies, and committees that make up the institutional policy bureaucracy. And, unlike the federal level, California's constitution requires that governmental authority be shared with voters through the initiative process, the recall, and the referendum. In addition, the vast network of organized citizen groups (parties, interest groups, and PACs), as well as the rise of the electronic media, political consultants, and other image-making professionals, further complicates the process. The role each actor plays, in combination with the relationship between actors in both policy bureaucracies, is ultimately what determines policy outcomes.

INSTITUTIONAL POLICY ACTORS

The State Legislature   The legislature is the central institution in the policy process because of its legislative authority. Within the legislature, power is centralized in the committees. Committee chairs have disproportionate influence over policy as a consequence of their power to determine committee agendas. Similarly, certain committees have more policy influence than others. The Assembly Rules Committee, for example, is responsible for determining which bills will be heard and in what order. The Appropriation Committees in both the assembly and senate are responsible for reviewing any legislation that requires funding. The power that members of such committees hold and the powers of committee chairs make them key players in the policy process.

Legislative staffers are another source of influence that is often overlooked. In *The Power Game*[9] Hedrick Smith describes staffers as "policy entrepreneurs." Staffers are important in two areas. First, the increasing use of staff to service constituents in district offices strengthens the legislator's stature among local voters, perhaps explaining in part the strength of incumbency. Second, staffers are the real expertise behind the legislator. With hundreds of bills introduced in an average session, legislators rely more and more on staff to analyze legislation, negotiate compromises, research issues, and meet with lobbyists. In their roles as legislative analysts and policy negotiators, as well as their role as political confidants and counselors, senior staffers have significant policy influence. And, with term limits now state law, staffers will have more experience than legislators, giving them even more power to influence.

The Governor and Executive Bureaucracy   The governor is mandated by the California constitution as a partner in the policy process. But, unlike the legislature, the governor can only approve or disapprove legislation, he or she has no power to amend. In addition, California's constitution requires that the seven nongubernatorial executive officers be directly elected, diluting the governor's power further. Thus, the policy priorities of the governor cannot be directly imposed. Rather, governors must rely on legislative partners in both houses, and on, what Richard Neustadt called, the "power to persuade."[10] This persuasion comes as a result of several factors. Paul Light suggests that executive policy is a result of the "stream of people and ideas" that flow through the executive office.[11] If public policy is a process of identifying problems, identifying solutions, and implementing those solutions, the identification of problems and solutions, Light argues, is tied to the assumptions held by players in that stream. The policy stream must accommodate the issues that percolate up through the systemic agenda, as well as those issues that may be on the executive agenda.

The implementation of gubernatorial policy objectives involves a different set of problems than those of the legislature. While the legislature makes laws, the governor can only recommend laws. Effective governors use the powers and perks of their office to maximize their policy agendas. Appointments are a major source of policy influence. By appointing individuals who share his or her political perspective and agenda, a governor is able to extend influence throughout the executive and judicial bureaucracies. Cabinet officers and heads of regulatory agencies establish policy priorities within their agencies. And, since most legislation allows for a significant measure of discretion among implementing and enforcement agencies, the cabinet officers and agency heads have wide latitude in defining, implementing, and enforcing policy.

The policy influence of regulatory agencies within the executive bureaucracy is substantial. Meier[12] describes the regulatory process as a combination of regulatory bureaucracies (values, expertise, agency subculture, bureaucratic entrepreneurs) and public interaction (interest groups, economic issues, legislative committees and subcommittees). Regulatory outcomes are a consequence of subsystem interaction between all of these influences. Those who are best able to influence these subsystems are best able to maximize their interests. As a result, policy subsystems are major points of access for policy influence.

The Courts   The influence of judges in interpreting laws has an equally significant impact on policy. And this impact is not free of political influence. Unlike the federal system, state judges are vulnerable to political scrutiny. This was most dramatically demonstrated in the expulsion of Chief Justice Rose Bird and two of her colleagues in 1984. The policy role of the judiciary is not universally appreciated. The current debate over judicial activism and judicial restraint is only the most recent in a long discourse. In "Towards an Imperial Judiciary?"[13] Nathan Glazer argues that judicial activism infringes on democratic policy institutions and that an activist court erodes the respect and trust people hold for the judiciary. Still, whether a court is active or passive, there are significant policy implications. Non-action is in itself a policy decision with substantial policy implications.

NON-INSTITUTIONAL ACTORS

Public policy is not merely the result of independent policymaking institutions. Non-institutional actors also play a significant role: The public elects legislators and executives; the media influences policy through its inherent agenda-setting function; parties influence policy through their role of drafting and electing candidates; and organized interest groups lobby elected officials and non-elected policy makers (e.g., agency staff). Policy, then, is a result of institutional processes influenced by non-institutional actors.

The Media   The media are influential to policy outcomes because they help define social reality. The work of McCombs and Shaw[14] suggests that the media influence the salience of issues. As Lippmann[15] observed in 1922, perceptions of reality are based on a tiny sampling of the world around us. No one can be everywhere, no one can experience everything. Thus, to a greater or lesser extent, all of us rely on media portrayals of reality. Graber[16] argues that the way people process information makes them especially vulnerable to media influence. First, people tend to pair down the scope of information they confront. Second, people tend to think schematically. When confronted with information, individuals will fit that information into pre-existing schema. Since news stories tend to lack background and context, schemata allow the individual to give the information meaning. In such a way, individuals re-create reality in their minds.

The data collected by Iyengar and Kinder[17] show that television news, to a great extent, defines which problems the public considers most serious. Iyengar and Kinder refine the agenda-setting dynamic to include what they call "priming." Priming refers to the selective coverage of only certain events and the selective way in which those events are covered. Since there is no way to cover all events, or cover any event completely, selective decisions must be made. But, there are consequences:

> By priming certain aspects of national life while ignoring others, television news sets the terms by which political judgements are rendered and political choices made.[18]

The implications for public policy are serious. If policy is a result of a problem recognition model, then the problems that gain media recognition are much more likely to be addressed.

California politics relies on the media to distribute political messages. With 32 million people, it is not possible for policy advocates to truly "meet" the voters as they might in New Hampshire or Iowa. Television, radio, and newspapers allow politicians, candidates, and interest groups to cover more ground with less money. In the Los Angeles television market alone, for example, policy advocates can reach 10 million people at once. As we will see in the following chapter, political parties and interest groups can translate their financial resources into air time to get their messages across.

Parties   Political parties are distinct from other citizen organizations. Rather than attempting to influence existing policymakers, parties seek to get their own members elected to policymaking positions. While interest groups seek influence on specific policy issues, parties seek influence on a wide spectrum of policy issues. Parties develop issue platforms, draft candidates, campaign on behalf of candidates, and mobilize voters. In short, parties work to bring citizens together under a common banner.

While most people may think of parties only during election cycles, their policy influence extends beyond campaigns. While the rise of the media over the last 30 years has deemphasized the power of parties in electoral politics, parties continue to play a dominant role in policy outcomes. Due to the institutional role parties play in the legislature, and the grassroots role that parties play at the local and county level, the party that emerges dominant often determines the direction policy will take. The governor is responsible to the party that got him or her elected, and therefore must pursue at least some of the policy objectives articulated at the party convention. The legislature continues to distribute committee membership and chairmanships according to party affiliation. While negotiation and compromise is typically necessary, the general direction of legislative policy is directly tied to the ideology of the larger party.

The strength of political parties has waned over the past three decades (see Chapter 11) but parties maintain policy influence in critical areas. Elections, patronage appointments, legislative committees, and policy discourses all reflect the influence of parties. In California, registered Democrats have outnumbered registered Republicans for the past generation. However, Republicans tend to turn out in higher numbers than Democrats. In 1994, for example, the Democratic party had 7,219,635 registered members in California, while the Republican party had 5,472,391 members. In that election, only 3,517,707 Democrats turned out to vote for governor, while 4,777,630 Republicans voted, re-electing a highly partisan chief executive. Thus, parties remain critical to the policy process.

Interest Groups   Interest groups are a fundamental partner in policymaking. Citizens participate in the policy process through communication with policymakers. Such communication takes place individually (e.g., letters to elected representatives), and collectively. Interest groups facilitate collective communication. James Madison recognized the propensity for individuals to factionalize in an effort to maximize political influence.[19] Robert Dahl further refined the analysis of Madisonian democracy, arguing that in an open society all persons have the right to press their interests. To the extent others share these interests, collective pressure may allow greater policy influence. Indeed, Dahl argued, those issues that have greater salience have greater interest group representation.[20]

The interest group dynamic, however, is not so simple. While it may be true that many salient issues have interest group representation, the strength of that representation is not tied to the strength of the issue salience. Further, the salience itself may be a consequence of interest group action. When studying policy outcomes it is necessary to identify the policy actors and the political resources they use. Maximizing policy interests —winning the policy game—requires specific political resources. The most common resources include bureaucratic knowledge, a network of contacts, citizen backing (size of constituency), an ability to make political contributions, and an ability to mount a public relations (media) campaign. Clearly, no group utilizes all of these resources. But the ability of an organized group to utilize one or more of these resources is critical for policy influence.

Political Consultants   Increasingly, political expertise is purchased by those with the need and the resources. In reviewing the rise and structure of the political consulting industry, Sabato[21] exposes the fragile relationship between articulating ideas in a political marketplace and manipulating public opinion. It is virtually impossible to win at the policy game without the marketing skills held by consultants and strategists. Like many other policy resources, political consultants are costly. As a consequence, those with greater economic resources enjoy a policy advantage.

The extremely competitive nature of California's political environment has made political consulting a growth industry in the state. There are 14 major political consulting firms in the state, representing candidates at all levels of government.[22] In addition, there are thousands of additional firms offering media consulting, public relations, survey research, direct mail, and fund raising. Critics argue that the selling of politics has become just as slick and self-interested as the selling of cars. Public policy has become just another commodity in a market environment. The implication, of course, is that the policy process may be less democratic as a consequence. It is often political consultants, rather than public-interested candidates, who are defining the political discourse in the state. Whether or not one perceives this as a problem might be related to an individual's access to the financial resources needed to purchase these services.

POLICY OUTPUTS: CALIFORNIA'S BUDGET AS A CASE STUDY

The California state budget provides one of the best case studies on the policy process. Since the budget defines fiscal allocations, it serves to define the state's policy priorities for the following year. As such, the budget process brings both institutional and non-institutional actors into passionate political battle. Legally, the formal budget process plays out as follows:

- January 10: Governor submits his or her budget to both houses of the legislature.
- February: Legislative analyst publishes its *Analysis of the Governor's Budget*.
- March and April: Senate and assembly budget subcommittees hold hearings on each budget item.
- May: Governor submits the "May revision," a revised estimate of revenues and expenditures. Subcommittee hearings end. Senate and assembly budget committees send bills to their full houses.
- June: Conference committee of both houses meets to reconcile differences between senate and assembly version of budget bills and ultimately sends recommendation to both houses for final vote.
- June 15: Budget goes to the governor for signature.[23]

While the process at first glance appears to include only the institutional policy actors, there are several points at which non-institutional actors become involved. Long before the governor's budget is submitted in June, citizens, interest groups, corporations, and legislators lobby the governor's office and each other in order to maximize the chances of receiving funding for policies they favor and for cutting funding for policies they are against. Once the governor's budget is made public, these groups direct their attention to the senate and assembly budget committees and subcommittees, lobbying and testifying at budget hearings.

Simultaneously, those groups with the economic resources will begin to lobby the public through both paid and non-paid media. Political advertising can be used to cue public concern, which may cue public budgetary demands. Similarly, policy advocates may seek media coverage through news or public affairs programming. Not only is this type of publicity free, it places a mantle of "objectivity" on the medium. As opposed to a paid political advertisement, news coverage of an event held by an interest group will carry more weight with the public if the messenger is a reporter or commentator.

SUMMARY

This chapter has explored the role and influence of actors in the policy process—both institutional (the legislature, the governor and executive bureaucracy, and the courts) and non-institutional (media, parties, interest groups, and political consultants). From the discussion it can be seen that policy outcomes are typically a result of institutional processes and non-institutional influence. As the previous chapters explain, California's political culture and structure is quite complex, representing the diverse interests of 32 million Californians. The policy game, therefore, is important to understand. As Californians navigate the ship of state, there is little consensus of who is at the helm. While the governor may be the captain, the crew are under little obligation to follow his course. With the multitude of destinations sought, it is little wonder that California politics are contentious and passionate. But that, after all, is what democracy is all about.

NOTES

1. B. Guy Peters, *American Public Policy: Promise and Performance*, 3rd ed. (Chatham, NJ: Chatham House Publishers, 1993), p. 4.
2. Harold Lasswell, *Politics: Who Gets What, When, and How* (New York: St. Martin's Press, 1988).
3. See Stella Theodoulou and Matthew Cahn, *Public Policy: The Essential Readings* (Upper Saddle River, NJ: Prentice Hall, 1995).
4. Niccolo Machiavelli, *The Prince*, in Peter Bondanella and Mark Muse, eds., *The Portable Machiavelli* (New York: Penguin Books, 1983).
5. Murray Edelman, *Constructing the Political Spectacle* (Chicago: The University of Chicago Press, 1988).
6. Kenneth Burke, *Language as Symbolic Action* (Berkeley: University of California Press, 1966), p. 5.
7. Murray Edelman, *Politics as Symbolic Action* (Chicago: Markham Publishing Co., 1971), p. 2.
8. G. William Domhoff, *Who Rules America Now?* (New York: Simon & Schuster, Inc., 1983).
9. Hedrick Smith, *The Power Game: How Washington Works* (New York: Ballantine Books, 1988).
10. Richard Neustadt, *Presidential Power* (New York: John Wiley and Sons, Inc., 1980).
11. Paul Light, "The Presidential Policy Stream," in Michael Nelson, ed., *The Presidency and the Political System* (Washington, D.C.: CQ Press, 1984).
12. Kenneth J. Meier, *Regulation: Politics, Bureaucracy, and Economics* (New York: St. Martin's Press, 1985).
13. Nathan Glazer, "Towards an Imperial Judiciary?" *Public Interest* (fall 1975).
14. Maxwell E. McCombs and Donald L. Shaw, *The Emergence of American Political Issues: The Agenda Setting Function of the Press* (Boston: West Publishing Company, 1977).
15. Walter Lippmann, *Public Opinion* (New York: The Free Press, 1922).
16. Doris Graber, *Processing the News: How People Tame the Information Tide*, 2nd ed. (New York: Longman, 1988).
17. Shanto Iyengar and Donald Kinder, *News That Matters: Television and American Opinion* (Chicago: The University of Chicago Press, 1987).
18. Ibid., p. 4.
19. James Madison, "Federalist #10," in Alexander Hamilton, James Madison, and John Jay, *The Federalist Papers* (New York: New American Library, 1961).
20. Robert Dahl, *Who Governs?* (New Haven, CT: Yale University Press, 1961).
21. Larry J. Sabato, *The Rise of Political Consultants: New Ways of Winning Elections* (New York: Basic Books, 1981).
22. Ibid.
23. Adapted from *California State Budget At-a-Glance*, published by the Senate Budget and Fiscal Review Committee, July 1992.

CHAPTER 11

Non-Institutional Players:
The Media,
Political Parties,
and Interest Groups

Communication is an essential feature of representative democracy. Citizens and leaders must be linked in order for the political system to function effectively. Leaders need to be aware of citizens' concerns so that they build policy accordingly and so they can mobilize policy support. Citizens must be aware of their representatives' actions so that they can provide policy feedback and so they can hold leaders accountable in elections. Democratic theory suggests that citizens know their local elected leaders, having worked with them at the local level. In some states, that may still be the case. California, however, is so large and complex, communication between elected leaders and the public is a carefully mediated process. The media, political parties, and interest groups are the vehicles through which these communication functions take place.

The role of parties in linking the public to their elected leaders has also changed over time. The influence of parties has declined as a consequence of several reforms—some going back to the Progressives and some more recent—as well as a consequence of the emergence of media power over the past 30 years. Commensurate with the rising power of the electronic media, and the rising costs associated with media politics, interest groups and political actions committees (PACs) have gained power through their ability to channel economic resources to campaign staff.

MEDIA POLITICS

Through political advertising, editorials and commentaries, and news and entertainment programming, media elites—those who exert a disproportionate influence over media content—are effectively able to control access to California's political discourse. The degree to which ordinary Californians and their grassroots organizations are able to compete in this arena may determine the extent to which they are able to affect policy outcomes. At the same time interest groups play a dominant role in providing direct pressure to the policy process and indirect influence through campaign contributions. The linkage between media politics, parties, and interest groups is made clear when correlating the costs of amplifying one's message through broadcast media and the significant role parties and interest groups play in financing campaigns. The media provide the vehicle through which candidates and elected officials communicate with the public: Parties and interest groups are vehicles that citizens use to communicate with elected officials.

MEDIA EFFECTS AND THE VULNERABILITY OF POLITICAL ATTITUDES

A significant body of research has been compiled on the question of mass media's effect on political attitudes. The initial research found little relationship. The discussion was reframed in the 1960s, when political scientist Philip Converse questioned the dominant notion that citizens are rational actors with fully developed attitudes on a wide variety of issues.[1] Walter Lippmann, after all, warned attitude researchers early in the twentieth century that individuals, like the media, simplify complex reality into a manageable representation. People simply cannot focus on every conceivable issue.[2]

Mass media, however, play a major role in defining the boundaries within which the public debate exists. The specific effect the media have on how individuals feel about specific issues is subtle. Rather than overtly propagandize, the media define the opinion choices citizens have. Over a lifetime, the cumulative effects of media messages are significant. Between 1946 and 1961 the Yale Program of Research on Communication and Attitude Change conducted numerous studies on the effect of communication on political attitudes. Shearon Lowery and Melvin DeFleur summarize the Yale findings:

> In summary, the many separate but related studies of the Yale Communication Research Program can be categorized as focusing on the communicators, the message, the audience, and the audience's responses to persuasive communications. In terms of the communicator, the program found that source credibility was an important factor in obtaining immediate opinion change. Low-credibility sources were seen as more biased and more unfair than were high-credibility sources. The researchers also found that the effects of the communicator's credibility diminish over time, because members of the audience tend to disassociate the message from the communicator. However, these credibility effects can be reinstated simply by reminding the audience who said what. Overall, however, most of the opinion change obtained was short rather than long term. Thus, while it is not difficult to change opinion immediately after a persuasive communication, when the change is measured a month later the audience has often reverted to its original position.[3]

These studies suggest that repeated exposure to a similar message agenda, especially when delivered by sources deemed to be highly credible, results in opinion change to reflect the message agenda.

Observational learning is the most widely cited process through which television affects attitudes. People internalize depictions of reality and form attitudinal responses. This exists both within entertainment programming and news programming. Entertainment programming creates roles that viewers often accept as accurate depictions of social interactions, with which they measure their own social interactions. News programming is much less subtle, in that it overtly articulates an interpretation of reality upon which viewers base political attitudes.

Numerous studies point out the inverse relationship between education levels and opinion influence by televised media. Nonetheless, issue awareness has always remained rather low among the whole population. People are simply too busy living their lives to follow politics closely. It is thus fair to assume that the influence of media on political attitudes is substantial, in that the media are the only access most individuals have to the world around them beyond their immediate community. The ability to determine the agenda and scope of media messages, then, may in fact translate into the ability to influence political attitudes.

THE MEDIA AND GOVERNMENTAL POLITICS IN CALIFORNIA

The ability to amplify one's message is critical in policy debates as well as elections. Electronic and print media, therefore, are necessary tools. The traditional family-owned newspapers played a major role in California's political history, reflecting the economic and political interests of their publishers. Families used their papers to push policies, candidates, and commerce that they favored. All the large publishing families held an interest in land speculation and industry, and therefore generated extremely favorable—some might say skewed—coverage of the land speculation and development that came to characterize the first half of the twentieth century. The Otis family's *Los Angeles Times* involvement in pressing for Owens Valley water to support sprawling residential development in the San Fernando Valley is merely one of the better known examples.[4] Hearst's *San Francisco Examiner*, the de Young brothers' *San Francisco Chronicle*, and McClatchy's *Sacramento Bee* all followed similar paths. It was not until the "Lou Grant" days of the 1970s that professional management and public ownership forced more professional balance.

The Vietnam War demonstrated the power of broadcast media over print media. Television coverage of the war brought home the gritty reality of combat like never before. Americans increasingly turned to their televisions to get their news. By war's end in 1974, television emerged as the primary source of information for Californians: Virtually all California households owned at least one television. The importance of television to politics was made clear in the Kennedy-Nixon debate in 1960.[5] But there remain serious questions as to the quality of information broadcast. In a state the size of California, statewide coverage is critical for keeping citizens informed. Yet no California station maintains a news bureau in the state capital. State politics receive less than 2 percent of newscast time, most of which is rehashed from newspapers and wire services.[6] Observers suggest that national political coverage, although much less relevant to the everyday life of most people, is much more in demand, as is the typical scandal, crime, and fire coverage of local news.

THE MEDIA AND ELECTORAL POLITICS IN CALIFORNIA

Since 1960 political advertising has emerged as a major determinant of outcomes in the electoral arena. It is also a major factor in the abstract area of attitude acquisition, defining for many voters who is more "presidential" or more "electable." Political advertising is successful in establishing an agenda both for the immediate election at hand, as well as the ongoing political climate. Several studies have found that political advertising can cause substantial change in voter attitudes.[7]

The need to advertise on television has increased the already colossal cost of mounting a statewide campaign in California. The 1994 gubernatorial race provides a case in point. The primary campaigns alone spent $29 million (see Table 11.1). The general election campaign between Democrat Kathleen Brown and Republican Pete Wilson was one of the most expensive governor's races ever. As Table 11.2 illustrates, the two campaigns spent $32 million in the general election.[8] Driving these figures is the high cost of advertising on television. To run a credible campaign for statewide office and to reach the voters from Alpine County to San Diego County, candidates must purchase massive amounts of paid TV ads to blanket the state.

TABLE 11.1   1994 PRIMARY ELECTION CAMPAIGN RECEIPTS AND EXPENDITURES

CANDIDATES FOR GOVERNOR	BEGINNING CASH ON HAND	CONTRIBUTIONS RECEIVED	MISCELLANEOUS CASH	EXPENDITURES MADE
DEMOCRATS				
Kathleen Brown	$2,132,768	$10,705,269	$305,773	$10,647,017
Mark Calney	70	335	0	253
John Garamendi	1,198	4,795,252	30,873	4,789,399
Tom Hayden	10,097	402,521	237	1,273
Charles Pineda	0	2,735	0	1,273
Jonathan Trip	0	2,700	0	2,566
Subtotal				**$15,829,521**
REPUBLICANS				
Louis D'Arrigo	$0	$0	$0	$0
Jim Hart	0	0	0	0
Ron Unz	0	2,328,649	1,199	7,114
Pete Wilson	21,426	15,112,050	258,257	4,713,194
Subtotal				**$12,999,843**
Total				**$28,829,364**

Source: Gerald Lubenow, ed., *California Votes: The 1994 Governor's Race* (Berkeley: Institute of Governmental Studies Press, University of California, Berkeley, 1995).

TABLE 11.2   GENERAL GUBERNATORIAL ELECTION CAMPAIGN, RECEIPTS
AND EXPENDITURES, 1978–1994

YEAR	CANDIDATE	RECEIPTS	EXPENDITURES
1978	Jerry Brown (D)	$3,485,328	$3,435,034
	Evelle Younger (R)	2,324,400	2,274,772
		$5,809,728	**$5,709,806**
1982	George Deukmejian (R)	$5,143,967	$4,972,389
	Tom Bradley (D)	6,627,492	6,803,633
		$11,771,459	**$11,776,022**
1986	George Deukmejian (R)	$4,774,842	$9,565,125
	Tom Bradley (D)	5,767,675	6,137,522
		$10,542,517	**$15,702,647**
1990	Pete Wilson (R)	$12,205,291	$16,028,590
	Dianne Feinstein (D)	12,718,038	13,227,930
		$24,923,329	**$29,256,520**
1994	Pete Wilson (R)	$14,828,808	$19,555,243
	Kathleen Brown (D)	9,294,145	12,251,634
		$24,122,953	**$31,806,877**

Source: Gerald Lubenow, ed., *California When The 1994 Governor's Race* (Berkeley: Institute of Governmental Studies Press, University of California, Berkeley, 1995).

PAID MEDIA

Broadcast media markets are defined by areas of dominant influence, or ADIs. ADIs are the geographic boundaries that encircle a common audience. California is divided into 15 ADIs. Due to the concentration of population in four urban centers, however, 85 percent of the state can be covered in four ADIs: Los Angeles, San Francisco, San Diego, and Sacramento.[9] The cost of advertising is dependent on an ADIs size and the Nielsen rating of a particular show, in addition to ad length. Los Angeles currently is the nation's most expensive ADI at $1,150 per rating point. A 30-second spot on a show with 10 rating points would cost $11,500. In the 1994 gubernatorial race, political "spots" in Los Angeles ranged between $12,000 and $30,000. The enormous costs of political advertising on television may be prohibitive for smaller races or challengers with small campaign war chests. The high prices charged for California ADIs encourage all candidates to seek free media.[10]

FREE MEDIA

Free media includes any news coverage a candidate might acquire through press conferences, photo opportunities, and staged spectacles. During campaign cycles, staged events tend to dominate political news coverage. Between cycles, elected officials hold news conferences to maximize visibility. Since candidates for office require extensive visibility, there often is a sense of spectacle to such events. The O. J. Simpson case provided ample opportunity for Los Angeles District Attorney Gil Garcetti to acquire statewide, and even nationwide, visibility. In the same way, elected officials are often tempted to pursue sensational policies in an effort to stimulate coverage. Within days of the death of Princess Diana, State Senator Tom Hayden was on the radio talk show circuit pushing for anti-paparazzi legislation. Certainly some elected officials will pursue symbolic policies that may attract political support, but may be extremely difficult to implement. Many observers suggest that Pete Wilson's support of Propositions 187 and 209 was targeted at maximizing free media coverage in an effort to gain national visibility for a possible second run for president.

POLITICAL PARTIES IN CALIFORNIA

One reason for the media's significant role in state politics is California's weak party system. Early in the twentieth century, Progressive reformers practically dismantled the parties in their zeal to fight corruption and the influence of special interests. California Progressives were concerned about the power of party machines, such as Boss Ruef's rule over San Francisco, and the domination of state government by the Southern Pacific Railroad. The introduction of nonpartisan local elections, cross-filing, the construction of a civil service system, and the end of patronage are all reforms that weakened the influence of state parties in government and in elections. Public loyalty to the two major parties has also been in decline, both in California and nationwide.

The California State Election Code provides detailed rules and structures that both the Democratic and Republican parties must follow. These guidelines, however, were created by elected legislators—Democrats and Republicans—and thus the parties themselves enjoyed great latitude in scripting the guidelines. Registered voters of both parties elect representatives to the county central committees in the primary elections. County central committees are the primary managers of local party activities. The workhorses of California's 58 county central committees are the assembly district committees, which are responsible for campaigns in the 80 assembly districts statewide. While these committees may appear independent, party affairs tend to be dominated by existing officeholders in each county who control the power, money, and resources locally. The state central committees have about 2,500–3,000 members on the Democratic party side and about 1,400 members on the Republican side. They coordinate state party affairs, orchestrate political campaigns for party designates, draft the state party platform (an agenda of major ideological principles and goals reflective of the party's stance), and select presidential electors. And, the state central committees, along with their executive board, nominate delegates to the national convention and serve as the state's party representatives on the national committee of each party.

THE ROLE OF PARTIES IN CALIFORNIA POLITICS

For many years, parties in the legislature maintained discipline by redistributing campaign money among members. This practice began under Assembly Speaker Jesse Unruh, who coined the overused phrase, "money is the mother's milk of politics."[11]

It continued under subsequent speakers, from Democrat Willie Brown to Republican Curt Pringle, whose domination of party campaign funds allowed them to maintain control of the institution and its agenda. However, the passage of Proposition 208 in 1996 limits the practice of redistributing campaign money, making the maintenance of party discipline more difficult.

The once-dominant role of the parties in campaigns and elections has been diminished since the Progressive era, and recent reforms have further weakened the parties. In 1974, in the aftermath of Watergate, California voters adopted Proposition 9, which was sponsored by Common Cause and Secretary of State Jerry Brown (then a candidate for governor). The initiative required politicians to disclose campaign contributions and expenditures of $100 or more as well as donations that could be potential conflicts of interest. It also established the California Fair Political Practices Commission (FPPC), an enforcement agency with the power to launch its own investigations into campaign finance abuse and to issue fines when violations occur.

In 1988, voters approved Proposition 73, which limited individual contributions to $1,000 and organizational and PAC contributions to between $2,500 and $5,000. The California Supreme Court struck down the measure in 1990. Voters approved Proposition 208 in 1996, which limits individual donors and groups to a maximum of $250 per candidate in an election, although they are allowed to donate more if the candidate agrees to a voluntary spending limit. It also imposes spending limits on parties and prohibits the transfer of funds between candidates. In short, Proposition 208 will severely restrict the role of the parties in state elections if it is allowed to stand. Currently, the measure is being held up in court.

The waning influence of parties may have begun during the Progressive era, but voters continue to view party influence as suspect. Although a 1996 federal court overturned the longstanding Progressive era prohibition keeping parties from officially endorsing candidates, both parties continue to be cautious about overstepping. While the Democrats have begun to carefully experiment with endorsements, Republicans, concerned about dividing their party, have thus far avoided endorsing individual candidates. The future of party politics in California continues to be in question.

INTEREST GROUP POLITICS

If broadcast and print media are used by elected officials and those seeking office to communicate with the public, interest groups are vehicles through which the public communicates with elected officials. Interest group politics is vilified by many, but it in fact represents a critical aspect of political participation. Interest groups participate in the governmental process by lobbying elected officials. They are also active in electoral politics by donating money and resources to candidates, and even by waging their own political campaigns.

All Californians are represented by several single-issue interest groups. Whether it be the local, county, school district, or favorite grassroots organization, all Californians benefit from the representation these groups provide. However, that representation is not equal, and some organizations benefit from much greater access than others. Interest group politics is a founding principle in American politics. We all recognize the problems of unequal access. James Madison argued 200 years ago that while factionalism represents a threat to democracy, the option to disallow such groups represents an even greater threat. Rather than outlaw interest groups, Madison argued persuasively that interest groups should be encouraged. In so doing, more groups will emerge, creating counterbalance to each other. If one group is bad, then two groups are better, and 2,000 groups are better yet. Problems emerge when powerful groups have coalescing interests.

The pluralist model of counterbalancing elites' mediating interests is inadequate. The theoretical work done by Mills, and empirical work done by Dye, Domhoff, and Presthus, among others, suggest that rather than competing, the interests of economic elites tend to cohere in key policy areas.[12] Lowi's *The End of Liberalism*[13] argues that this interest group influence threatens the democratic basis of government. If interest groups provide the framework for government–citizen interaction, and these groups are based on individual self-interest, there may be little opportunity for pursuing a meaningful public interest.

There are currently 1,024 registered lobbyists and over 350 registered lobbying firms representing some 1,956 paying interest groups throughout the state and beyond.[14] As Table 11.3 shows, almost $267 million was spent lobbying California state government in the 1994–1996 legislative session. Not surprisingly, this is up from prior sessions, and if past performance is an indicator, the expenditures during the 1996–1998 and 1998–2000 sessions will be even higher. As Table 11.4 illustrates, lobbying efforts are not restricted to private corporations. The industry with the highest expenditures was government. Between 1994 and 1996 local and county governments spent $37 million lobbying the state. Oil and gas corporations spent less than half that—$15 million. Still, the single largest expenditure was by the Western States Petroleum Association—$3,883,845 (see Table 11.5).

Interest groups have long influenced the California political landscape. The Central Pacific Railroad, for example, dominated California politics from the 1860s through 1910 when the Progressive movement successfully won constitutional amendments and new statutes to limit railroad influence. Today, lobbyists advocate on everything from agriculture to organized labor to university student services to theme parks.

TABLE 11.3   LOBBYING EXPENDITURES FOR LEGISLATIVE SESSIONS, 1988–1996

SESSION	EXPENDITURES
1988–1990	$193,575,480
1990–1992	233,872,097
1992–1994	250,119,667
1994–1996	266,939,559

Source: Bill Jones, Secretary of State, *Lobbying Expenditures and the Top 100 Lobbying Firms 1995–1996* (Sacramento, CA: Secretary of State's Office, June 1997).

TABLE 11.4   LOBBYING EXPENDITURES FOR 1994–1996 LEGISLATIVE SESSION (RANKED HIGH TO LOW)

Local and County Government	$36,947,670
Health	30,831,647
Finance and Insurance	28,965,837
Miscellaneous	28,569,220
Manufacturing/Industrial	28,459,113
Professional/Trade	18,722,322
Education	16,117,939
Utilities	15,636,128
Oil and Gas	15,220,828
Labor Unions	8,736,787
Entertainment and Recreation	6,727,759
Agriculture	6,153,211
Real Estate	6,087,409
Legal	5,714,396
Transportation	5,170,784
Public Employees	4,038,691
Merchandise/Retail	3,173,226
Lodging/Restaurants	938,092
Political Organizations	728,496
Total	**$266,939,559**

Source: Bill Jones, Secretary of State, *Lobbying Expenditures and the Top 100 Lobbying Firms 1995–1996* (Sacramento, CA: Secretary of State's Office, June 1997).

TABLE 11.5   ORGANIZATIONS SPENDING THE MOST ON LOBBYING ACTIVITIES, 1994–1996 LEGISLATIVE SESSION

Western States Petroleum Association	$3,883,845
California Healthcare Association and affiliated entities	2,686,270
California Cable Television Association	2,627,989
Pacific Telesis Group and subsidiaries	2,567,223
California Medical Association, Inc.	2,449,664
Chevron Corporation and subsidiaries	2,408,031
Consumer Attorneys of California	2,147,192
Edison International and subsidiaries	2,125,701
California Chamber of Commerce	2,100,380
California Teachers Association	1,985,108

Source: Bill Jones, Secretary of State, *Lobbying Expenditures and the Top 100 Lobbying Firms 1995–1996* (Sacramento, CA: Secretary of State's Office, June 1997).

When successful, the interest group dynamic allows Madisonian democracy to flourish, allowing the public access to politics and policy in a direct and meaningful way. When unsuccessful, the group dynamic maximizes the power and influence of those interests most able to pay.

Interest groups have learned to exploit the ballot initiative process in order to circumvent elected representatives altogether. By placing legislative proposals directly before the voters, groups have more control over final policy outcomes. Even when an initiative's chances of victory are slim, interest groups have strong incentives to pursue this type of strategy.[15] These reasons revolve around mobilization and group cohesion. First, a controversial ballot measure can help mobilize group members, whose participation is crucial for the group to be effective. Second, an initiative campaign can invigorate the group itself—regardless of outcome. Even a futile campaign for an unpopular ballot measure is an opportunity to attract and recruit new members. Third, groups have an unparalleled opportunity to influence public opinion in the context of an election. Groups can take advantage of free media to get their message out and possibly influence public opinion in advance of the next legislative session or election. Finally, the issue may entice enough sympathetic voters to go to the polls to influence the outcome of other races on the ballot. The increasing use of the initiative by deep-pocket interests threatens to destabilize the democratic equilibrium Madison was so concerned about.

INTEREST GROUPS AND ELECTORAL POLITICS

Stepping into the void that was left by the weakened parties, interest groups are asserting an ever-greater role in the state's political campaigns. Key to their influence are campaign donations from PACs. Much of the money that used to be distributed by parties is now filtered to candidates through PACs, which are controlled by interest groups. In contrast to parties, many of these groups are motivated by narrow agendas, to which candidates must cater in order to secure contributions. This reliance on single-issue groups, it is argued, contributes to the fragmentation of politics.[16] Even though individual donors are still the largest source of donations to political campaigns, PACs are growing in significance.

Even without PAC money, the augmented role of interest groups means that in some races, groups can outspend the candidate's own organizations, hijacking the political debate and rendering the parties irrelevant. The influence of interest groups in one recent election gained national attention. A special election was held in 1998 to replace the late U.S. Representative Walter Capps, a Democrat whose 22nd District encompassed San Luis Obispo and Santa Barbara Counties along the central coast. Two Republicans faced the late congressman's widow, Democrat Lois Capps, who was running to succeed her husband. Initially, the campaign revolved around local and state issues, including the future of a nearby Air Force base, HMO reform legislation, and a school construction bond. However, the contest took place in a competitive district, and national interest groups poured hundreds of thousands of dollars into the race in order to influence the outcome. The AFL-CIO, Planned Parenthood, and the Wisconsin-based Americans for Limited Terms spent money on ads and direct mail intended to help Capps. The Republicans competing for the seat benefited from similar activities, financed by the Christian Coalition, the Foundation for Responsible Government (an anti-tax group), and the Campaign for Working Families (a conservative group opposed to late-term abortions).[17] Capps won the election, but only after she and her opponents had lost control of the campaign agenda. They spent most of the campaign debating abortion and term limits, not the issues of primary concern to the voters of the central coast.

SUMMARY

This chapter has explored the role of the media, political parties, and interest groups in California's political process. In this media age the escalating costs of political campaigns have encouraged interest groups and the media to play an enhanced role in governmental politics and elections, filling the vacuum left behind by weakened political parties. Print and broadcast media— particularly television—have emerged as the dominant tools with which elected officials and those seeking elected office amplify their voices to the public. Interest groups have emerged as the tools of sophisticated citizens who seek to maximize individual participation and influence. However, the major parties still play an important role in the electoral process, as we will see in the next chapter. This chapter began by exploring the impacts and effects of media messages, as well as the markets and costs of political advertising. It then examined the role and impacts of parties and interest groups in California. Ultimately, parties, interest groups, and the media are powerful tools in the policy process. Those individuals and organizations—whether public or private, for profit or non-profit—who can best utilize these tools will enjoy greater influence.

NOTES

1. Philip E. Converse, "The Nature of Belief Systems in Mass Publics," in *Ideology and Discontent*, David Apter, ed. (New York: Free Press, 1964).
2. See Walter Lippmann, *Public Opinion* (New York: Free Press, 1922).
3. For a full discussion, see Shearon Lowery and Melvin DeFleur, *Milestones in Mass Communication Research: Media Effects* (New York: Longman, 1983).
4. The film *Chinatown* depicts the role of Los Angeles elites, in particular the *Los Angeles Times*, in foisting a false water emergency on Los Angeles residents in order to influence bond measures to fund the Owens Valley water grab.
5. The Kennedy–Nixon debate in 1960 was a turning point for demonstrating the power of television in politics. The debate was both televised and broadcast over radio. Television viewers widely credited Kennedy with "winning" the debate while radio listeners credited Nixon with "winning." The ability to convey nonverbal cues through a television debate or advertisement has become extremely important—and more so now that most people get most of their information from television.
6. Dan Walters, "Stations Ignore State Capitol," *San Jose Mercury News*, 22 November 1988, B5. In Gerston and Christensen, *California Politics and Government* (San Francisco: Wadsworth, 1995).

7. Blumber & McQuail, 1969; Patterson & McClure, 1976. Further, there is a positive relationship between advertising exposure and levels of political information (Hofstetter & Buss, 1980; Hofstetter, Zukin, Buss, 1978; Mendelsohn & O'Keefe, 1976). Political advertising communicates an issue agenda that defines the political debate (Bowers, 1973; Kaid, 1976).

8. Gerald Lubenow, ed., *California Votes: The 1994 Governor's Race* (Berkeley: Institute of Governmental Studies Press, University of California, Berkeley, 1995).

9. Gerston and Christensen, *California Politics and Government* (San Francisco: Wadsworth, 1995).

10. See Stephen Ansolabehere, Roy Behr, and Shanto Iyengar, *The Media Game: American Politics in the Television Age* (New York: MacMillan Publishing Company, 1993).

11. Unruh's advisors date the earliest use of that phrase in print to the article, "Big Daddy's Big Drive," *Look*, 25 September 1962.

12. See C. Wright Mills, *The Power Elite* (Oxford: Oxford University Press, 1956); Thomas Dye, *Who's Running America? The Conservative Years*, 4th ed. (Englewood Cliffs, NJ: Prentice-Hall, 1986); G. William Domhoff, *Who Rules America Now?* (New York: Simon and Schuster, 1983); Robert Presthus, *Elites in the Policy Process* (Cambridge, MA: Cambridge University Press, 1974).

13. Theodore Lowi, *The End of Liberalism*, 2nd ed. (New York: W. W. Norton, 1979).

14. Bill Jones, Secretary of State, *1997–1998 Directory of Lobbyists, Lobbying Firms, and Lobbyists Employers* (Sacramento, CA: Secretary of State's Office, 1997).

15. See Mark J. Rozell and Clyde Wilcox, *Interest Groups in American Campaigns* (Washington, D.C.: Congressional Quarterly Press, 1999).

16. See Ross Baker, *The New Fat Cats* (New York: Priority Press, 1989).

17. Todd S. Purdum, "Interest Groups Run Own Race in California," *New York Times*, 7 March 1998, A3.

CHAPTER 12

The Electorate as Players: Elections and Political Participation

California voters have the opportunity to exercise a great deal of power at the ballot box. Every two years, Californians choose the entire state assembly, half of the state senate, and the state's delegation to the U.S. House of Representatives, the largest delegation of any state. In non-presidential election years, Californians must choose candidates to fill the state's executive offices, including the governor and secretary of state. Besides electing candidates for office, the voters are regularly called upon to amend the state's constitution, to reverse legislative acts, or to decide other weighty issues brought to ballot through the initiative process. This chapter examines the role of the electorate as players in the policy process. It first examines California's election cycle and then goes on to explore the role of declining voter turnout. The chapter considers the implications of voter decline in political participation.

THE ELECTION CYCLE

Parties have played an increasingly minimal role in the recruitment of candidates, the selection of nominees, and even in the general election campaign. Consequently, in California's candidate-centered politics, candidates must build their own campaign organizations, raise money, and purchase media time with little or no coordination or support from the state party committees. There are few constitutional restrictions governing who may run for office. One must be a U.S. citizen and a resident of the state. In legislative offices such as the state assembly or senate, the candidate must live in the district that the seat represents. Since there are no explicit regulations as to how district residency must be established, some candidates have been attacked as "carpetbaggers" who move into a district in order to file nomination papers. One must also be a registered voter of the party whose nomination is being sought, although independents can run for partisan offices.

In order to file for candidacy, anyone seeking public office must first file a declaration of intent with the county clerk or register recorder. Nomination papers must be returned within the specified time frame, with a completed petition among a limited amount of voters and a small filing fee (usually 1 percent of the annual salary for most offices; 2 percent of the annual salary for statewide offices). Upon certification by the elections clerk, the name of the candidate is put on the ballot. Ballots carry with them some inherent biases. The candidate's full name appears, followed by the candidate's party affiliation if the election is partisan. In the absence of other information about candidates, voters look for cues in assessing candidates by their occupational designation. Attorneys and other professionals with impressive titles tend to do well. Another inherent bias is the position of the candidate names. Research has demonstrated that at least some voters simply choose the name on the top of the list. Prior to 1974, all incumbents would be listed first thus giving them unfair advantage. Today, ballot position is determined by a lottery.

THE PRIMARY

Primaries were pushed by Progressive reformers early in the twentieth century to give average people a voice in the nomination of candidates. It was thought that allowing citizens to register their preferences at the polls would reduce the power of party bosses and special interests to wield undue influence at state party nominating conventions. Allowing the voters to choose candidates in a direct primary has become the only legitimate method for the two major parties to decide their candidates for the general election in California.

Two recent changes in California's primary election process are likely to have lasting consequences for politics in the state and the nation. One is the "open primary," created by voters in 1996 with the passage of Proposition 198. The second change is the adoption of an early primary, which could make California the decisive battleground in the presidential prenomination campaign. In most states with an open primary, voters decide which party's ballot to cast in the privacy of the voting booth. California's version of the open primary (also called a "blanket" primary) is modeled after similar systems in Washington state and Alaska, where every voter is issued an identical ballot at the polling place on Election Day. The ballot allows voters to choose among any of the candidates of every officially recognized party, regardless of the voter's own party affiliation. In June 1998, for example, voters in California's first open primary had the opportunity to choose among 17 candidates (in seven parties) for governor. Under the old system, a voter was issued a ballot only for the party with which he or she had registered.

Proposition 198 passed overwhelmingly with 60 percent of the vote, despite vigorous opposition by both major political parties. The initiative was sponsored by Representative Tom Campbell, a moderate Republican who had lost a bid for his party's nomination for the U.S. senate to conservative media personality Bruce Herschensohn. In the general election, Herschensohn was defeated by liberal Democrat Barbara Boxer. Ironically, Boxer secured the Democratic nomination after defeating a moderate opponent in a closed primary. Supporters of the open primary claim that the old system of nominations was dominated by the extreme wings of the two parties. They argue that allowing independents and crossover voters to participate will stimulate interest by offering voters more choice and help moderate consensus-building candidates win nomination.[1] Critics fear that the new rules may create opportunities for mischief in the nomination process—with voters of one party crossing lines to help nominate the weaker candidate of the opposing party.

California's "early" primary was adopted by the legislature in 1998 in order to move up the date of California's primary to March, making it one of the earliest in the nation. In past election years, California's contest had been held at the end of the primary season in June. By that late date, the nominees for president had already been determined. Holding a March 7, 2000 primary—on the heels of the Iowa caucus and New Hampshire primary—is sure to give the Golden State a greater voice in presidential nominations because of the state's huge share of electoral votes. It was also believed that the move was designed to give former Governor Pete Wilson an advantage, should he attempt a second run for president.

Of course, not all races are partisan. Nonpartisan elected offices such as judges, local officials, and the superintendent of public instruction also appear on the primary ballot. During the primary, and without the designation of any party label, all the candidates for a particular nonpartisan elected position are placed on the ballot. The one who receives the majority vote (50 percent plus one) wins outright in the primary. If no one receives the majority vote, the top two vote-getters will face off in the general election.

THE GENERAL ELECTION

California holds its general elections on the first Tuesday after the first Monday in the month of November for both state and national offices. The period between the primary and the general election is typically an intense political season in which candidates work to secure their party loyalists and try to attract crossover votes from the ranks of the opposition party and from independent voters. Gubernatorial candidates Gray Davis and Dan Lungren, for example, spent much of the 1998 general election campaign trying to position themselves at the political center, attempting to appeal to the "median" voter. In an October debate in Sacramento, *both* Davis and Lungren spent time talking about how they were pro-death penalty, against assault weapons, pro-abortion rights, pro-HMO reform, in favor of targeted tax cuts for business, and supportive of public schools while acknowledging that education needed reform. Republican Lungren wanted to eliminate the car tax; Democrat Davis wanted it reduced. At the same time, each candidate tried repeatedly to show that his opponent held positions on these issues that were out of the mainstream.[2]

SPECIAL ELECTIONS

A special election is called when there is a vacancy during the term of a member of the state legislature or congressional delegation due to death, retirement, resignation or some other reason. When a special election becomes necessary, the governor decides when to schedule the vote. These elections are infrequent, but they come with a hefty price tag: approximately $40–$50 million. One type of special election, the recall, was designed by Progressive reformers to remove corrupt politicians from office. In recent years, it has been used as a partisan instrument. In 1995, former Assembly Speaker Doris Allen and another Republican assembly member were removed from office after some of their conservative Orange County constituents, upset over Allen's power-sharing arrangement with assembly Democrats, gathered enough signatures for a recall.[3] Generally, voters who participate in special elections tend to be highly motivated by partisanship or have passionate feelings about a candidate or issue at hand. Turnout in these contests is low and the electorate tends to be whiter, older, and more ideologically conservative than in the general election.

Special elections have characteristics of both primary and general elections. Voters are given a choice of all candidates from all parties on a single ballot. If a candidate gets a simple majority of the vote, he or she is the winner. If no one receives a clear majority, the top two vote-getters face each other four weeks later in a run-off election. Given the state's term limits initiative that passed in 1990, one might expect to see more special elections in the future as legislators leave office midway through their terms for other political offices or more lucrative positions in the private sector.

CALIFORNIA'S ELECTORATE

California's electorate is one of the most complex in the nation. While the state has had more registered Democrats than Republicans for most of the postwar era, this partisan balance has not always been reflected in electoral outcomes. Gray Davis was only the third Democrat to be elected governor since the end of World War II. Similarly, in nine of the last 13 presidential elections, California voted for Republican presidential candidates (the Republican ticket in seven of those contests included either Richard Nixon or Ronald Reagan—both Californians). One reason why California has remained competitive is that voters have always been willing to cross party lines. The antipartyism of the Progressive era has remained a powerful force in state politics, causing voters to shun party labels in statewide elections and to choose candidates on the basis of multiple criteria. In the last gubernatorial election, nearly one out of five (18 percent) Republican voters cast their ballots for Davis in 1998. While crossover votes were key to the victories of Republican governors in the four previous elections, this time the Democratic candidate reaped the benefits of a campaign that successfully appealed to this crossover constituency.

As Table 12.1 illustrates, party registration tells only part of the story. The exit poll data also reveal that the largest ideological category in the electorate (43 percent) was not "liberal" or "conservative," but "moderate." More than two-thirds of these self-identified moderates (68 percent) supported Davis over his conservative opponent, Attorney General Dan Lungren. In contrast, Lungren won a majority of the votes in just a few key Republican constituencies: conservatives, registered Republicans, Protestants, and voters in the Central Valley. Senator Barbara Boxer, a liberal Democrat running for re-election on the same ballot, did slightly worse among "moderates" than Davis.

TABLE 12.1 PROFILE OF THE 1998 ELECTORATE

		GOVERNOR		SENATOR	
	% OF VOTERS	DAVIS (D)	LUNGREN (R)	BOXER (D)	FONG (R)
Gender					
Male	51	53	42	47	49
Female	49	62	35	57	39
Age					
18–29	10	63	29	59	33
30–49	40	58	38	53	43
50–64	21	56	39	55	42
65 +	29	56	42	46	51
Ethnicity					
White	64	51	45	47	49
Black	13	76	22	64	34
Latino	13	71	23	69	24
Asian	8	65	35	48	51
Education					
High School	20	61	34	56	37
Some College	26	59	38	52	43
College Grad.	36	54	43	50	47
Adv. Degree	18	59	37	53	45
Party					
Democrat	48	90	9	86	12
Independent	8	60	28	48	43
Republican	39	18	80	13	85
Ideology					
Liberal	23	87	6	85	11
Moderate	43	68	28	48	43
Conservative	34	24	74	16	81
Income					
Less than $20,000	10	70	26	65	30
20,000–39,999	19	63	31	56	37
40,000–59,999	21	60	38	56	42
60,000–74,999	17	58	39	52	44
More than 75,000	33	50	46	47	50
Religion					
Protestant*	43	47	51	41	56
Catholic	26	58	38	54	42
Jewish	5	80	19	72	27
Region					
LA County	23	69	27	64	32
Other S. Cal.	31	49	48	42	54
Cen. Valley	17	43	52	38	56
SF Bay Area	14	72	24	70	27
Other N. Cal.	15	62	34	59	39

*Includes all non-Roman Catholic Christians.

Source: *Los Angeles Times* Exit Poll, November 5, 1998.

The size and impact of these self-identified moderates may reflect a growing frustration with partisan politics. Nonetheless, California's electorate is growing ever more reluctant to identify with either of the two major political parties. The proportion of the state's electorate registered as Democrats and Republicans has been shrinking over time. While the Democrats and Republicans remain dominant, increasing numbers of independent and minor-party voters have the potential to influence election outcomes, threatening the hegemony of the two major parties. Growing dissatisfaction with the two major parties has fueled the growth of alternative parties nationwide.

MINOR PARTIES

In the 1996 general election, no fewer than six minor parties joined the Republicans and Democrats on the ballot in California. Among these parties were the laissez-faire, anti-tax Libertarian Party and the pro-environment, pro-social justice Green Party. Two minor parties that developed from the social movements of the 1960s were the anti-war Peace and Freedom Party and the conservative, pro-segregationist American Independent Party, which was inspired by the candidacy of former Alabama Governor George Wallace. Finally, two new parties that qualified for the ballot in time for the 1996 election were the Natural Law Party, which was a political offshoot of Maharishi Mahesh Yogi's Transcendental Meditation movement, as well as the Reform Party, founded by Texas billionaire and presidential candidate H. Ross Perot.

A party can qualify for the ballot and field candidates in California if it can gather the signatures of 1 percent of the state's registered voters (890,064 signatures) on petitions seeking "official" status for the party. Prior to seeking official status, new parties normally hold a party caucus, select party nominees, agree on a party plank, and design a campaign strategy. To remain an official party, it must get at least 2 percent of the statewide vote for at least one candidate and retain $\frac{1}{15}$ of 1 percent of registered voters. In some states, minor parties have had a limited impact as "spoilers," skimming enough votes away from one of the two major parties to effectively hand a victory to the other party. So far, these minor parties have had little impact on the duopoly of the two major parties in California. As Table 12.2 shows, the Democrats and Republicans accounted for 46 percent and 35 percent of the state electorate, respectively, in 2000. By comparison, none of the six minor parties could claim more than 2 percent of California voters. Voters with no party affiliation, on the other hand, accounted for 14 percent of the electorate.

THE RISE OF INDEPENDENT VOTERS

Despite the proliferation of alternative parties, many voters have shunned party politics altogether. Americans have been less willing to identify themselves as Republicans or Democrats ever since the late 1960s. Mirroring national trends, voters in California have been registering as independents in higher rates. According to the registration figures in Table 12.2, independents comprise 14 percent of California's registered voters—the third largest group after Democrats and Republicans.

Combined, independents and minor-party voters comprise just 19 percent of the state electorate. Because no single party can claim a clear majority of the voters, this

TABLE 12.2   VOTER REGISTRATION BY PARTY, FEBRUARY 2000

PARTY	REGISTERED VOTERS	% OF TOTAL
Democratic	6,684,668	45.69
Republican	5,140,951	35.14
American Independent	295,387	2.02
Green	108,904	.74
Libertarian	87,183	.60
Natural Law	62,183	.42
Reform	85,869	.59
Misc./Non-Qualified	133,997	.92
Declined to State	2,032,663	13.89

Note: Of the 21,220,772 citizens eligible to register to vote, a total of 14,631,805 (68.95 percent) actually registered.
Source: Bill Jones, Secretary of State, *2000 Statement of the Vote.*

sizeable block has significant power to decide the outcome of close elections. This might seem like a sizeable uncommitted block with the potential to challenge the two-party dominance of state politics. In reality, independents tend to be reliable support-ers of one of the two major parties at the ballot box. Voting researchers have found that many independents vote for either the Republican or Democratic parties so con-sistently that they may be considered "closet" Republicans and Democrats.[4] Under Cal-ifornia's weak-party system, the benefits of aligning oneself with a party are not always clear. Until recently, independents were effectively disenfranchised from the primary election stage of the process. That obstacle to participation has been removed with the elimination of the closed primary in 1996. One possible side effect of the open primary, though, is the further weakening of the two major parties in California.

VOTER TURNOUT

Because of California's weak parties, its system of directly deciding policy through the ballot initiative, and its overwhelming significance in presidential elections, the state's voters have considerable power and relevance in comparison to voters in other states. Yet when compared to the national average, California's turnout is quite low. Because of this low turnout, electoral outcomes are often determined by the success a campaign has in getting out the vote. That is, the winning side in a campaign is the one that is more successful at persuading supporters to go to the polls. This rule ap-plies to interest groups as well as candidates. In California's ballot initiative indus-try, proposition sponsors build strategies around the recognition that they only need a simple majority of voters to approve a measure. Once the paid signature gatherers have succeeded in placing the measure on the ballot, strategic advertising can mo-bilize enough potential supporters to make the proposition law. To the firms that sponsor these initiatives, low turnout is actually desirable because a predictable num-ber of voters coupled with targeted advertising is enough to guarantee the success of a ballot measure.[5] Therefore, one consequence of low voter turnout is that California's ballot initiative process is more vulnerable to manipulation by interest groups.

THE DISAPPEARING CALIFORNIA VOTER

Consistent with national trends, participation in California's elections has been declining in recent years. Only 14.6 million of California's 32 million residents are registered to vote. Still fewer actually exercise that right on Election Day. In the 1992 presidential election, 54.5 percent of eligible voters in California made it to the polls. Four years later, that figure was 52.6 percent. In 2000, 67 percent voted in one of the closest presidential contests ever. Turnout in gubernatorial elections has been even more dismal. Since 1982, gubernatorial elections have failed to attract even half of all eligible voters. California now has one of the lowest turnout rates in the nation. Out of all 50 states and the District of Columbia, California ranked 47th in turnout in the 1992 presidential election, despite the unique opportunity that voters had that year to decide two U.S. senate contests.

One option that has made it easier for many people to vote is the absentee ballot. Any Californian is permitted to register to vote in this manner. Prior to 1978, only voters who had a specific reason—such as illness—were permitted to vote absentee. By the 1993 special statewide election, some 22 percent of the electorate were voting absentee. Modern campaign tactics helped fuel the increase of absentee vote-by-mail. Political parties and candidates routinely try to get their identified loyal constituents to vote by absentee ballot. To the campaigns, absentee votes are analogous to money in the bank, gaining interest. If your absentee voter base is secure, you can expend the rest of your limited campaign resources on mobilizing other sympathetic voters. Although growing in popularity, voting by absentee ballot has not succeeded in increasing participation among traditionally underrepresented groups and classes. Absentee voters tend to be older, more affluent, and conservative than the average voter.

VOTER REGISTRATION

Chief among the factors that suppress voter turnout are the nation's restrictive voter registration laws. The United States is one of the only democracies that make its citizens register before they can actually vote. In other Western democracies, where there are no registration requirements, turnout rates of 80–90 percent are not uncommon. Thus, voter registration is somewhat of an anachronistic impediment to full democratic participation. Supporters of the registration process claim that it reduces potential voting fraud. Critics claim that it is an archaic remnant of earlier colonial America and is a burden that drives some voters away from their electoral right. The two-step nature of the voting process creates an additional obstacle, raising the cost of the act of voting for many individuals who are too busy working and living their lives to meet the registration deadline. As a consequence of this impediment, some states in the United States have begun experimenting with Election-Day registration. This has not yet caught on in California.

In order to be eligible to vote, California residents must register and designate a home address at least 29 days before an election. Once a person registers, he or she stays permanently on the voting rolls until changing party affiliation, changing residence, changing name, or is ruled ineligible to vote by a court decision. Of the 14 million or so registered voters in the state, there is a substantial number of nonvoters whose names remain on the state's voting rolls. These names will remain until the state's election officials orchestrate some procedures to remove this "deadwood." Various efforts have been attempted, such as a "negative purge," whereby nonvoters are contacted by postcards via the U.S. mail. If the cards are returned as undeliverable, then the nonvoter's name is dropped. Needless to say this is a cumbersome, highly ineffective means of keeping the voting rolls current. There are also political reasons for the deliberately slow pace of this process. Campaign experts believe that Democrats comprise the lion's share of these chronic nonvoters. Thus, the Democrats have not been particularly eager to assist in purging the voter rolls.

Since turnout is key to the outcome of close contests, successful campaigns must mobilize supporters to register to vote well before Election Day. Thus, voter registration drives are constant fixtures of California politics. The state's two major political parties spend millions of dollars in "soft money" each election cycle to bolster their registration numbers. Professional campaign firms are subcontracted to collect partisan registrations and are paid $3–$6 per head for a valid completed form. Individual candidates in certain legislative districts have been known to set aside a chunk of money to orchestrate their own voter drive—either solo or in cooperation with an adjoining or overlapping member's jurisdiction. Finally, civic groups, churches, nonprofit organizations, colleges, civil rights groups, and other interest groups also help register voters.

In an attempt to encourage voter participation, in 1995 Congress passed the so-called "motor-voter" law, which allows states to take a more active role in registering voters. State and local service providers at the Department of Motor Vehicles or at the County Department of Social Services may provide registration forms and technical assistance in completing them in order to encourage more registration. This law remains highly controversial in a partisan sense because it is assumed that more Democrats than Republicans will be registered in this manner. Even after the law was passed, the Wilson administration dragged its heels for months in implementing the law, until forced by court order to comply.

DEMOGRAPHICS AND VOTER TURNOUT

In addition to the registration requirement, there are socioeconomic factors that affect turnout. Not all groups or classes are equally likely to vote. Generally, the socially and economically disadvantaged are less likely to participate in the political process. Hence, these groups are less likely to make their voices heard at the ballot box. One of the key factors that helps predict whether a person is likely to vote is income. Wealthy and middle-class individuals are more likely to vote than working class individuals. Another factor, which correlates with income, is education. College graduates are significantly more likely to vote than people with no more education than a high school diploma. Paradoxically, increasing rates of education in the general population since the 1950s have not increased turnout overall, although individuals with more education are still more likely to vote. Political scientists have grappled for some time with this puzzle.[6]

Partisanship also matters. Republicans are slightly more likely to vote than Democrats, though this may be a function of income more than party affiliation since Republicans have historically been more affluent than Democrats. In addition, people with strong ideological commitments are more likely to vote than those with weak partisan loyalties. Age is another factor: Individuals between the ages of 35 and 55 are considered more likely to vote than younger or older persons. In California, only one-third of people between the ages of 18 and 24 are registered to vote. Men are still slightly more likely to vote than women, although that difference has been shrinking over time.

A final generalization is that ethnicity matters. Whites are more likely to vote than people of color. Of the white population in California, 65 percent are registered to vote, compared with 58 percent of African Americans, 42 percent of the Latino population, and only 39 percent of the Asian population. These inequalities in registration rates have consequences at the ballot box. A study of political participation by ethnic groups in Southern California found that African Americans vote in approximately the same rates as whites, while Latinos and Asians vote in significantly lower rates. One reason why Latinos and Asians vote in lower rates than whites and African Americans is that immigrants comprise a larger proportion of these communities. Even though it is their right as U.S. citizens, naturalized immigrants tend to vote in lower rates than native-born citizens.

Much of the difference in turnout rates among these groups can be explained by the factors already discussed. The Latino population, on average, tends to be younger than the white population, with lower levels of income and education. When controlling for these differences, the gap in voting disappears. As the average age of the Latino population increases, and as the community becomes more affluent and more highly educated over time, it is projected that the participation gap between Latinos and whites will disappear.[7] At the same time, ethnic identification is believed to increase turnout among Latinos. The mobilization of young Latinos in support of Alex Padilla's (District 7) candidacy in the 1999 Los Angeles city council race demonstrates the potential of the emerging Latino vote. At 26, Padilla was one of the youngest people ever to be elected to a major California city. While still lagging behind white and African-American participation levels, Latino participation grew drastically in the 1990s. This translated directly into benefits for many Latino politicians, including California's first statewide elected Latino leader, Lieutenant Governor Cruz Bustamante.

Among Asian Americans turnout has also been low, even though the Asian community on average is slightly older, with higher rates of income and education. This has been explained by the fact that the Asian community in California is dispersed around the state. Because they are not as geographically concentrated as Latino voters, the diverse and diffuse Asian communities are more difficult to mobilize. But, voting is only one form of political participation. As Latinos and Asians continue to assert political and economic power, their influence and representation will only improve. That increase may further drive up levels of voting in these communities.

IMMIGRATION AND PARTICIPATION

California's status as the leading gateway for new immigrants into the United States has impacts on participation and turnout. Naturalized immigrants, regardless of national origin, are less likely to participate in politics if they are from nations without a democratic tradition, although that difference disappears over time. Immigrants who read newspapers and watch the news on television tend to be more informed and engaged in local politics. Across the state, numerous foreign-language media outlets provide the information that helps new immigrants make this transition. For example, KMEX, one of the Spanish-language television stations in Los Angeles, draws larger audiences for its local newscasts than any of the English-language alternatives. Another example is the *Korea Times*. This international newspaper has a circulation of 50,000 in the Los Angeles area, to which it reports local news as well as news from Korea.

Both organizations boast a dedication to help their audience become citizens by educating them about policy issues, particularly those that affect their communities, such as immigration and welfare reform proposals that would have cut benefits to legal immigrants.[8] English-language television also plays an important role in this process. A study of media use by Korean immigrants in the San Francisco Bay area found that exposure to television news was an important predictor of political learning, because the language barrier is not as severe as in reading English-language newspapers.[9] This suggests that television news has the potential to facilitate the assimilation of immigrants, enticing the state's diverse population into becoming more active and involved citizens.

IMPLICATIONS FOR UNEQUAL PARTICIPATION

The participation gap has serious implications for a state as diverse as California. It raises questions about the legitimacy of a political system that is based upon the principle of majority rule. When six out of ten eligible adults stay away from the polls, it also casts doubt on the ability of a democratically elected legislature to accurately represent public needs, which it must translate into effective policy outputs.[10] If certain subgroups of the electorate are routinely underrepresented at the ballot box, then the bias introduced at the polls may result in inequitable public policies that favor the interests of the majority at the expense of the minority.

Unequal participation is particularly dangerous when there are issues on the public agenda that disproportionately affect minorities. Proposition 187 provides a case in point. In 1994, a sizeable majority of California's voters registered their support for the initiative, which was designed to cut off services to undocumented immigrants. While the initiative was approved by a 20-point margin, Californians were clearly divided along ethnic lines. White voters accounted for most of the initiative's support. African Americans and Asian Americans split their votes. In contrast, 77 percent of

Latinos were opposed to the measure.[11] This made little difference in the outcome, however. Latinos comprised only 8 percent of the voters on Election Day in 1994, even though they made up over one-fourth of the state's population. Whites accounted for 80 percent of voters on Election Day, but they were only 57 percent of the state's population. Given the high turnout among the white majority, it was no surprise which policy preference prevailed on Election Day.

SUMMARY

Political participation in California, as across the country, is on the decline. There are reasons to be hopeful, however. Recent changes in the way the state conducts its primary elections may renew interest in the electoral process. The early primary may energize Californians by the feeling that they could make a difference in choosing the president. The open primary, though a bane to the parties, may stimulate interest in the process by giving voters greater choice.

Thanks to reforms such as the "motor-voter" law and voter registration drives, it has become easier for those eligible to register to vote. Most importantly, however, as California's ethnic communities continue to assert their political will, more equitable participation will emerge, with more equitable policy outcomes as a result. California's electorate may prove to be the most important policy player—given greater levels of participation and fewer stumbling blocks.

NOTES

1. Jennifer Warren, "Voters Seem to Enjoy Chance to Shop Around," *Los Angeles Times*, 3 June 1998, A3.
2. Nicholas Lemann, "Government of, by and for the Comfortable," *New York Times Magazine*, 1 November 1998, 37–42.
3. Dan Bernstein, "Allen Recalled by Huge Margin," *Sacramento Bee*, 29 November 1995, A1.
4. See Bruce Keith, David Magleby, Candice Nelson, Elizabeth Orr, Mark Westlye, and Raymond Wolfinger, *The Myth of the Independent Voter* (Berkeley: University of California, 1992).
5. Peter Shrag, *Paradise Lost: California's Past, America's Future* (San Francisco: Public Policy Institute, 1998).
6. See, for example Richard Brody, "The Puzzle of Participation," in *The New American Political System*, Anthony King, ed. (Washington, D.C.: American Enterprise Institute, 1978).
7. Carole Uhlaner, Bruce Cain, and D. Roderick Kiewiet, "Political Participation of Ethnic Minorities in the 1980s," *Political Behavior* 11 (1989): 195–231.
8. Susan Rasky, "The Media Covers Los Angeles," *California Journal* (July 1997): 42–45.
9. Steven H. Chaffee, Clifford J. Nass, and Seung-Mock Yang, "The Bridging Role of Television in Immigrant Political Socialization," *Human Communication Research* 17 (1990): 266–288.
10. For a classic expression of this argument, see E. E. Schattschneider, *The Semisovereign People* (Philadelphia: Harcourt Brace Jovanovich, 1975).
11. Patrick J. McDonnell, "State's Diversity Doesn't Reach Voting Booth," *Los Angeles Times*, 10 November 1994, A1.

CHAPTER 13

Education Policy

Featured Reading / Pages 141–142
Susan E. Brown
The Zip Code Route into UC

California's goal has been a dramatic one of making higher education available to one and all. The reality, however, reveals a system that favors the rich and the few.

—Susan E. Brown, from *The Zip Code Route into UC*

Not content with traditional answers to public problems, Californians have incorporated creative and innovative tools to supplement the traditional policy structures. Not surprisingly, these innovations are both praised and condemned, depending on which communities of interest one resides in. California's willingness to experiment and its reputation as a trendsetter have made the state a leader for the rest of the nation in several key policy areas: Education is one of these policy areas. The 1960 Master Plan for Higher Education, which promised a heavily subsidized public university education to all students, represents California policy innovation at its best.

In statewide polls, Californians continue to identify education as the most important issue facing the state.[1] This should come as no surprise, considering that California is home to the nation's largest public school system, serving 5.7 million students. Public schools are the nexus of all community issues and concerns: civic responsibility, cultural literacy, tolerance, job skills, economic growth, and crime are all related to our educational system. Additionally, schools provide the initial point of access to our civic institutions and political bureaucracy. This is true for children, as well as for adults with children. As a consequence, schools have become the battleground for civic discourse. This has been abundantly illustrated over the past several years with school busing in the 1970s, Proposition 13 (1978), and a trio of more recent ballot initiatives: Proposition 187 (1994), Proposition 209 (1996), and Proposition 227 (1998).

Public education provides a critical service to any society. Basic literacy—including the ability to read, write, perform quantitative functions, and critically assess the world around us—is a necessity in any complex society. This is especially true in

California. With one of the world's largest economies, California's economic and political success has been based on a skilled workforce. Manufacturing industries and skilled agriculture dominated California's growth years from the 1940s to 1970s. The basic skills taught in California's primary schools, the vocational skills taught in California's secondary schools, and the professional skills taught in California's colleges and universities gave California's industrial sector a highly skilled labor pool at no cost.

CALIFORNIA'S PUBLIC K–12 INSTITUTIONS

California's public K–12 institutions are administered in autonomous school districts around the state, with oversight coming through the office of the State Superintendent of Public Instruction. The state superintendent has limited authority to see that individual school districts comply with state and federal mandates. Local districts are charged with administering school policy as well as day-to-day operations. School districts are run by locally elected school boards, bringing together local—and often provincial—concerns with state and federal concerns.

The clash between localism and statist concerns is often harsh. This is explained, in part, by the relative inexperience of local district boards. School boards are typically the first point of entry to politics. Board members are generally inexperienced but highly motivated. State and federal legislators and staff, on the other hand, tend to be politically well seasoned, but somewhat cynical. This creates serious tension in communicating across institutional lines, making partnerships between state agencies and local boards difficult. State agencies tend to view local districts as inefficient, ideological, and marginally competent. Local districts tend to view state agencies as inefficient, coercive, and self-motivated.

The K–12 school boards are autonomous, on the one hand, but dependent on state and federal resources on the other. While both the federal and California constitutions recognize the need to respect local control, larger questions have come to dominate federal–state–local relationships. Desegregation, anti-racism and anti-sexism policies, affirmative action, and special education all represent federal interests, while curriculum issues represent state interests. Local issues tend to focus on class size, crime, and cost, and on occasion, provide a forum for ideologically driven reform. Since federal and state agencies maintain the power of the purse, and the state asserts the right of fiscal and managerial oversight, local districts are often in resentful compliance. At best, the policy structure driving K–12 education policy is combative and confusing.

CALIFORNIA'S PUBLIC COLLEGES AND UNIVERSITIES

California's public institutions of higher education are defined by the state's Master Plan for Higher Education (1960). The Master Plan was unique in defining the most comprehensive system of public colleges and universities in the nation. The plan devised a three-tiered system of community colleges, state universities, and research universities. According to the plan, any California resident who desired a college education would have a place in the system. The top 10 percent of California high-school seniors would be eligible for the University of California (UC) (although not necessarily their campus of choice), the top one-third of high-school students would be eligible for the California State University (CSU), and everyone, regardless of GPA, would be eligible to attend their local community college. This system revolutionized higher education by democratizing college attendance. Unlike traditional universities, the typical CSU student is the first of their family to attend a university. The result: Blue-collar workers who built California's industrial economy in the 1940s and 1950s were able to educate their children to compete in the increasingly skilled economy of the 1960s and 1970s, and beyond. California's economic success in the 1990s is directly linked to the three-tiered system of higher education.

THE POLICY QUESTIONS

The challenges facing both K–12 and postsecondary institutions are similar: declining investment in education, overcrowding, an increasing proportion of underprepared students, increasing racial and cultural tensions, increasing violence in communities and schools, declining community support, and—not surprisingly—a consequential drop in student performance. The emerging policy questions focus on these issues. How can schools do more with less? Will higher "standards" and testing to those standards create higher performance? Is violence in the community seeping into schools, or is juvenile crime causing violence in the community? Does community support follow school performance, or does school performance follow community support? Regardless of how people "feel" about public schools, there is little question that the vexing problems facing our school system will only become more severe.

THE FUNDING INFRASTRUCTURE

The primary tool of educational policy is budgetary allotment. While economic conservatives have long held that "you can't solve a problem by throwing money at it," one can certainly exacerbate problems by withdrawing appropriate financial support. Per student spending has dropped at a precipitous rate in the state. California ranks 40th among the states in per student expenditures, a drop from 26th a decade ago, and last among the 10 largest states.[2] California spends nearly $1,000 less per student than the national average. Several factors lead to an even greater disparity among urban districts. Schools are traditionally funded by local communities through property taxes. Since different communities have different property values, tax revenues vary widely. Similarly, supplemental economic support from a local school's parents varies according to the neighborhood's median income. This has created systemic inequities in the delivery of education.

California's educational funding woes are impacted by two significant events. First, in *Serrano v. Priest* (1972), the state supreme court held that an educational system financed by disparate property tax revenues was by definition contrary to the equal protection clause. This placed an extra burden on the state legislature to reduce disparities through state funding. Proposition 13 (1978) reduced property tax revenues by 57 percent, forcing counties to deeply cut services. This placed an even greater burden on the state to provide replacement dollars. Where the state provided 30 percent of educational funding in 1972, by the mid-1990s the state was responsible for 60 percent.

As a consequence of shrinking property tax revenues and greater reliance on state dollars, K–12 educational funding has become extremely vulnerable. As the state has confronted increasing pressure for scarce resources, school funding has declined. When the state's long boom began to wane in the mid-1970s, educational dollars dropped precipitously. By 1988 the proportion of general fund dollars committed to K–12 education fell to a low of 37 percent. This period of decline paved the way for the success of Proposition 98 (1988), which required a minimum 40 percent general fund commitment.

POLICY RESPONSES

With over 5.5 million students in California's K–12 system, the difficulties facing public education have not gone unnoticed by policymakers. Unfortunately, differing political ideologies and divided government have often kept the state from developing corrective policies. The most significant educational policy to emerge was the Educational Reform Act of 1983 (SB 813). This bill emerged during a brief period of congeniality between then State Superintendent of Public Education Bill Honig—a Democrat with strong support from teachers' unions—and Republican Governor George Deukmejian. SB 813 required increased standards for high-school graduation; more basic subject requirements in math, English, science, and foreign language; and additional hours of instruction over the year. The bill also required increased statewide testing, higher teacher salaries, and the California Basic Educational Skills Test (C-BEST) as an entrance exam to teach.

While these get-tough approaches have achieved some success, the overall quality of public schools continues to decline. The reforms of 1983 were not enough to keep up with decreasing per student expenditures, overcrowding, and increasing drop-out rates. Further reform came in 1991 with the California Learning Assessment System (CLAS). CLAS was a testing program that asked students to read various literature and respond to it. The intent was to get students personally involved in reading and writing by relating the material to events in their personal lives. CLAS sparked contentious debate by conservatives and the religious right. Since CLAS presented students with stories representing the diversity of California families and encouraged independent thought, critics argued that the program was anti-family, pro-homosexuality, intrusive into family privacy, and wishy-washy pedagogy. The bill to reauthorize CLAS was vetoed by Governor Wilson in 1994.

By 1993 the school voucher movement succeeded in getting a privatization initiative on the ballot. The voucher would have given California parents a set amount of money to spend on their children's education, whether in public or private institutions. The voucher issue added fuel to the contentious education debate by suggesting that public schools will never improve and that the only rational response was mass exodus. Proponents argued that this competition for public dollars would force public schools to improve, while critics argued that vouchers would simply subsidize private schools at the expense of public schools, further eviscerating the public school expenditures.

In the end there is a policy paradox at play. While "reformers" continue to call for higher standards, tighter discipline, and more narrow academic curricula, California's emerging demographics suggest that bilingual education, greater remedial instruction, and cultural breadth is, in fact, more appropriate. It is estimated that 1.4 million students in California have limited English skills.[3] Fully one-third of California students speak a primary language other than English, with one-fifth speaking little or no English at all. The response to this challenge was Proposition 227, sponsored by Silicon Valley businessman Ron Unz, banning bilingual education in public schools. Voters approved the "English for the Children" initiative overwhelmingly in 1998. It is expected that California will continue to diversify and that language minorities will continue to present challenges to educators.

At best, public policy can be understood as a public action directed at resolving some public problem.[4] Education policies, however, tend to encompass far more values and ideologies than other policy areas. Since public education provides a structure for social reproduction and basic civic education to all members of society, it is, by definition, an extremely politicized arena.

The following case studies illustrate the tensions inherent in education policy.

CASE STUDIES

Different school districts around the state confront different types of problems and have provided different types of responses. The following case studies explore the rise of the religious right in the Vista Unified School District in northern San Diego County, the economic collapse of the Richmond Unified School District in the northeast San Francisco Bay Area, and the movement to split up the huge Los Angeles Unified School District.

VISTA UNIFIED SCHOOL DISTRICT

Vista, in suburban San Diego County, is 35 miles north of San Diego and 90 miles south of Los Angeles. Its Web page boasts:

> Vista is probably best known for its wonderful climate with an average daily temperature of 74 degrees. But Vista is more than just weather! It is only 10 minutes from the Pacific Ocean, has one of the top ranked high schools in the State, has six

times the national average number of parks, and enjoys a long tradition of strong community involvement. And don't forget California's best organic Farmer's Market every Saturday morning and Thursday afternoon![5]

Vista's population of 82,000 is 67 percent white, 25 percent Latino, 4 percent black, and just under 4 percent Asian. The median age is 29.7, the median house value is $183,000, and the median family income is $35,098.[6] Incorporated in 1963, Vista is an archetypal California edge city.

Controversy arose in January 1992 when this sleepy town elected a school board with a three-member conservative Christian majority. The new board enacted several policies that many feared would inject a conservative Christian agenda into the classroom. In May the board sent to committee a policy that would allow the discussion of "scientific evidence" that would challenge dominant scientific theories of evolution and encourage "appropriate … discussions of divine creation, ultimate purposes, or ultimate causes (the 'why')" in social studies and English classes.[7] Later that summer in a 2–3 vote, the board passed a policy stating that "scientific evidence that challenges any theory in science should be presented" in science classes and that "no theory of science shall be taught dogmatically and no student shall be compelled to believe or accept any theory presented in the curriculum."[8] This policy was widely seen as an attack on the statewide curriculum on evolution and an attempt to open the door to the teaching of creationism.

The Vista debate has exacerbated tensions between local ideologues and the state Board of Education. Since the state tends to avoid these kinds of conflicts, state officials left it to community members and the ACLU to file suit should the Vista Unified School District actually put creationism on the curriculum. Since Vista is a bedroom suburb with 86 percent of the working population leaving town daily for work, few residents follow school board decisions closely. Ultimately, it became a contest between the Christian Right, led by the Institute for Creation Research, and concerned parents mobilized by Larry Lovell, a local marine biologist. As the fundamentalist flavor of the debate emerged, many Vista parents became involved, effectively ending the fight. The conservatives lost the board in the following election.

The Vista case is important in illustrating the complex relationship between the various levels of government. The local district has autonomy, up to a point. But state and local governments are loath to intervene in local political skirmishes. Ultimately, the Vista experience worked just the way democratic theory suggests it should: robust discourse at the local level, culminating with open elections.

THE RICHMOND UNIFIED SCHOOL DISTRICT

The Richmond case illustrates a fundamentally different aspect of education policy and state–local relations. Unlike Vista, Richmond is an extremely diverse urban city, in the east San Francisco Bay Area, ten miles north of Oakland. Chartered in 1909, Richmond's population of 93,000 is 43.4 percent black, 31 percent white, 12 percent Asian, 12.15 percent Latino, and 0.5 percent Native American. The median household income is $32,165, median age of resident is 34.3, and median housing unit value is $142,600.[9] The Richmond Unified School District serves some 31,000 students, speaking 70 different languages in 5 north East Bay cities. In the early 1990s the district experienced severe financial distress as a result of continuing financial problems. The case is of interest not because of the fiscal strife, but because of the state–local relationship that emerged.

In the late 1980s and early 1990s, at least 20 school districts in California were facing financial collapse. It was common for the state to bail out ailing districts. But by 1991 Governor Wilson refused to sign any legislation bailing out Richmond unless the district granted the state broad managerial authority.[10] Without state assistance, the district would have to shut down for summer six weeks early. The Richmond district was an interesting choice for a showdown. First, the district is predominantly black. Second, although Richmond had a history of financial trouble, its innovative enrichment programs had achieved national acclaim for resolving many of the problems that plague urban districts. As the stand-off between the governor and the state dragged on, Contra Costa County's Superior Court ordered the state to do whatever was necessary to ensure that the Richmond Unified School District remain open. In the end the state loaned the Richmond district $19 million.[11]

In its oversight role, the state maintains the right to audit school district finances. In auditing Richmond, the state controller's office uncovered serious problems, including an inability to properly track debts and payments. The audit found that 7 of the 12 district accounting department employees were working in substitute roles, with little or no training. In summarizing the Richmond situation, a spokesman for the controller's office commented, "Richmond is a worst-case example of what happens when a school board does not meet its fiscal responsibility.... There is no remedy for deficit financing in a district of finite means than to go broke eventually."[12] The district ultimately went into receivership with a court-appointed trustee. In 1993 the Richmond Unified School District was reorganized into the West Contra Costa Unified School District.

The relationship between the state and Richmond illustrates the fiscal responsibility the state asserts over local districts. Unlike the ideological and curricular issues involved in the Vista case, when financial questions emerge the state is likely to act quickly and affirmatively. Where the state allowed Vista to resolve its own programmatic and constitutional dilemmas, the leash was tightened around Richmond much more quickly. Different areas of education policy rely on different types of partnerships among local, state, and federal agencies. In this way there may be fundamentally differential levels of autonomy and control simultaneously present in state–local relations.

LOS ANGELES UNIFIED SCHOOL DISTRICT

The Los Angeles Unified School District is the second largest school district in the nation. Its 668,000 K–12 students and 136,000 adult students are drawn from 708 square miles in Los Angeles County. LAUSD currently employs over 64,000 people,

including 32,000 teachers.[13] Clearly, the district has exploded since it was originally chartered in 1853, covering 28 square miles. LAUSD is one of the nation's most
diverse districts: Latino 68 percent, black 14 percent, white 11 percent, Asian 4.4
percent, Filipino, 1.9 percent, Pacific Islander 0.4 percent, and Native American 0.3
percent.[14]

Over the last decade several movements have erupted to break the district up.
The shear vastness of the bureaucracy make the district cumbersome and slow to respond. Critics argue that the district is too large to properly serve students and that the
central administration is nonresponsive to parents. Further, they argue that smaller
districts would allow students to attend classes closer to home. Between 1995 and
the present movements to break up the district have emerged in vastly different areas
in the district, from core city neighborhoods to the suburbs.[15] The most salient demands for breaking up the district have emerged from the largely white, affluent corridor between Encino and Woodland Hills in the San Fernando Valley. Not surprisingly,
this is precisely the same area calling for secession from the City of Los Angeles.

Angelenos, particularly affluent suburban Angelenos, are dissatisfied and angry.
Many feel that they are not getting their fair share from downtown, that their concerns
are not taken seriously, and that the education of their children—correctly seen as a local
issue—has been highjacked by bureaucrats sitting in gray buildings an hour's drive
away. High visibility mishaps—such as the development of the ill-fated $200 million
Belmont High site and the school board's attempt to dislodge then Superintendent
Ruben Zacarias—highlight the problems facing the district. The Belmont High School
site was to be the LAUSD's signature school site. Costing upwards of $200 million,
the construction has been plagued by mismanagement, not the least of which was approval of the site itself, which is contaminated with toxic pollution, making the school
uninhabitable without significant mitigation. Ruben Zacarias was hired to resolve many
of these problems, but was pushed out by a new school board majority—backed by the
mayor. The board could not fire Zacarias, so instead hired a district C.E.O., who would
have direct control of the district. This essentially removed any day-to-day authority
from the superintendent. The high profile insult to Zacarias was also seen as an insult
to the district's Latino majority. Critics argued both that Zacarias was not given sufficient time to fix the problems he was hired to fix and that if he were white rather than
Latino he would have been replaced in a much more low-profile, respectful way. The
articulation of this type of dissatisfaction is clearly behind the efforts to reform both the
district structure and Los Angeles' city charter.

The LAUSD conflict is fundamentally an issue of control. Will schools be controlled locally or by a large regional district? If the LAUSD is broken up into smaller districts, will parents have more control or will the smaller districts simply be more
vulnerable to ideological meddling? Will breaking up the district break the back of the
32,000 member United Teachers of Los Angeles (UTLA)? Will it make teachers "more
accountable" to local parents? These questions reflect the classic concerns of local politics. Unlike both the Vista case and the Richmond case, the LAUSD issue is exclusively local. Since day-to-day education policy is necessarily a local issue, the structure
of the local district is beyond the reach of the state.

The Zip Code Route into UC   *Susan E. Brown*

California's system of higher education has been celebrated as the nation's model system, providing equal access to the American dream. But a look at who's admitted to the prestigious University of California campuses shows that ZIP code may be as critical as grade point averages in determining who gets in and who stays out.

This is how the system works. The top 12.5 percent of the state's high school graduates are eligible for the University of California; the top 33.5 percent are eligible for the state universities; for everyone else there is open access to community colleges with the option, after two years, of transferring into a four-year institution.

California's goal has been a dramatic one of making higher education available to one and all. The reality, however, reveals a system that favors the rich and the few. The list of the feeder high schools that send more than one hundred students each to UC reads like a social register. It includes Beverly Hills, Palos Verdes, Santa Monica, Rolling Hills, Palisades, and in the San Fernando Valley, Granada Hills, Birmingham, and Taft. With the exception of San Francisco's Lowell and University High Schools, the UC feeders are in predominately, if not exclusively, white, affluent, enclaves. Not surprisingly, the mean family income for freshman at UC Berkeley last fall was nearly sixty thousand dollars, well above the national average.

Both the California Master Plan and Education Code are structured in such a way that students not ordinarily eligible for a state university may be able to transfer after two years at a community college. But, to the extent that transfer from a community college to UC works at all, it works primarily for the select, the affluent— and principally the white—community college. The top ten community college feeder campuses to UC for Fall 1986 were mainly in affluent residential communities: Santa Monica (252 transfers), Diablo Valley (241), Santa Barbara (227), Orange Coast (207), Cabrillo (151), El Camino (143), De Anza (139), San Diego Mesa (138), American River (132), and Saddleback (132).

By contrast, consider Fresno City College, which serves large numbers of minority students from a predominately agricultural region. Only one black and four Latinos (out of a student body of thirteen thousand) transferred to UC in 1986. Imperial Valley Community College, serving a similar student body, sent only three Latinos to UC campuses out of a freshman class of 1,341 that year. At predominately black Compton College, only two blacks transferred to UC campuses in 1986.

Statewide, the 106 community colleges in California sent a total of 189 blacks and 485 Latinos to the eight UC campuses, an average of six minority students from each college. Yet approximately 80 percent of underrepresented minorities who enter college in the state begin their studies in a community college.

While it is surely important to maintain high standards, the goal of a tax-based state educational system should be the development of talents and skills from all socio-economic groups. Public education by its very nature must reflect the entire population that supports it. What California has, instead, is a perfectly correlated system of family income to educational benefits—that is, the wealthiest are rewarded with access to the University of California; middle-income students end up at the California State University; low-income students begin and end their higher education at community colleges.

One possible solution to the perpetuation of a hereditary elite is to expand eligibility to UC and CSU to the top 12.5 percent and top 33.5 percent of students at every high school. There is nothing in state law or the California Master Plan to prevent this more egalitarian approach. Without such a remedy, California will merely continue to favor students from those schools with honors courses, enriched curriculums, well-equipped science laboratories, and optimal learning conditions.

Shouldn't a serious student at an inner-city school who graduates in the top 10 percent of his or her class have the same access to the benefits of California's postsecondary system as his or her counterpart in an exclusive private or magnet public school? If not, we should recognize that we are rewarding accidents of birth and that our current system of admissions to the University of California is, in truth, determined by ZIP code.

Editor's note: Though this piece appeared in 1989, the observations are still largely accurate. And, this predates the raucous debate around affirmative action in 1996. The recommendation of assessing performance on a campus by campus basis rather than statewide is being explored in several quarters.

Source: Sonia Maasik and Jack Soloman, eds., *California Dreams and Realities*, 2nd ed. (Boston: Bedford/St. Martin's, 1999). Originally published in 1989 by Pacific News Service. Reprinted by permission.

SUMMARY

This chapter has explored the policy framework surrounding California's public education system. Education policy is a function of local decision making within a framework defined by the state and heavily influenced by the federal government. Further influence is ensured through funding agencies that require specific actions and policies in exchange for grant dollars. While the state maintains fairly tight control over postsecondary education (community colleges, the California State Universities and University of California campuses), K–12 education remains fundamentally a local issue. The federal government is responsible for assuring equality of access; the state is responsible for establishing curricular priorities and financial oversight; and local K–12 districts are primarily responsible for short- and long-term policies affecting their students. The case studies illustrate how different districts pursue different challenges, emphasizing the idiosyncratic nature of education policy.

NOTES

1. Nick Anderson, "Davis Promises Fast Start on Sweeping Education Agenda," *Los Angeles Times*, 5 November 1998, S1.
2. *CAL FACT: California's Economy and Budget in Perspective* (Sacramento, CA: Legislative Analysts Office, 1996): 50.
3. Maria L. LaGanga, "Bilingual Ed Initiative Wins Easily," *Los Angeles Times*, 3 June 1998, A1.
4. See, for example, Stella Theodoulou and Matthew Cahn, *Public Policy: The Essential Readings* (Upper Saddle River, NJ: Prentice Hall, 1995).

5. San Diego Association of Governments, Regional Census Data Center, 19 August 1997 <http://www.vista.org/f2life.htm>.
6. San Diego Association of Governments, Regional Census Data Center, 19 August 1997 <http://www.vista.org/f2life.htm>.
7. Peter West, "California Board Defers Action on Religious Tenets in Science Classes," *Education Week on the Web*, 2 June 1993 <http://www.edweek.org>.
8. Peter West, "New Tactic Used to Push Teaching Creation Theory," *Education Week on the Web*, 8 September 1993 <http://www.edweek.org>.
9. 1990 U.S. Census.
10. Peter Schmidt, "Judge Halts Plan to Close Schools in California District," *Education Week on the Web*, 8 May 1991 <http://www.edweek.org>.
11. Peter Schmidt, "State Auditors in California Discover 'Serious' Flaws in Troubled District's Financial-Management," *Education Week on the Web*, 22 May 1991 <http://www.edweek.org>.
12. Ibid. Jay Ziegler, spokesman for Controller Gray Davis, May 1991.
13. Los Angeles Unified School District, "1996–1997 Fingertip Facts," 21 August 1997 <http://www.lausd.k12.ca.us/lausd/finger.html#a2.1>.
14. Los Angeles Unified School District, Ethnic Survey (fall 1996).
15. Peter Schmidt, "L.A. Breakup Plans Gather Head of Steam," *Education Week on the Web*, 25 October 1995 <http://www.edweek.org>.

CHAPTER 14

Environmental Policy

Featured Reading / Pages 158–161
Barry Commoner
The Closing Circle: Nature, Man, and Technology

Ecology has become the political substitute for the word "motherhood."

—Jesse Unruh, former Democratic Leader of the California State Assembly

We have met the enemy and he is us.

—Pogo

Environmental policy provides another example of policy success in California. Rich in both environmental resources and environmental problems, California has long battled environmental challenges. From its pristine coastal redwood forests in the north to the warm sandy beaches of the south, from the Sequoias in the Sierra Nevada to the desolate beauty of Joshua Tree, Mojave, and Death Valley, from the ruggedness of the Channel Islands to the windswept Monterey Peninsula, from the muddy Sacramento Delta to the fertility of the Central Valley, California overflows in natural beauty and biological diversity. Yet at the same time, California's vast industrial and agricultural infrastructure, its massive urban areas and encroaching sprawl, its densely populated coastline, its military bases, and its transportation corridors, all present significant environmental challenges that the state is only now coming to terms with. California's environmental dilemma is, at its core, a contest over scarce resources.

California has the largest population, the largest economy, and the most serious environmental problems of any state in the nation. These issues are, of course, interrelated. The challenge facing policymakers is how to accommodate an increasing population while maintaining healthy economic growth and simultaneously improving environmental quality. This discourse, not surprisingly, is extremely divisive, with different interests pushing in very different directions. This chapter explores California's environmental challenges and the policies that have succeeded—at least in part—in stemming the tide of environmental degradation. Specific attention is paid to air pollution policy in Southern California, water quality in the San Francisco Bay–Delta Area, and evolving transportation policy in the greater Los Angeles area.

AIR QUALITY

Air quality throughout the state differs widely. Los Angeles and its neighbors in the south coast basin experience the most degraded air quality in the nation after Houston. Yet a significant portion of the state remains out of compliance with Federal Air Quality Standards. As Figure 14.1 (on page 146) illustrates, ozone levels vary widely throughout the state. The southern California basin is "extreme" in its nonattainment status, representing the most severe air pollution in the nation. But northern and central California are not smog free. The metropolitan Sacramento area, including Sacramento, Yolo, and Solano Counties are designated "severe," and California's Central Valley is designated "serious." Ventura, San Bernardino, and Riverside Counties are "severe," Santa Barbara County is "moderate," San Diego "serious," Butte, Yuba, and Imperial are "transitional." The remaining areas are in compliance with federal ozone standards.[1]

Air pollution provides a challenging policy area because of ambient emissions travel. The San Francisco Bay Area tends to appear smog free, but this is in large measure due to its prevailing west winds. Emissions are extremely high in the Bay Area, with its 5.6 million residents. However, its ambient air quality tends to be quite good. Just as East Bay cities suffer through San Francisco's smog contribution, Yolo and Solano Counties suffer through Bay Area emissions.

California's smog problems are a result of two primary factors: its dense population with its reliance on individual automobile transit and its industrial economy. Air pollution is caused by a variety of factors and carries severe health consequences. Carbon monoxide is emitted from vehicle and stationary source exhaust. It is an odorless gas that replaces oxygen in red blood cells. It can cause angina, impaired vision, poor coordination, and dizziness. While the earth releases CO naturally, the expansive release of industrial CO emissions contributes to the greenhouse effect, throwing off the equilibrium of the earth's temperature (global warming).

Hydrocarbons, or volatile organic compounds, are released by the incomplete combustion of gasoline and evaporation from petroleum-based fuels, solvents, and paints. Hydrocarbons react in the sunlight with oxygen and nitrogen dioxide to form ozone, peroxyacetyl nitrate (PAN), and other photochemical oxidants. Ozone, the main component of smog, irritates the mucous membranes (eyes, nasal passages, throat, lungs) causing coughing, choking, reduced lung capacity, as well as aggravating asthma, bronchitis, and emphysema. Smog, containing hundreds of chemicals including ozone and peroxyacetyl nitrate, damages trees, crops, and building materials.

Lead is used as an anti-knock additive in some gasolines, as well as a stabilizing agent in household and industrial paints and as a structural component of pipes

FIGURE 14.1 AIR QUALITY ATTAINMENT DESIGNATIONS FOR OZONE LEVELS IN CALIFORNIA

Sources: 1990 Bureau of Census TIGER files; 40 CFR Part 1; 1985 USGS DLG files.

and roofing. Nonferrous smelters and battery plants also emit lead into the atmosphere. Lead, like other heavy metals, accumulates in the fat, bone, and other soft tissues of the body. The most common symptoms of lead poisoning include nausea and severe stomach pains. Larger accumulations cause deterioration of blood-forming organs, kidneys, and, ultimately, the nervous system. As well, lead has been tied to learning disabilities in young children.

Nitrogen dioxide is a product of industrial and vehicle exhaust. It attacks the lungs, causing cellular changes resulting in lowered resistance to respiratory infections. NO_2 is a main contributor to acid rain and, when mixed with hydrocarbons, creates ozone. Particulate matter is the smoke, dust, and soot that is emitted from industrial processes, heating boilers, gasoline and diesel engines, coal and diesel-burning utilities, cigarette smoke, and both organic and synthetic dusts. Larger particulates clog the lung sacs causing bronchitis and more serious pneumoconioses (diseases related to inhalation of organic and inorganic dusts), irritate mucous membranes, and clog tear ducts, damaging the surface of the eye. Microscopic particulates pass into the bloodstream, introducing carcinogens and heavy metals. Sulfur dioxide is released in coal- and oil-burning processes. SO_2 is a corrosive, poisonous gas that is associated with coughing, colds, asthma, and bronchitis, and, like nitrogen dioxide, contributes to acid rain.[2]

While few would argue that California has solved its air problems, the California Environmental Protection Agency reports that there has been meaningful improvement in California's air over the last fifteen years, as Figure 14.2 illustrates. While population has increased by 27 percent and vehicle-miles traveled by 27 percent, carbon monoxide has decreased by 14 percent and ozone by 25 percent since

FIGURE 14.2   STATEWIDE AMBIENT AIR QUALITY, 1983–1994

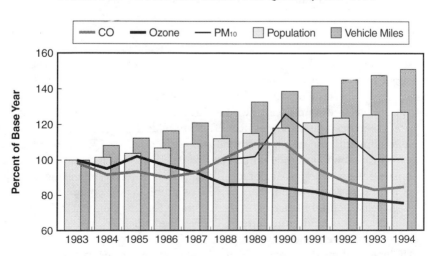

Note: Ozone and CO values reflect the highest values statewide. PM_{10} reflects the highest values excluding two rural air basins.

1983. Particulate matter (PM_{10}) had an increase followed by a reduction.[3] The areas of most significant improvement include Monterey Bay, Chico, and Yuba City for ground-level ozone (O_3); Sacramento, Mojave Desert, and Mono Lake for particulate matter (PM_{10}); and the San Francisco Bay Area, San Diego, Sacramento, Fresno, Stockton, Modesto, Bakersfield, Chico, and Lake Tahoe for carbon monoxide (CO). The areas where serious problems remain include most of Southern California, the San Joaquin Valley, the San Francisco Bay Area, and the greater Sacramento Area for ground-level ozone (O_3); the greater Los Angeles basin and the San Joaquin Valley for particulate matter (PM_{10}); and the greater Los Angeles basin for carbon monoxide (CO).[4]

WATER QUALITY

California's water quality is a major concern as well. The same factors contributing to the poor air quality contribute to poor water quality. And as the largest farm state in the nation, California surface waters and aquifers must absorb millions of tons of pesticides and chemical fertilizers. California's manufacturing industries dump millions of gallons of contaminated waste water, and California's cities and suburbs pump out tens of millions of gallons of sewage and polluted run-off. In addition, in seeking to maximize arable land, California has lost more that 80 percent of its wetlands. Wetlands are critical tidal zones that, when healthy, keep water clean by filtering out contaminants. Wetlands provide essential habitat for threatened and endangered plant and wildlife. Forty-five percent of the nation's listed endangered animals and 26 percent of its endangered plants rely on wetlands to survive.[5] California is among only seven states with this degree of loss, as Figure 14.3 illustrates.

California water quality is degraded through a variety of pollution sources. As sewer systems continue to age and deteriorate, growing populations produce increasing demands. The result is the seepage of raw sewage into aquifers. Improper discharge from septic tanks exacerbates the problem, making sewage the single largest polluter of drinking water. Waste disposal sites also pose special dangers.

Agriculture sprays millions of tons of fertilizers and pesticides on crops, which ultimately seep into water sources. Runoff from fields, feedlots, and barnyards carries potassium and nitrogen into ground and surface waters. Water diverted from rivers for irrigation is returned with excessive levels of salt and minerals, degrading drinking water sources. Colorado River water becomes increasingly sodium rich as it makes its way south, causing serious problems for communities such as Los Angeles, which rely heavily on the Colorado for drinking water. Mine runoff brings high levels of acid, iron, sulfates, copper, lead, uranium, and other hazardous materials into aquifers and streams.

The potential health effects of water pollution are serious. Nitrates from agricultural runoff can cause birth defects in infants and livestock. Chlorinated solvents

FIGURE 14.3 HISTORICAL WETLAND LOSS BY STATE

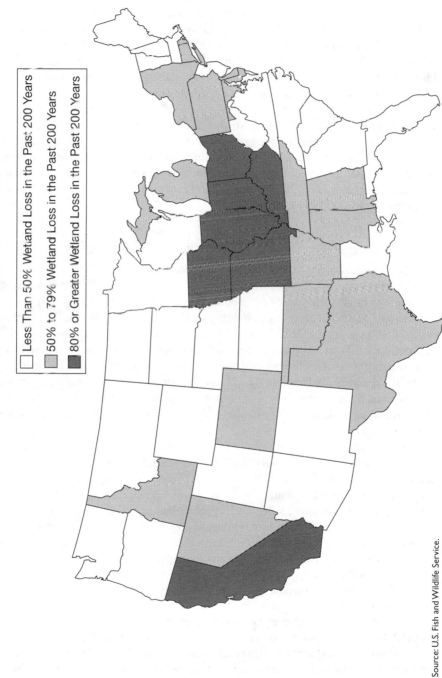

Less Than 50% Wetland Loss in the Past 200 Years

50% to 79% Wetland Loss in the Past 200 Years

80% or Greater Wetland Loss in the Past 200 Years

Source: U.S. Fish and Wildlife Service.

from chemical degreasing agents, machinery maintenance, and chemical production are known carcinogens. Trihalomethanes, produced by chemical reactions with chlorinated water, may cause liver and kidney damage and are similarly carcinogenic. Polychlorinated biphenyls (PCBs) are produced as waste from outmoded manufacturing facilities and may cause liver damage and possibly cancer. Lead etching from old piping and solder in water systems may cause nerve damage, learning disabilities, birth defects, and possibly cancer. Coliform and pathogenic bacteria and viruses from leaking sewers and septic tanks spread gastrointestinal illnesses.

California's water quality is monitored by the State Water Resources Control Board (SWRCB). The SWRCB reports that discharges of contaminants is decreasing, the number of leaking underground storage tanks (USTs) is decreasing, and that fewer organic chemicals and pesticides are found in California's drinking water.[6] Although water quality issues vary throughout the state, as the point of estuarial destination for the state's largest watershed, the greater San Francisco Bay–Delta provides a useful barometer to statewide water quality.

BAY AREA WATER QUALITY: A STATEWIDE BAROMETER

The San Francisco Bay Regional Water Quality Control Board tracks the water quality for rivers, streams, estuaries, and bays in the Bay Area. They report that fish populations have suffered serious declines in all areas, with major reductions of striped bass, delta smelt, splittail, longfin smelt, and salmon. This is due to spawning habitat losses in the Delta region.[7] Bay sport fish have been impacted by chemical pollutants. White croaker, shiner surfperch, walleye surfperch, leopard sharks, brown smoothhound sharks, striped bass, sturgeon, and halibut have all tested high for PCBs, mercury, dieldrin, total DDT, total chlordane, and dioxin/furans, prompting the state to warn that Bay fish consumption should be limited (adults should consume no more than two Bay-caught fish meals per month, pregnant women and children no more than one).[8]

Water and sediment is routinely tested at 16 sites around the Bay. PCB concentrations exceeded safe levels at all sites. Pesticides DDT, dieldrin, and chlordane exceeded safe levels at several sites. Trace metals (copper, nickel, lead, mercury, and chromium) were above safe levels at many sites, particularly in the North Bay. On the positive side, the Regional Water Quality Control Board found no toxicity to fish and other aquatic organisms due to the water quality. However, sediment toxicity was widespread, even though only nickel concentrations exceeded guidelines.[9] The control board also tests groundwater around the Bay Area. Pollution is widespread, primarily due to 7,500 known leaking underground fuel tanks. There are an additional 500 sites estimated where industrial solvents have leaked into aquifers.

The most significant water quality issue in the Bay Area is aquatic habitat loss. In 1850 there were about 545,000 acres of tidal wetlands in the Bay and Delta. Today there are about 45,000 acres.[10] Historically, most of these lost wetlands were taken for agriculture. Increasingly, however, urban development is taking a serious toll, both as a consequence of habitat loss and the rise of urban creeks and non-point runoff. Urban runoff is responsible for carrying wastewater, chemical contaminants, and trash into riparian habitat, causing further water pollution and sediment problems.

Rural creeks in Marin and Sonoma Counties are polluted by dairy and agricultural runoff, bringing manure, fertilizers, and pesticides into rivers and other surface waters. Sediment "hot spots" have been created by heavy metals, solvents, pesticides, and toxic organics introduced into sediment around the Bay Area by waste water discharges and industrial runoff. The Water Control Board cautions that these hotspots may be directly toxic to any organisms in them, and the contaminants can "bioaccumulate," becoming toxic to other animals higher up the food chain.[11]

PUBLIC TRANSIT IN LOS ANGELES: A CASE STUDY IN ENVIRONMENTAL AMBIVALENCE

The Los Angeles area continues to experience the worst air quality in the nation. As such, it provides a useful case study in air quality management. This section explores the evolution of the southern California basin into its current quagmire. Public transit in Los Angeles provides perhaps the best illustration of environmental ambivalence. Los Angeles public transit began as a private venture of Henry Huntington, president of Southern Pacific. Between 1895 and 1905, Huntington's Pacific Electric built the first interurban lines servicing Pasadena and Los Angeles. By the late 1920s Pacific Electric created a significant web throughout the region, stretching to all cities within a 75-mile radius of Los Angeles. Ridership grew from 68 million passengers in 1919, to 85 million in 1920, and over 100 million in 1924.[12] Unfortunately, the early success of L.A.'s public transit was not to last. By the 1930s reliance on public transit began to wane.

Three dynamics led to the rising use of individual transportation: increasing affluence, dropping automobile prices, and building out of regions between rail lines. By 1929 there was a car for every three people in the area.[13] While in the 1910s homebuilders would advertise that new tracts were within walking distance to the trolleys, by the 1920s homebuilders were advertising that new homes came complete with garages and easy road access.[14]

As early as 1924 it was clear that cars and trolleys sharing the same roads was both a congestion problem and a safety problem. Two proposals were put out for a vote in 1926: One—the transit proposal—called for a series of elevated lines and subways; the second called for intensive highway development on north-south and east-west arterial boulevards capable of handling three lanes in each direction.[15] The outcome is obvious.

During the 1940s Pacific Electric was acquired by Pacific City Lines (PCL), a regional subsidiary of National City Lines (NCL). NCL was a holding company established in 1936 by General Motors, along with Greyhound, Standard Oil of California, and Firestone Rubber, with the intent of buying local transit companies, and replacing electric railcars and buses with diesel buses—buses built by

GM, with tires by Firestone, operated by Greyhound, and fueled by Standard Oil. After acquiring Pacific Electric, PCL dismantled the tracks in downtown Los Angeles, the nucleus of the system, replacing them with loud, smokey buses.

This had two immediate effects. First, it made it impossible to utilize fully the remaining tracks. It also made travel by mass transit an uncomfortable, cumbersome experience. PCL's Pacific Electric reduced lines further to cope with dropping ridership.[16] In the end, National City Lines bought and dismantled over 100 electric transit systems in cities from 16 states, including New York, Philadelphia, Baltimore, St. Louis, Oakland, Salt Lake City, and, of course, Los Angeles. In *U.S. v. National City Lines* (1949), the federal courts found that NCL colluded to dismantle rail lines to thwart competition to automobile, bus, and truck sales.

By the early 1950s Los Angeles's public transit system was in serious disrepair and financial ruin. Pacific Electric sold the system to the Los Angeles Metropolitan Coach Lines—later the Metropolitan Transit Authority (MTA)—which systematically replaced all electric trolley lines left with diesel buses.[17] The early MTA becomes the first public agency to operate LA's public transit. In 1955 the Glendale-Burbank line, begun in 1904, was abandoned. By 1958 LA's last electric Red Car was removed.

Southern California's growing reliance on private cars came as a direct result of GM's actions. The impact on air quality is clear; vehicle traffic alone accounts for roughly 50 percent of airborne pollutants.[18] By 1973, when urban mass transit again became a local issue, Los Angeles estimated it would cost $6.6 billion for a system one-sixth the size of the original Pacific Electric system.[19] By 2002 when LA's new light rail is scheduled for completion, the costs of rebuilding LA's transit lines are estimated to exceed $8 billion for a system that covers substantially less area.[20]

THE ENVIRONMENTAL CONNECTION:
TRANSPORTATION IMPACTS ON AIR, WATER, TOXICS, AND LAND USE

The environmental impacts of private transit are serious. As Table 14.1 illustrates, onroad vehicle traffic alone accounts for 52 percent of hydrocarbon emissions, 63 percent of nitrogen dioxide emissions, 81 percent of carbon monoxide emissions, 33 percent of sulfur dioxide emissions, and 8 percent of particulate matter emissions. Coastal water impacts are equally serious. Every year millions of pounds of lead, oil and grease, and garbage wash down storm drains and out to sea in non-point runoff. Environmentalists estimate that more than 4.5 million pounds of oil products from cars washes out of the Los Angeles Coast Basin to sea yearly.[21]

The phenomenal growth in cars has led to an equally phenomenal growth in gas stations, with associated toxic and hazardous materials spills. The EPA estimates on a nationwide level that 30 percent of underground storage tanks (USTs) leak, and the American Petroleum Institute estimate that 40 percent of USTs leak nationwide.[22] This has led directly to contamination of several aquifers in the region. The combined impacts of USTs at gas stations, airports, and industry sites have seriously impacted

TABLE 14.1   VEHICLE IMPACTS ON AIR QUALITY IN THE LOS ANGELES BASIN

1990 BASE YEAR (EMISSIONS IN TONS PER DAY)

SOURCE	VOCs	NO_X	CO	SO_X	PM_{10}
Stationary	658	209	131	36	447
Mobile	990	1,204	8,092	68	59
Onroad					
Vehicles Only	863	891	6,679	34	39
Total					
Onroad Vehicle Emission Share	52.4%	63.1%	81.2%	32.7%	7.7%

2000 BASE YEAR (ESTIMATED EMISSIONS IN TONS PER DAY)

SOURCE	VOCs	NO_X	CO	SO_X	PM_{10}
Stationary	429	113	172	18	410
Mobile	462	769	4233	48	31
Onroad					
Vehicles Only	350	521	2963	14	16
Total					
Onroad Vehicle Emission Share	39.3%	59.1%	67.3%	21.2%	3.7%

Source: South Coast Air Quality Management District—SCAQMD, 1997.

groundwater. As if to underscore the point, aquifers in the San Fernando and San Gabriel Valleys have been listed as Superfund Sites.[23]

Finally, the vast reliance on private cars has had significant land use impacts. The vast majority of public space is taken up by roads and freeways. There are approximately 52,000 miles of nonresidential roadways in the Southern California basin. Roadways in residential subdivisions consume more space than parks, schools, public squares, and malls combined. Not surprisingly, most Californians grew up playing in the street.

POLICY RESPONSES

Environmental policy responses in California are textbook illustrations of federalism in action. Like most other states, California only acted to improve environmental quality after the federal government required the state to do so. As a consequence, most of California's environmental policy responses are state elements of federal programs. Responses to the policy areas of air quality, water quality and water quantity, and solid and hazardous waste follow.

AIR POLICY

California Air Policy is facilitated at the state level by the California Air Resources Board (CARB) and addressed locally by 34 air pollution districts. As a consequence of the variation in air quality throughout the states, CARB and the EPA requires that regional air quality control districts create plans specifically designed for problems in their area. The local air pollution control districts set emission levels and grant emission permits for stationary sources, as well as managing transportation control measures for their respective regions. Each district develops its own air policy management plan to combat the unique air quality problems in its region. Depending on the level and type of airborne pollutants in a district, the local control board may regulate manufacturers, power plants, refineries, gasoline service stations, and auto body shops. If the Bay Area is the barometer for statewide water quality, the Los Angeles Basin is surely the barometer of air quality management in the state.

LOS ANGELES: A CASE IN POINT

Like many other jurisdictions, California was slow to comply with the 1970 Federal Clean Air Act amendments. California's State Implementation Plan (SIP), accepted by the EPA under the Reagan administration, argued that Southern California simply could not meet federal standards. Ironically, it was this weak SIP that initiated California's evolution as the leader in innovative clean air policy. The acceptance of California's SIP allowed environmentalists to challenge the EPA's weak implementation of the Clean Air Act in court. Perhaps as a consequence of its growing urban density and increasingly degraded environment, California has emerged as a leader in creative environmental policymaking. This is especially true in Southern California's air quality policy.

In 1987, after discussions with the EPA broke down, the Ninth Circuit Court of Appeals in San Francisco ordered the EPA to reject California's 1984 SIP. Facing potential sanctions, including the loss of federal highway and sewer funds, and with prodding from Rep. Henry Waxman (D-Los Angeles), the California Air Resources Board (CARB), the South Coast Air Quality Management District (SCAQMD), and the Southern California Association of Governments (SCAG), created the initial Air Quality Management Plan for Southern California in 1989 (SCAQMP).

The plan mandates specific controls to be in place by 2010. The first part of the plan (Tier I) includes 123 immediate controls to be implemented by the year 2000. These controls focus on immediate changes based on current technologies, such as reformulating commercial and household paints and solvents to reduce hydrocarbon emissions, regulating charcoal broilers in restaurants, requiring emission control equipment for bakeries and dry cleaners, and more effective inspection of motor vehicles. In addition, the SCAQMP requires large employers— those employing 100 people or more—to provide employees with incentives for carpooling and public transit use.

The second section of the plan (Tier II) depends on the development of new technologies, and requires implementation over a 15-year period. This portion of the plan mandates that 40 percent of private vehicles and 70 percent of commercial trucks and buses be required to run on nonpetroleum fuels, such as methanol, by 1999. Two percent of all cars sold in 1998, and 10 percent sold in 2003, must meet zero-emission standards. With available technology, only electric vehicles are able to meet that standard. The plan also includes the construction of housing hubs closer to job centers and improved mass transit and carpooling.

The final portion of the plan (Tier III) requires the further evolution of new technologies, and therefore focuses on research and development and includes the establishment of an Office of Technology Assessment. The specific controls in this section of the plan include the conversion of motor vehicles to "extremely low-emitting" engines, which may preclude the use of the internal combustion engine.

By 1991 the SCAQMD adopted a revised SCAQMP. The 1991 plan maintains the basic structure of the 1989 plan, but establishes several new control measures that include the application of more advanced technologies, such as the Phase 2 reformulated fuels program, for reducing stationary and mobile emissions. Additionally, the 1991 plan included eight specific measures for controlling transportation-related emissions by reducing government-related vehicle miles and vehicle trips. In 1994 the plan was redesigned to fulfill the requirements of federal Clean Air Act Amendments (1990) and the California Clean Air Act (1988). Structurally, the 1994 plan is similar to the earlier versions. Tier I measures are now divided into "short-term" and "medium-term" measures (to be implemented between 1994 and 2005). Tier II and III measures are now consolidated as "long-term" measures. Control changes are a little more substantial. In addition to the controls mentioned, the plan imposes more stringent emissions and fuel quality standards, accommodating the California Air Resources Board—the statewide agency—Low Emission Vehicle (LEV) and Clean Fuels regulations. Stationary sources require greater application of "technologically feasible" control equipment. The plan also requires the adoption of new technologies that "may reasonably be expected to be utilized by the year 2010."

Ships, trains, aircraft, and farming and construction equipment continue to be regulated primarily by the federal EPA and state Air Resources Board (CARB). A court-ordered Federal Implementation Plan (FIP) was released by the EPA in February 1994, requiring greater federal air quality standards. The standards were adopted by the new SCAQMP. Although the FIP was ultimately withdrawn as a concession to the new Republican Congress, the SCAQMP continues to require additional measures for non-road sources, including recreational boats and vehicles to meet these standards. As well, several new implementation strategies were included in the 1994 plan, including increased use of market incentives, greater use of permitting, greater education programs, equipment standards, and greater communication between the local agency (the SCAQMD), and state (CARB) and federal (EPA) agencies. Several market incentives have been written into the plan. The plan expands the RECLAIM (Regional Clean Air Incentives Market) program, a "bubble" policy requiring aggregate control of a facility's emissions rather than command and control of specific emissions within the facility. RECLAIM also creates a pollution permit market where participants can sell unused pollution rights. Further, the plan establishes a wider program of tax credits for companies that reduce vehicle emissions. Perhaps most creative is the plan to develop a model of emission-based registration fees and sales taxes to encourage financial incentives for emissions reduction.

Educational outreach programs are utilized to help bring newly regulated small source categories (e.g., dry cleaners and bakeries) into compliance. Since the district is attempting to create a better working relationship with the business community in the south coast basin, information on alternative products, cleaner processes, and equipment modifications is being distributed so as to encourage greater emissions reductions. In addition, the plan encourages public education campaigns in order to encourage environmentally friendly behavior changes, including maximizing mass transportation use and minimizing residential emissions such as BBQs and fireplaces. The most recent version, adopted in 1997, scales back the innovative approaches that characterized the earlier versions. Placing a greater emphasis on "flexible, alternative approaches," the 1997 version backs off from some standards (e.g., ozone) and replaces remaining command and control structures with incentive-based regulations. On the positive side, the new version accommodates the new federal requirements for particulate matter (PM_{10}).

Southern California's South Coast Air Quality Management Plan (SCAQMP) leaves the federal air quality model and institutes a stringent 20-year plan to reduce smog. The commitment of the South Coast Basin to lower emissions through a four-point plan of conservation, alternative fuels, mass transit, and a shift in residential and economic social patterns, makes the plan the strongest clean air program in the world.

WATER POLICY

The State Water Resources Control Board (SWRCB) was established in 1967 with the mission of ensuring the "highest reasonable quality of waters of the state, while allocating those waters to achieve the optimum balance of beneficial uses."[24] The board is made up of five full-time members, appointed to four-year terms by the governor and confirmed by the senate.

The state board shares authority with the nine regional water quality control boards. The regional boards are responsible for developing and enforcing water quality basin plans consistent with the state's water policies and objectives, and addressing the local differences in climate, topography, geology, and hydrology. The regional boards each have nine part-time members appointed by the governor and confirmed by the senate. The regional boards have specific authority to "issue waste discharge requirements, take enforcement action against violators, and monitor water quality."[25] Water quality problems throughout the state necessitate strong policy, but the state requires that these policies balance the need to improve quality with the needs of industry, agriculture, and municipal districts.

State water agencies are currently implementing several programs aimed at specific problems. The Federal Clean Water Act (1987) provides the standards and framework through which the state must operate. The Clean Water Act requires the state to improve waste treatment facilities, manage and treat non-point runoff (urban runoff), and develop estuary management programs. In addition, the state has developed an aggressive watershed management program, an underground storage tank cleanup program, and through the California Coastal Act and the resulting Coastal Commission, an aggressive coastal management program.

WASTE POLICY

Californians generate over 37 million tons of municipal solid waste every year, about 90 percent of which is buried in the state's 670 landfills. Waste policy has traditionally been seen as a local issue, resulting in widespread landfills and incinerators. This has created serious problems over time: Toxic lechate percolates from landfills, posing serious groundwater threats; escaping gases have been shown to contain toxic contaminants and noxious odors. Most existing landfills are in violation of state and federal operating requirements. All of this is exacerbated by California's increasingly dense population, making open spaces more and more rare. As a result, the state has stepped in and taken charge of solid waste policy.

The Integrated Waste Management Act of 1989 (IWMA, also referred to as AB 939) identifies five components to an integrated waste management program for the state: source reduction; recycling; composting; waste to energy; and continued landfilling, albeit at lower volumes. The law requires cities and counties to divert at least 25 percent of their waste by 1995 and 50 percent by 2000, relative to the 1990 waste stream. IWMA establishes source reduction, recycling, and composting as policy priorities over landfilling and incineration. The statute replaces the old industry-oriented waste management board with six full-time members. The governor is required to appoint one member representing the solid waste industry, one member representing the environmental community, and two "public" members; the Speaker of the Assembly and the Senate Rules Committee each have one discretionary appointment. The new Integrated Waste Management Board holds greater authority to enforce compliance through punitive fines of as much as $10,000 per day to noncompliant jurisdictions.

The rate of waste diversion in 1989 was 12.5 percent. Most counties were able to exceed the 25 percent reduction by 1995. The question, remains, however, as to whether the 50 percent reduction will be achieved. By January 2000 the statewide rate of diversion was 33 percent, short of the 50 percent goal, but well above the 27 percent national average.[26] As counties have come into compliance, municipal recycling centers have increased by 155 percent. But, this may be the easy part. Reducing incoming waste remains a major challenge. Creating markets for recovered materials continues to be a major effort for the board.

The Closing Circle: Nature, Man, and Technology   *Barry Commoner*

The environment has just been rediscovered by the people who live in it. In the United States the event was celebrated in April 1970, during Earth Week. It was a sudden, noisy awakening, School children cleaned up rubbish; college students organized huge demonstrations; determined citizens recaptured the streets from the automobile, at least for a day. Everyone seemed to be aroused to the environmental danger and eager to do something about it.

They were offered lots of advice. Almost every writer, almost every speaker, on the college campuses, in the streets and on television and radio broadcasts, was ready to fix the blame and pronounce a cure for the environmental crisis. Some regarded the environmental issue as politically innocuous:

> Ecology has become the political substitute for the word "motherhood."
>
> —Jesse Unruh, Democratic Leader of the State of California Assembly

But the FBI took it more seriously:

> On April 22, 1970, representatives of the FBI observed about two hundred persons on the Playing Fields shortly after 1:30 P.M. They were joined a few minutes later by a contingent of George Washington University students who arrived chanting "Save Our Earth."... A sign was noted which read "God Is Not Dead; He Is Polluted on Earth."... Shortly after 8:00 P.M. Senator Edmund Muskie (D), Maine, arrived and gave a short anti-pollution speech. Senator Muskie was followed by journalist I. F. Stone, who spoke for twenty minutes on the themes of anti-pollution, anti-military, and anti-administration.
>
> —FBI Report entered into Congressional Record by Senator Muskie on April 14, 1971

Some blamed pollution on the rising population:

> The pollution problem is a consequence of population. It did not much matter how a lonely American frontiersman disposed of his waste.... But as population became denser, the natural chemical and biological recycling processes became overloaded.... Freedom to breed will bring ruin to all.
>
> —Garrett Hardin, Biologist

> The causal chain of the deterioration [of the environment] is easily followed to its source. Too may cars, too many factories, too much detergent, too much pesticide, multiplying contrails, inadequate sewage treatment plants, too little water, too much carbon dioxide-all can be traced easily to *too many people.*
>
> —Paul R. Ehrlich, Biologist

Some blamed affluence:

> The affluent society has become an effluent society. The 6 percent of the world's population in the United States produces 70 percent or more of the world's solid wastes.
>
> —Walter S. Howard, Biologist

And praised poverty:

> Blessed be the starving blacks of Mississippi with their outdoor privies, for they are ecologically sound, and they shall inherit a nation.
> —Wayne H. Davis, Biologist

But not without rebuttal from the poor:

> You must not embark on programs to curb economic growth without placing a priority on maintaining income, so that the poorest people won't simply be further depressed in their condition but will have a share, and be able to live decently.
> —George Wiley, Chemist and Chairman, National Welfare Rights Organization

And encouragement from industry:

> It is not industry *per se*, but the demands of the public. And the public's demands are increasing at a geometric rate, because of the increasing standard of living and the increasing growth of population.... If we can convince the national and local leaders in the environmental crusade of this basic logic, that population causes pollution, then we can help them focus their attention on the major aspect of the problem.
> —Sherman R. Knapp, Chairman of the Board, Northeast Utilities

Some blamed man's innate aggressiveness:

> The first problem, then, is people.... The second problem, a most fundamental one, lies within us—our basic aggressions...., As Anthony Storr has said: "The sombre fact is that we're the cruelest and most ruthless species that has ever walked the earth."
> —William Roth, Director, Pacific Life Assurance Company

While others blamed what man had learned:

> People are afraid of their humanity because systematically they have been taught to become inhuman.... They have no understanding of what it is to love nature. And so our airs are being polluted, our rivers are being poisoned, and our land is being cut up.
> —Arturo Sandoval, Student, Environmental Action

A minister blamed profits:

> Environmental rape is a fact of our national life only because it is more profitable than responsible stewardship of earth's limited resources.
> —Channing E. Phillips, Congregationalist Minister

While a historian blamed religion:

> Christianity bears a huge burden of guilt.... We shall continue to have a worsening ecologic crisis until we reject the Christian axiom that nature has no reason for existence save to serve man.
> —Lynn White, Historian

A politician blamed technology:

> A runaway technology, whose only law is profit, has for years poisoned our air, ravaged our soil, stripped our forests bare, and corrupted our water resources.
> —Vance Hartke, Senator from Indiana

While an environmentalist blamed politicians:

> There is a peculiar paralysis in our political branches of government, which are primarily responsible for legislating and executing the policies environmentalists are urging.... Industries who profit by the rape of our environment see to it that legislators friendly to their attitudes are elected, and that bureaucrats of similar attitude are appointed.
>
> —Roderick A. Cameron, Environmental Defense Fund

Some blamed capitalism:

> Yes, it's official—the conspiracy against pollution. And we have a simple program—arrest Agnew and smash capitalism. We make only one exception to our pollution stand—everyone should light up a joint and get stoned.... We say to Agnew country that Earth Day is for the sons and daughters of the American Revolution who are going to tear this capitalism down and set us free.
>
> —Rennie Davis, Member of the Chicago Seven

While capitalists counterattacked:

> The point I am trying to make is that we are solving most of our problems ... that conditions are getting better not worse ... that American industry is spending over three billion dollars a year to clean up the environment and additional billions to develop products that will *keep* it clean ... and that the real danger is *not* from the free-enterprise Establishment that has made ours the most prosperous, most powerful and most charitable nation on earth. No, the danger today resides in the Disaster Lobby—those crepe-hangers who, for personal gain or out of sheer ignorance, are undermining the American system and threatening the lives and fortunes of the American people. Some people have let the gloom-mongers scare them beyond rational response with talk about atomic annihilation.... Since World War II over one *billion* human beings who worried about A-bombs and H-bombs died of other causes. They worried for nothing.
>
> —Thomas R. Shepard, Jr., Publisher, *Look* magazine

And one keen observer blamed everyone:

> We have met the enemy and he is us.
>
> —Pogo

Earth Week and the accompanying outburst of publicity, preaching, and prognostication surprised most people, including those of us who had worked for years to generate public recognition of the environmental crisis. What surprised me most were the numerous, confident explanations of the cause and cure of the crisis. For having spent some years in the effort simply to detect and describe the growing list of environmental problems—radioactive fallout, air and water pollution, the deterioration of the soil—and in tracing some of the links to social and political processes, the identification of a single cause and cure seemed a rather bold step.

After the excitement of Earth Week, I tried to find some meaning in the welter of contradictory advice that it produced. It seemed to me that the confusion of Earth Week was a sign that the situation was so complex and ambiguous that people could read whatever conclusions their own beliefs—about human nature, economics, and politics—suggested. Like a Rorschach ink blot, Earth Week mirrored personal convictions more than objective knowledge.

Earth Week convinced me of the urgency of a deeper public understanding of the origins of the environmental crisis.... [They] can be organized into a kind of informal set of "laws of ecology...."

The First Law of Ecology: *Everything Is Connected to Everything Else* ...
The Second Law of Ecology: *Everything Must Go Somewhere* ...
The Third Law of Ecology: *Nature Knows Best* ...
The Fourth Law of Ecology: *There is No Such Thing as a Free Lunch* ...

In ecology, as in economics, the law is intended to warn that every gain is won at some cost. In a way, this ecological law embodies the previous three laws. Because the global ecosystem is a connected whole in which nothing can be gained or lost and which is not subject to overall improvement, anything extracted from it by human effort must be replaced. Payment of this price cannot be avoided; it can only be delayed. The present environmental crisis is a warning that we have delayed nearly too long.

Source: Barry Commoner, *The Closing Circle*. Copyright © 1971 by Barry Commoner. Reprinted by permission of Alfred A. Knopf, a division of Random House, Inc.

SUMMARY

Perhaps as a consequence of the state's poor environmental quality, California has developed innovative approaches in a variety of areas. The regional Clean Air and Clean Water Plans, as well as the statewide solid waste plan, are promising innovations. Most innovative, perhaps, is the state's response to air pollution. The South Coast Air Quality Management District's plan for bringing Southern California into compliance with federal standards is widely recognized as the most aggressive approach in the nation. Unlike the federal air quality model, it institutes a stringent 20-year plan to reduce smog through a four-point plan of conservation, alternative fuels, mass transit, and a shift in residential and economic social patterns. Urbanized states across the nation are watching California's air policy approach to see whether it provides a model worth emulating.

California's environmental future will depend on the success of its current generation of environmental policy responses. The degree to which California's aggressive policy approaches can withstand political opposition will determine statewide environmental quality over the next 30 years. As a community of diverse interests, the benefits of environmental improvement—and the costs of that improvement—will be experienced differentially by different sectors. This is the basis of politics, and in a state as contentious as California it would be foolhardy to predict the future direction of any policy area. California's environmental future may in large measure depend on the ability of the state's environmental constituency to persuade rank and file Californians that cleaner air and water are more to their benefit than an unrestrained, market-driven economy.

NOTES

1. U.S. Environmental Protection Agency, "PM-10 Non-attainment State/Area/County Report" <http://134.67.104.12/e-drive/CAAA/TL1/ bgilbert/ 1996)>.
2. Matthew Cahn, *Environmental Deceptions* (Albany: State University of New York Press, 1995).
3. Cal-EPA, Environmental Indicators Report <http://www.calepa.cahwnet.gov>.
4. US-EPA Region 9, *Breathing Easier 1996* <http://www.epa.gov/region09>.
5. World Resources Institute, *The 1993 Information Please Environmental Almanac* (New York: Houghton Mifflin Co., 1992).
6. Cal-EPA, *Environmental Indicators Report* <http://www.calepa.cahwnet.gov/graphx/ eitable.gif>.
7. San Francisco Bay Regional Water Quality Control Board <http://www.abag.ca.gov/ abag/other_gov/rwqcb/rwqcb.htm#gp>.
8. Ibid.
9. *Regional Monitoring*, San Francisco Bay Regional Water Quality Control Board <http:// www.abag.ca.gov/abag/other_gov/rwqcb/rwqcb.htm#gp>.
10. *Habitat Loss*, San Francisco Bay Regional Water Quality Control Board <http://www. abag.ca.gov/abag/other_gov/rwqcb/rwqcb.htm#gp>.
11. *Sediment Hotspots,* San Francisco Bay Regional Water Quality Control Board <http://www.abag.ca.gov/abag/other_gov/rwqcb/rwqcb.htm#gp>.
12. Michael Bernick and Robert Cervero, *Transit Villages in the 21st Century* (New York: McGraw Hill, 1997).
13. Genevieve Giuliano, "Transporting Los Angeles," in *Rethinking Los Angeles* (Thousand Oaks, CA: Sage, 1996).
14. Bernick and Cervero, 1997.
15. Bernick and Cervero, 1997.
16. Bradford Snell, "American Ground Transport," in *Crisis in American Institutions*, 6th ed., Jerome Skolnick and Elliott Currie, eds. (Boston: Little, Brown, and Company, 1985).
17. Ruth Cavin, *Trolleys: Riding and Remembering the Electric Interurban Railways* (New York: Hawthorne Books, Inc., 1976).
18. South Coast Air Quality Management Plan (SCAQMD), 1997.
19. Bradford Snell, "American Ground Transport," in *Crisis in American Institutions*, 6th ed., Jerome Skolnick and Elliott Currie, eds. (Boston: Little, Brown, and Company, 1985).
20. Metropolitan Transit Authority, 1997 <http://www.mta.net>.
21. Mary Nichols and Stanley Young, *The Amazing LA Environment: A Handbook for Change* (Los Angeles: Living Planet Press and Natural Resources Defense Council, 1991).
22. Steven Cohen and Sheldon Kamieniecki, *Environmental Regulation through Strategic Planning* (Boulder: Westview Press, 1991).
23. Nichols and Young.
24. California State Water Resources Control Board, 5 July 1997 <http://www.swrcb.ca.gov>.
25. Ibid.
26. California Integrated Waste Management Board (IWMB), Publication #530-99-007, January 2000.

CHAPTER 15

Immigration Policy

Appendix / Pages 170–175
Proposition 187 (1994, Full Text)

The New Colossus

Not like the brazen giant of Greek fame,
With conquering limbs astride from land to land;
Here at our sea washed, sunset gates shall stand
A mighty woman with a torch, whose flame
Is the imprisoned lightning, and her name
Mother of Exiles. From her beacon-hand
Glows world-wide welcome; her mild eyes command
The air-bridged harbor that twin cities frame.
"Keep ancient lands, your storied pomp!" cries she
With silent lips. "Give me your tired, your poor,
Your huddled masses yearning to breathe free,
The wretched refuse of your teeming shore.
Send these, the homeless, tempest-tost to me,
I lift my lamp beside the golden door!"

—Emma Lazarus, engraved on the pedestal of the Statue of Liberty

Immigration policy[1] provides insight into one of California's less innovative areas. The question of immigration has challenged Californians since the state first joined the Union in 1850. Some argue that immigration is essential to the continued prosperity of California and the nation, while proponents of stricter immigration laws have long argued that the influx of new Californians takes a heavy toll on the state's resources and dilutes its culture. The United States admits more immigrants across its borders than any other nation; more, in fact, than all other nations combined. Immigration has always played a significant role in U.S. population growth; it is estimated that one-third of the nation's annual population increase is the result of immigration alone.[2] California has emerged as the gateway state for new immigrants. This chapter explores the development of immigration policy in California.

IMMIGRATION IN CALIFORNIA'S HISTORY

Ever since its founding as a state in 1850, California has been the epicenter of the immigration debate and to a large degree has led the national policy discourse. As early as 1870, drawn by the Gold Rush, fully 37 percent of California residents were foreign born.[3] By the turn of the century, 25 percent of all Californians were foreign born. This declined subsequently to a low point of 9 percent by 1960.[4] Today, 22 percent of Californians, and one-third of the residents of Los Angeles County, are foreign born. Up to one-quarter of all immigrants to the United States have settled in the Southern California region.

California followed much of the classic patterns of ethnocultural cleavages spinning out of the East and Midwest of the United States as territorial expansion took place. White Protestant nativists aligned themselves politically against the newly arrived urban immigrant class, composed of European ethnics (Irish, Polish, Italians), Catholics, and East European Jews. The political reaction in most of the nation's older cities was the rise of "ethnic party machines," which not only delivered the ethnic vote during local elections, but guaranteed that immigrant communities would receive a proportionate amount of the spoils of the public largess—from pork-barrel projects to government jobs.

As quickly as the window opened for ethnic political empowerment and coalition building during the machine era, so too did the door slam on the expansion of political rights with tighter immigration restrictions and the launching of the "good government" reforms during the Progressive era. The wave of immigrants from non-European nations into California and the West produced an even stronger political response. These included the large numbers of Asian and Mexican immigrants arriving to build the railroads and harvest the fields. Western state legislatures passed a series of constitutionally suspect measures—ranging from restrictions on property rights to the denial of education, health, and economic protection. The western states—California in particular—called on Congress to enact strict immigration quotas for certain groups and eventual exclusion from entry into the United States. From the Workingmen's Party, formed in 1877 and organized against Chinese immigrants in San Francisco, to the later "fringe" movements like the Asiatic Exclusion League of California, whose sole purpose was to pressure Congress to cut off Japanese immigration in the 1920s, California has been a wellspring for nativist and exclusionary movements since statehood.

The major political parties and West Coast state legislatures maintained a rigid system of exclusion and discrimination against Asian immigrants. Early Chinese and Japanese immigrants to California were politically disenfranchised and excluded from full participation in American life because of discriminatory laws and policies. As the major port of entry for these initial groups, California led the way in racially tinged discriminatory practices that were emulated by other states and even the national government. In 1854, for example, Chinese immigrants were prohibited from testifying in court against whites. In 1855, the state legislature imposed a $50 "head tax" on Chinese immigrants. San Francisco passed an ordinance that same year referred to as the "pigtail ordinance," requiring Chinese lawbreakers to cut their hair within one inch of the scalp. In 1871, a Los Angeles mob, which included many prominent citizens of the time, tortured and lynched Chinese men. In 1879, the new California state constitution barred corporations from hiring Chinese employees and prohibited the employment of people of Chinese descent in any public works "except for punishment of a crime." This so-called Chinese exclusion provision remained in the state constitution until it was repealed in 1952. Also repealed in 1952 was a measure put into effect in 1913 by the Progressives called the Alien Land Law, which prohibited Asians—but not Europeans— who were not citizens from owning land in California. In 1882 pressure from California was instrumental in the passage of national legislation barring Chinese from acquiring citizenship and banning the entry of Chinese workers for decades.[5]

With the federal exclusion of Chinese from entering the United States, California's agricultural interests started to recruit imported Japanese workers to its fields. In the vast Central Valley over 250 crops are grown, and cheap dependable labor to harvest the crops has always been a state mandate. In the end, however, the Japanese fared no better that did their Chinese predecessors, bearing the brunt of "yellow-peril" discriminatory policies that robbed the Japanese of their due process and citizenship rights. In 1906, for example, the San Francisco school board issued a mandatory order segregating Japanese schoolchildren in the system. During the same year, the State of California barred marriages between whites and "Mongolians." Just a few years later, an open political quarrel arose on the "Japanese question" between the Republican leadership of the state and Democratic President Woodrow Wilson. Wilson ultimately dispatched his Secretary of State, William Jennings Bryan, to cajole California not to pass anti-Japanese immigrant legislation. While the state backed off, California later passed legislation in 1913 to bar non-citizen Japanese from owning property or leasing farmland. Things were no better on the jurisprudential level, with the U.S. Supreme Court deciding in *Ozawa v. United States* (1922) that Asian immigrants could be barred from becoming naturalized citizens.[6]

This dual pattern of economic recruitment and social demonization played out through the development of California, the West, and indeed the rest of the United States. By 1924, immigration from Japan was effectively halted and new immigrant communities were recruited to replace them, including Filipino and Mexican laborers. When the Great Depression hit California, nativist sentiments awoke once again—resulting in the deportation of hundreds of thousands of Mexican agricultural workers. This exclusionary impulse is in constant tension with the insatiable desire for cheap labor to fuel the state's economic growth. Not long after the mass deportation of Mexicans during the depression, California's agricultural sector—the state's largest and most politically powerful industry—persuaded Congress during World War II to establish the Bracero guest worker program that brought Mexican immigrants back across the border. This flip-flopping policy toward immigrants followed the nation's economic cycles of expansion and contraction, with California and the West leading the nation's immigration policy thrust.

California's phenomenal growth over the past century was a direct consequence of a constant supply of cheap immigrant labor. During the 1980s, nearly one-fourth of all immigrants to the United States settled in California, and more than half of the 3 million undocumented immigrants granted amnesty under the 1986 Immigration Reform and Control Act (IRCA) settled in California. Overall, California's foreign-born population has increased from 1.3 million in 1960 to 6.45 million in 1990—from about 9 percent to 22 percent of the population. In Los Angeles County alone, estimates are that nearly 33 percent of the population is foreign born—up from 11 percent in 1970. More immigrant arrivals entered California in the 1980s than in the previous three decades combined.[7] California's historic immigration patterns have created a dysfunctional political culture that continues to be unable to successfully integrate new waves of immigrants as policy stakeholders.

THE CURRENT CLIMATE: PROPOSITION 187 AND BEYOND

> Every now and then, an initiative comes along that galvanizes the public to such an extent that it becomes the engine that drives an entire election. Proposition 13 (property tax relief) served that function in 1978. So did ... Proposition 140 (term limits) in 1990. This year it was Proposition 187—the initiative that denies educational, social, and medical services to those who cannot prove American citizenship.[8]

Nativist sentiments have again risen up in California to carry the immigration issue onto the national agenda. This is more than just a debate over legal status. Nation-states throughout the world are puzzling over the impacts of migration. Many nations that once welcomed immigrants freely are now ambivalent. This includes Australia, Canada, New Zealand, Germany, and the United States—to mention a few. In the case of the United States, individual states are sometimes at odds with the federal government's immigration policies. In California, Nancy H. Martis captures this tension:

> As certain as the seasons, issues surrounding illegal migrants and their rights in society come around again and again.... In 1913, the Legislature made no apologies when it ultimately passed a law designed to prevent Asian immigrants from owning and leasing land despite its clear intention to suppress undocumented residents. The law was signed by Progressive Governor Hiram Johnson over the objection of President Woodrow Wilson.[9]

PROPOSITION 187

In 1994, Governor Pete Wilson made Proposition 187 a cornerstone of his successful reelection campaign. Proposition 187—entitled "SOS" (Save Our State) by proponents—was designed to stop "illegal aliens" from entering the state. But, like past immigration reforms, the policy goes well beyond attacking the problem of undocumented immigration. There are three major provisions to the measure. First, it makes undocumented immigrants ineligible for public social services, public health care services (unless emergency services mandated by federal law), and public school education at the elementary, secondary, and postsecondary levels. Second, it requires that "all persons employed in the providing of (public) services shall diligently protect public funds from misuse" by excluding anyone who has not been "verified" to be in the country legally. State and local agencies are required, under the measure, to report persons who are *suspected* undocumented immigrants to the California Attorney General and the Immigration and Naturalization Service, and maintain records of such reports. The law states:

> If any public entity in this state to whom a person has applied for public social services determines *or reasonably suspects*, based upon the information provided to it, that the person is an alien in the United States in violation of federal law, the following procedures shall be followed by the public entity: (1) The entity shall not provide the person with benefits or services. (2) The entity shall, in writing, notify the person of his or her apparent illegal immigration status, and that the person must either obtain legal status or leave the United States. (3) The entity shall also notify the State Director of Social Services, the Attorney General of California, and the United States Immigration and Naturalization Service of the *apparent* illegal status, and shall provide any additional information that may be requested by any other public entity. (emphases added)[10]

Finally, Proposition 187 makes it a felony to manufacture, distribute, sell, or use false citizenship or residency documents. (The full text of Proposition 187 appears on pages 170–175.)

Proponents of Proposition 187 argued that the proposal would end "the illegal alien invasion" and ultimately "save our state."[11] For them, this "invasion" has cost taxpayers in excess of $5 billion a year for welfare and medical and educational benefits, which acts as "magnets" to draw undocumented immigrants to the state in the first place. Further, the federal government has been derelict in its duties to control the nation's borders, so the people of California must "send a message" to Washington. Opponents of Proposition 187 argued that while undocumented immigration may be a problem for the state, 187 is not the solution. Further, they point out that under *Plyler v. Doe* (1982), denying children of undocumented immigrants educational services is unconstitutional. Further, opponents were concerned about the ethical and practical implications of cutting medical services to this population, pointing out that untreated health problems would exacerbate existing public health concerns. But most importantly, the Proposition's vague language of "reasonable suspicion" underscored the concern of many that Latinos and other ethnic minorities—immigrant or not—would become a vulnerable class of citizens.

THE 1994 VOTE AND THE ISSUE OF ILLEGAL IMMIGRATION

Voters in the general election of 1994 produced an electoral earthquake in the body politic, shifting control of Congress to the Republicans, and throwing many incumbent Democrats from the state legislature. Clearly, voters were angry with "politics-as-usual," and eager to upset the status quo, much as they did two years prior with the election of President Clinton. California's divided government between a sitting Republican governor and a Democratically controlled legislature produced little substantive policy momentum. One year before the 1994 election, Pete Wilson trailed his Democratic challenger, Kathleen Brown, by 23 percentage points. In an amazing comeback, Wilson went on to defeat Brown by close to 1.4 million votes (Wilson 55 percent to Brown's 41 percent). Wilson's win was credited to his ability to associate his campaign with crime and anti-immigration themes—specifically through two ballot initiatives: Propositions 184 and 187. Wilson effectively controlled the campaign agenda, deflecting attention away from the state's early 1990s recessionary economy, an issue on which he ordinarily would have been extremely vulnerable.

Wilson's campaign message clearly resonated with the electorate. Stressing the themes of less government spending, law and order, lower taxes, and controlling illegal immigration appealed to groups that were overrepresented at the polls—older white voters. Teaming up with conservative assemblyman Richard Mountjoy and reactionary congressman Dana Rohrabacher, Wilson made Proposition 187 the foundation of his campaign. The campaign whipped up a dormant xenophobia that is never far from California's political culture. Campaign literature screamed: "Proposition 187 will ultimately end the ILLEGAL ALIEN invasion" (emphasis in the original).[12]

As late as November 1993, the California Opinion Index barely measured immigration as a voter's concern. In fact, of the 28 major issues California voters identified as a concern, immigration came in at 19. Crime, the state's economy, the spread of AIDS, and public schools all ranked above it. In September 1986, the Field Poll measured immigration to be 15th in importance out of 27 issues, with only 53 percent registering it was "extremely important."[13] Still, by the end of the campaign, voters believed that the issue of illegal immigration was important, and (by a margin of 49 percent to Brown's 22 percent) that Wilson was better equipped to tackle the problem.[14] Sixty-four percent of white voters favored 187, while 73 percent of Latino voters voted against it. African-American and Asian voters were almost evenly split. Clearly, voters sought to "send a message," as Table 15.1 illustrates.

TABLE 15.1   REASONS GIVEN FOR SUPPORTING PROP. 187

	LIKELY YES VOTERS
It will send a message to federal government to do more to protect our national borders	90%
It will send a message to federal government to pay for the costs associated with illegal immigrants	74
State government will save millions of dollars that are now being spent on illegal immigrants	61
It will reduce the number of illegal immigrants who move here to have their children born as U.S. citizens	76
It will free up money for the education of the children of legal residents	78
It will deter illegal immigrants from coming to California in the first place	71
It will create more job opportunities for legal residents	69
It will help reinforce English as our common language	62
It will make it easier to preserve the American way of life	56

Source: *The Field Poll*, no. 1734 (October 17, 1994): 5.

THE DEATH OF PROPOSITION 187

In November 1995, U.S. District Judge Mariana R. Pfaelzer threw out significant portions of Proposition 187, ruling them unconstitutional and setting in motion a protracted legal battle. Judge Pfaelzer ruled that Sections 4, 5, 6, 7, and 9 of the initiative were invalid because they were preempted by federal laws. In these sections, Judge Pfaelzer found that the state could not bar illegal immigrants from health care and social welfare services (since most of these services were federally funded), to which they were otherwise entitled under existing federal laws. The judge also ruled that the prior precedent, *Plyler v. Doe* (1982), should be followed in application to this initiative and therefore the exclusion of children of illegal immigrants from public elementary and secondary schools under Section 7 was invalid.

At the same time Judge Pfaelzer only partially struck down Section 8 of the initiative, which would have excluded illegal immigrants from public postsecondary educational institutions. She ruled that the state does not have to provide postsecondary education to persons who are not authorized under federal law to be in the United States. However, a subsection that required admissions officials to report any illegal immigrant to authorities was ruled to be preempted by federal law. Beyond this, the judge let stand three other sections pertaining to severability and the criminal sanctions applying to the manufacture, sale, and use of false citizenship documents. On the sections ruled invalid Pfaelzer stated that the measure's provisions "directly regulate immigration by creating a comprehensive scheme to detect and report the presence and affect the removal of illegal aliens ..." and that "the state is powerless to enact its own scheme to regulate immigration."[15]

In short, Proposition 187 has been effectively ruled unconstitutional. All that remains are two relatively minor laws that establish state criminal penalties for the manufacture and use of false documents. In July 1999, Governor Gray Davis reached an agreement with civil rights organizations and agreed to drop litigation and further appeal, effectively killing 187 for good.[16]

As California's economy has rebounded from recession, people seem less concerned about immigration—legal or otherwise. Republican presidential candidate Robert Dole counted on a tough immigration reform proposal to win the state in the 1996 election (as Pete Wilson had done so successfully two years earlier) but the issue won him little support outside the ranks of the most dedicated Republican faithful. Dole lost the California vote to Bill Clinton in an election in which just 7 percent of Californians identified illegal immigration as a major issue influencing their vote.[17] Two years later, Attorney General Dan Lungren tried the same Wilson-style campaign in his bid for governor, losing by a landslide to Democrat Gray Davis.

SUMMARY

Because of the disproportionate impact of immigration upon the Golden State, the nation's immigration policies have been especially important here. California has been a destination of choice for immigrants from around the globe as well as for migrants from other states. The state's opportunities, resources, and promise of a better life have guaranteed that people will continue arriving here, even during those times when shifting political attitudes create a chilly climate for immigrants. From statehood on, California's immigration policy has swung between extremes, reflecting dual realities: Immigrants are essential components of the state's economic growth; and, California's political culture has long demonized newcomers. "Welcome to California—Now Go Home!"[18] California remains an ideal, to be pursued by people seeking a better life— whether native born or foreign born. This is unlikely to change any time soon.

APPENDIX: PROPOSITION 187 (1994, FULL TEXT)

SECTION 1. Findings and Declaration.

The People of California find and declare as follows:

That they have suffered and are suffering economic hardship caused by the presence of illegal aliens in this state.

That they have suffered and are suffering personal injury and damage caused by the criminal conduct of illegal aliens in this state.

That they have a right to the protection of their government from any person or persons entering this country unlawfully.

Therefore, the People of California declare their intention to provide for cooperation between their agencies of state and local government with the federal government, and to establish a system of required notification by and between such agencies to prevent illegal aliens in the United States from receiving benefits or public services in the State of California.

SECTION 2. Manufacture, Distribution or Sale of False Citizenship or Resident Alien Documents: Crime and Punishment.

Section 113 is added to the Penal Code, to read:

113. Any person who manufactures, distributes or sells false documents to conceal the true citizenship or resident alien status of another person is guilty of a felony, and shall be punished by imprisonment in the state prison for five years or by a fine of seventy-five thousand dollars ($75,000).

SECTION 3. Use of False Citizenship or Resident Alien Documents: Crime and Punishment.

Section 114 is added to the Penal Code, to read:

114. Any person who uses false documents to conceal his or her true citizenship or resident alien status is guilty of a felony, and shall be punished by imprisonment in the state prison for five years or by a fine of twenty-five thousand dollars ($25,000).

SECTION 4. Law Enforcement Cooperation with INS.

Section 834b is added to the Penal Code, to read:

834b. (a) Every law enforcement agency in California shall fully cooperate with the United States Immigration and Naturalization Service regarding any person who is arrested if he or she is suspected of being present in the United States in violation of federal immigration laws.

(b) With respect to any such person who is arrested, and suspected of being present in the United States in violation of federal immigration laws, every law enforcement agency shall do the following:

(1) Attempt to verify the legal status of such person as a citizen of the United States, an alien lawfully admitted as a permanent resident, an alien lawfully admitted for a temporary period of time or as an alien who is present in the United States in violation of immigration laws. The verification process may include, but shall not be limited to, questioning the person regarding his or her date and place of birth, and entry into the United States, and demanding documentation to indicate his or her legal status.

(2) Notify the person of his or her apparent status as an alien who is present in the United States in violation of federal immigration laws and inform him or her that, apart from any criminal justice proceedings, he or she must either obtain legal status or leave the United States.

(3) Notify the Attorney General of California and the United States Immigration and Naturalization Service of the apparent illegal status and provide any additional information that may be requested by any other public entity.

(c) Any legislative, administrative, or other action by a city, county, or other legally authorized local governmental entity with jurisdictional boundaries, or by a law enforcement agency, to prevent or limit the cooperation required by subdivision (a) is expressly prohibited.

SECTION 5. Exclusion of Illegal Aliens from Public Social Services.

Section 10001.5 is added to the Welfare and Institutions Code, to read:

10001.5. (a) In order to carry out the intention of the People of California that only citizens of the United States and aliens lawfully admitted to the United States may receive the benefits of public social services and to ensure that all persons employed in the providing of those services shall diligently protect public funds from misuse, the provisions of this section are adopted.

(b) A person shall not receive any public social services to which he or she may be otherwise entitled until the legal status of that person has been verified as one of the following:

(1) A citizen of the United States.

(2) An alien lawfully admitted as a permanent resident.

(3) An alien lawfully admitted for a temporary period of time.

(c) If any public entity in this state to whom a person has applied for public social services determines or reasonably suspects, based upon the information provided to it, that the person is an alien in the United States in violation of federal law, the following procedures shall be followed by the public entity:

(1) The entity shall not provide the person with benefits or services.

(2) The entity shall, in writing, notify the person of his or her apparent illegal immigration status, and that the person must either obtain legal status or leave the United States.

(3) The entity shall also notify the State Director of Social Services, the Attorney General of California, and the United States Immigration and Naturalization Service of the apparent illegal status, and shall provide any additional information that may be requested by any other public entity.

SECTION 6. Exclusion of Illegal Aliens from Publicly Funded Health Care.

Chapter 1.3 (commencing with Section 130) is added to Part 1 of Division 1 of the Health and Safety Code, to read:

Chapter 1.3. Publicly-Funded Health Care Services

130. (a) In order to carry out the intention of the People of California that, excepting emergency medical care as required by federal law, only citizens of the United States and aliens lawfully admitted to the United States may receive the benefits of publicly-funded health care, and to ensure that all persons employed in the providing of those services shall diligently protect public funds from misuse, the provisions of this section are adopted.

(b) A person shall not receive any health care services from a publicly-funded health care facility, to which he or she is otherwise entitled until the legal status of that person has been verified as one of the following:

(1) A citizen of the United States.

(2) An alien lawfully admitted as a permanent resident.

(3) An alien lawfully admitted for a temporary period of time.

(c) If any publicly-funded health care facility in this state from whom a person seeks health care services, other than emergency medical care as required by federal law, determines or reasonably suspects, based upon the information provided to it, that the person is an alien in the United States in violation of federal law, the following procedures shall be followed by the facility:

(1) The facility shall not provide the person with services.

(2) The facility shall, in writing, notify the person of his or her apparent illegal immigration status, and that the person must either obtain legal status or leave the United States.

(3) The facility shall also notify the State Director of Health Services, the Attorney General of California, and the United States Immigration and

Naturalization Service of the apparent illegal status, and shall provide any additional information that may be requested by any other public entity.

(d) For purposes of this section "publicly-funded health care facility" shall be defined as specified in Sections 1200 and 1250 of this code as of January 1, 1993.

SECTION 7. Exclusion of Illegal Aliens from Public Elementary and Secondary Schools.

Section 48215 is added to the Education Code, to read:

48215. (a) No public elementary or secondary school shall admit, or permit the attendance of, any child who is not a citizen of the United States, an alien lawfully admitted as a permanent resident, or a person who is otherwise authorized under federal law to be present in the United States.

(b) Commencing January 1, 1995, each school district shall verify the legal status of each child enrolling in the school district for the first time in order to ensure the enrollment or attendance only of citizens, aliens lawfully admitted as permanent residents, or persons who are otherwise authorized to be present in the United States.

(c) By January 1, 1996, each school district shall have verified the legal status of each child already enrolled and in attendance in the school district in order to ensure the enrollment or attendance only of citizens, aliens lawfully admitted as permanent residents, or persons who are otherwise authorized under federal law to be present in the United States.

(d) By January 1, 1996, each school district shall also have verified the legal status of each parent or guardian of each child referred to in subdivisions (b) and (c), to determine whether such parent or guardian is one of the following:

(1) A citizen of the United States.

(2) An alien lawfully admitted as a permanent resident.

(3) An alien admitted lawfully for a temporary period of time.

(e) Each school district shall provide information to the State Superintendent of Public Instruction, the Attorney General of California, and the United States Immigration and Naturalization Service regarding any enrollee or pupil, or parent or guardian, attending a public elementary or secondary school in the school district determined or reasonably suspected to be in violation of federal immigration laws within forty-five days after becoming aware of an apparent violation. The notice shall also be provided to the parent or legal guardian of the enrollee or pupil, and shall state that an existing pupil may not continue to attend the school after ninety calendar days from the date of the notice, unless legal status is established.

(f) For each child who cannot establish legal status in the United States, each school district shall continue to provide education for a period of ninety days from the date of the notice. Such ninety day period shall be utilized to accomplish an orderly transition to a school in the child's country of origin. Each school district shall fully cooperate in this transition effort to ensure that the educational needs of the child are best served for that period of time.

SECTION 8. Exclusion of Illegal Aliens from Public Postsecondary Educational Institutions.

Section 66010.8 is added to the Education Code, to read:

66010.8. (a) No public institution of postsecondary education shall admit, enroll, or permit the attendance of any person who is not a citizen of the United States, an alien lawfully admitted as a permanent resident in the United States, or a person who is otherwise authorized under federal law to be present in the United States.

(b) Commencing with the first term or semester that begins after January 1, 1995, and at the commencement of each term or semester thereafter, each public postsecondary educational institution shall verify the status of each person enrolled or in attendance at that institution in order to ensure the enrollment or attendance only of United States citizens, aliens lawfully admitted as permanent residents in the United States, and persons who are otherwise authorized under federal law to be present in the United States.

(c) No later than 45 days after the admissions officer of a public postsecondary educational institution becomes aware of the application, enrollment, or attendance of a person determined to be, or who is under reasonable suspicion of being, in the United States in violation of federal immigration laws, that officer shall provide that information to the State Superintendent of Public Instruction, the Attorney General of California, and the United States Immigration and Naturalization Service. The information shall also be provided to the applicant, enrollee, or person admitted.

SECTION 9. Attorney General Cooperation with the INS.

Section 53069.65 is added to the Government Code, to read:

53069.65. Whenever the state or a city, or a county, or any other legally authorized local governmental entity with jurisdictional boundaries reports the presence of a person who is suspected of being present in the United States in violation of federal immigration laws to the Attorney General of California, that report shall be transmitted to the United States Immigration and Naturalization Service. The Attorney General shall be responsible for maintaining on-going and accurate records of such reports, and shall provide any additional information that may be requested by any other government entity.

SECTION 10. Amendment and Severability.

The statutory provisions contained in this measure may not be amended by the Legislature except to further its purposes by statute passed in each house by rollcall vote entered in the journal, two-thirds of the membership concurring, or by a statute that becomes effective only when approved by the voters.

In the event that any portion of this act or the application thereof to any person or circumstance is held invalid, that invalidity shall not affect any other provision or application of the act, which can be given effect without the invalid provision or application, and to that end the provisions of this act are severable.

NOTES

1. Portions of this chapter on immigration policy have been printed in Michael Preston, Bruce Cain, and Sandra Bass, eds., *Racial and Ethnic Politics in California* (Berkeley: Institute for Intergovernmental Studies, 1997).
2. William O'Hare, "America's Minorities: The Demographics of Diversity," *Population Bulletin* 47, no. 4 (Washington, D.C.: Population Reference Bureau, 1992).
3. Doris Marion Wright, "The Making of Cosmopolitan California: An Analysis of Immigration 1848–1870," *California Historical Society Quarterly* XIX (December 1940): 332.
4. Dowell Myers, "The Changing Immigrants of Southern California," *Research Report LCRI-95-94R* (University of Southern California, School of Urban and Regional Planning) (October 25, 1995): 1.
5. Morton Grodzins, *Americans Betrayed* (Chicago: University of Chicago Press, 1949); Roger Daniels, *The Politics of Prejudice* (New York: Atheneum, 1968).
6. Yuji Ichioka, "Early Japanese Quest for Citizenship: The Background of the 1922 Ozawa Case," *Amerasia Journal* 4 (1977): 1–22.
7. Ronald Brownstein and Richard Simon, "Hospitality Turns Into Hostility," *Los Angeles Times*, 14 November 1993, A6–7.
8. Nancy Martis and A. G. Black, "Proposition 187," *California Journal* (December 1994): 20.
9. Nancy Martis and A. G. Black, "Proposition 187," *California Journal* (November 1994): 9.
10. Ballot text of California's Proposition 187 (1994), now state law. Several elements of the law are under review by federal courts.
11. California 1994 Voter's Guide: Argument in Favor of Proposition 187.
12. California 1994 Voter's Guide: Argument in Favor of Proposition 187.
13. *The Field Poll* 5 (September 1986).
14. Weintraub.
15. Paul Feldman, "Major Portions of Proposition 187 Thrown Out By Federal Judge," *Los Angeles Times*, 21 November 1995, A1.
16. Patrick J. McDonnell, "Davis Won't Appeal Prop. 187 Ruling, Ending Court Battles; Litigation," *Los Angeles Times*, 29 July 1999, A1.
17. Maria La Ganga and Dave Lesher, "Dole to Push Tough Stand in California Swing," *Los Angeles Times*, 26 October 1996, A1.
18. Bumper sticker popular during the summer of 1984, when Los Angeles hosted the Summer Olympics.

CHAPTER 16

Civil Rights Policy

Featured Reading / Pages 181–182
Tom Brokaw
Shame
Appendix / Pages 182–188
Korematsu v. United States (1944)

There were small acts of cruelty to go with the larger violations of constitutional rights. Norman Mineta, later a congressman from California, was just ten years old when his family was loaded onto a train in the San Jose freight yards. He was wearing his Cub Scout uniform and carrying his baseball bat and glove, the American-born son of a prominent Japanese businessman who had lived in the area for forty years. Several of young Norman's schoolmates came to the tracks to say good-bye, just in time to see the armed guards confiscate his baseball bat because, they said, it could be used as a weapon. It was a world turned upside down for these law-abiding, productive, and respectable families.

—Tom Brokaw, from *Shame*

Because California was not admitted to the Union until 1850, many of the controversies over slavery and civil rights that had troubled the rest of the nation were avoided. Its acceptance into the Union as a free state meant that it would never experience the institutional dehumanization of a slave society. California's role in the Civil War was as banker for the Unionist side, providing rich gold reserves but avoiding the bloody human cost. By 1876, just a few years before California drafted its second constitution, the U.S. Constitution had been permanently altered by the addition of the Thirteenth, Fourteenth, and Fifteenth Amendments. Equal protections were thus handed to California as a fundamental legal principle.[1]

Still, life was not easy for people of color in the latter part of the 1800s. In the areas of suffrage, education, and the right to provide testimony in court, equality was delayed for many of the state's minority communities.[2] From the passage of its first public school laws in 1851, California exhibited an unwillingness to provide schools that would "mix the races." By 1870 California segregated white students from black, Indian, Chinese, and Latino students. While minorities had the right to vote after 1870, the Fifteenth Amendment was not formally ratified by the state legislature until as late as 1962, 92 years after it became part of the U.S. Constitution. Legislative roadblocks were established to prohibit blacks, Native Americans, and later Chinese residents from testifying in court. Public law required the following:

No black or mulatto person or Indian shall be permitted to give evidence in favor or against any white person. Every person who shall have one-eighth part or more Negro blood shall be deemed a mulatto, and every person who shall have one-half Indian blood shall be deemed an Indian.[3]

These impediments demonstrate how the drama of differentness played out early in California's development and how concomitant political power was distributed or denied.

CIVIL RIGHTS POLICY IN CALIFORNIA

The fight for civil rights in California is not merely pro forma. Though avoiding the Jim Crow past of many states, California's racial demons are just as dark.[4] The most dramatic, perhaps, was the internment of Japanese Americans during World War II. Roosevelt's Executive Order #9066 (1942) authorized the Secretary of War to exclude "all persons of Japanese ancestry, both alien and non-alien" from the Pacific Coast area on a plea of military necessity. Though not a state law, the exclusion order resulted in curfews, detention, and ultimately relocation of Japanese Americans and Japanese residents throughout California and Hawaii. It is widely recognized that the military justification was suspect and that local interest groups fought hard to remove the Japanese for nonmilitary reasons. Supreme Court Justice Murphy argued as follows:

This exclusion of "all persons of Japanese ancestry, both alien and non-alien," from the Pacific Coast area on a plea of military necessity in the absence of martial law ought not to be approved. Such exclusion goes over "the very brink of constitutional power" and falls into the ugly abyss of racism.[5]

Mr. Austin E. Anson, managing secretary of the Salinas Vegetable Grower-Shipper Association, stated the following in the *Saturday Evening Post*:

We're charged with wanting to get rid of the Japs for selfish reasons.... We do. It's a question of whether the white man lives on the Pacific Coast or the brown men. They came into this valley to work, and they stayed to take over.... They undersell the white man in the markets.... They work their women and children while the white farmer has to pay wages for his help. If all the Japs were removed tomorrow, we'd never miss them in two weeks, because the white farmers can take over and produce everything the Jap grows. And we don't want them back when the war ends, either.[6]

It was not until the 1960s that California embarked on an explicit path to remedy discrimination. With the passage of the federal Civil Rights Act in 1964 and the Voting Rights Act of 1965, the state responded with its own antidiscriminatory legislation. Under the Unruh Civil Rights Act, the state reaffirmed federal civil rights mandates. The act prohibited discrimination in public accommodations on the grounds of race, color, religion, gender, or national origin—sexual orientation was later added in the 1990s. It further prohibited discrimination in employment hiring, firing, and prohibited discrimination in the sale or rental of housing. *De jure* ("under the law") legal guarantees tell only part of the story, however. *De facto* ("in fact") bigotry and discrimination on the community level is just as important. Despite the significance of *Brown v. Board of Education of Topeka* (1954), *Green v. School Board of New Kent County* (1968), and *Swann v. Charlotte-Mechlenburg Board of Education* (1971), California's public schools remained largely segregated well into the 1970s. The result was court-ordered integration through a program of mandatory busing.

Busing created a backlash that continues today. Anti-busing leaders in California argued that busing conflicted with neighborhood rights and that integrating less-prepared "inner city" students into high-performing suburban campuses would "dumb-down" educational standards. Bobbi Feidler, an anti-busing activist from Los Angeles' San Fernando Valley, used the issue as a launching pad to win a congressional seat. Anti-busing sentiment had a profound impact on California communities across city-suburban-rural lines. White families started leaving the integrated school districts in droves to avoid forced busing—establishing "white flight" as the *de facto* response to *de jure* protections.

The battles over urban secession, school standards, and district control that are common today are a direct outgrowth of the busing controversy. What we are left with is a profound reflection about government's ability to sustain civil and human rights legislation in the face of a hostile majority. Subsequent supreme courts have retreated from pressing full integration and equality of education in the face of the hostile majorities. School desegregation has remained a back burner issue in the 1980s and 1990s, not only within the courts but also in Congress and in the state legislatures.

ENDING DISCRIMINATION THROUGH AFFIRMATIVE ACTION

The phrase "affirmative action" was first used by President Lyndon Johnson. Johnson argued that discrimination was sufficiently ingrained in American culture that taking affirmative (rather than passive) action was necessary. His 1965 Executive Order 11246, required federal contractors to

> take affirmative action to ensure that applicants are employed, and that employees are treated during employment, without regard to their race, creed, color, or national origin.

In 1967, Johnson expanded the Executive Order to include women. Affirmative action has come to refer to specific programs that were designed to expand access to education and the workplace to members of historically underrepresented groups. The National Organization for Women suggests that "Affirmative Action levels the playing field so people of color and all women have the chance to compete in education and in business."[7] Affirmative action programs have sought to expand the number of applicants from underrepresented groups and have given preference to members of specified communities in an effort to bring the numbers of women, African Americans, Latinos, and Asians up in competitive educational and professional environments. Thus, if equality under the law sags under the weight of *de facto* discrimination, proponents argue "affirmative action is the bridge between changing the laws and changing the culture."[8] Since the late 1960s, affirmative action has taken many forms and has proven quite controversial.

THE BAKKE CASE

Affirmative action was first challenged in the *Bakke* (1978) case. Allan Bakke was rejected from UC Davis Medical School although his grades and test scores were higher than those for students accepted to 16 slots held for underrepresented applicants. UC Davis had a special-admissions program that held aside 16 of the 100 medical school slots for members of underrepresented communities. Bakke filed suit in state court, claiming he was a victim of racial discrimination. The California Supreme Court upheld Bakke's legal challenge, and the state—on behalf of the University of California—appealed the case to the U.S. Supreme Court. In *Regents of the University of California v. Bakke* (1978),[9] the Court ruled 5–4 that while racial preference can be used as a factor, a specific quota like UC Davis' 16 percent was unconstitutional and that Bakke should be admitted. Four justices supported the constitutionality of racial quotas (or set-asides) as a remedy for historical discrimination under the Civil Rights Act of 1964. Four justices opposed the quota system under their test of the Fourteenth Amendment. Justice Lewis F. Powell, Jr. was the swing vote. The final legal result was that while Bakke was admitted as an individual, the system of admissions used at UC Davis Medical School was constitutionally flawed. However, the *Bakke* decision was extremely important in determining that race and other factors could be used to allow a "preferential admission" program to ensure a diverse student body. A more refined affirmative action program would therefore be constitutionally maintained, not only in California's higher educational system but throughout the nation.

By the late 1980s several court cases undercut *Bakke*, giving greater standing to claims of reverse discrimination, invalidating minority set-asides in cases where past discrimination against minority contractors was unproven, and limiting the use of statistics to demonstrate past discrimination since statistics are aggregate and cannot prove intent.[10] While the Civil Rights Act of 1991 confirmed a belief in many of the principles of affirmative action as an important remedy to discrimination, the future of affirmative action is in jeopardy.

PROPOSITION 209: "THE CALIFORNIA CIVIL RIGHTS INITIATIVE (CCRI)"

In the midst of the rancor over California's role in the 1996 presidential elections, opponents of affirmative action turned in some 1.1 million signatures on a ballot proposition to prevent race, ethnicity, or sex from being used as the basis for "discriminating against, or granting preferential treatment to, any individual or group."[11] 209 seeks to dismantle the state's longstanding commitment to affirmative action. The law states that

> The state shall not discriminate against, or grant preferential treatment to, any individual or group on the basis of race, sex, color, ethnicity, or national origin in the operation of public employment, public education, or public contracting.[12]

Critics argue that 209 is disingenuous, arguing that discrimination is already banned by federal civil rights laws and pointing out that the third clause of the initiative presents an explicit attack on the protections against sexual discrimination ensured by Title X of federal civil rights law. The third clause of 209 declares that

> Nothing in this section shall be interpreted as prohibiting bona fide qualifications based on sex which are reasonably necessary to the normal operation of public employment, public education, or public contracting.[13]

What "bona fide qualifications" are "reasonably necessary" has not been defined. Since public safety agencies (e.g., police and fire departments) have traditionally used this line of argument to exclude women, this language has elicited protest.

The initiative continues to stir controversy because it targets equity programs that are largely responsible for giving traditionally underrepresented communities (women, blacks, Latinos, Asians) greater access to education, business, and the professions. Advocates of 209 argue that affirmative action programs have served their purpose, but that they no longer are appropriate. Opponents—mainly Democrats—saw the initiative as a wedge issue, as Proposition 187 had been. California was critical of Clinton's election victory four years earlier, and this issue threatened to divide the state electorate, which was leaning toward Clinton once again.

THE FUTURE OF PROPOSITION 209

As California goes, so goes the nation. Two years after Proposition 209 was ratified in California, Washington state became the second state to abolish affirmative action when voters approved Initiative 200. After the vote, UC Regent Ward Connerly—who help finance and campaign for the Washington initiative—announced that the initiative process provided the best vehicle to further the anti-affirmative action movement. He also announced that he was setting his sights on Nebraska as the next battleground.[14] However, a nationwide grassroots movement to roll back affirmative action is still far from certain. Voters in Houston, Texas, rejected a citywide initiative to ban affirmative action, and activists in Florida failed to gather enough signatures to place a version of Proposition 209 on that state's ballot.

Although Proposition 209 became state law, the battle over affirmative action programs in California is far from over. In 1998, San Francisco's Board of Supervisors balked at CCRI, voting to extend—and even expand—the city's affirmative action program. In a plan backed by Mayor Willie Brown, San Francisco upheld its Business Enterprise program, giving preferences to minority- and women-owned businesses, as well as local businesses in the awarding of city contracts. Even under the ten-year-old program, 89 percent of construction dollars go to firms owned by white men. Supervisor Amos Brown, who sponsored the plan, remarked: "It's not about giving anyone anything they don't deserve in a just society. This legislation is about inclusion."[15] Charging that the San Francisco program contradicts the will of the majority of the state's voters, Ward Connerly vowed a legal challenge.

At the University of California, where the rollback of affirmative action began, there are also signs that policy may change once again. Governor Gray Davis, a moderate, is not expected to directly challenge 209. However, he has pledged to appoint an ethnically-diverse group of individuals to important posts. *Sacramento Bee* columnist Peter Schrag speculated that the five UC regents that Davis appoints will work to reverse many of the policies of Wilson's appointees, even though they cannot overturn the restrictions of Proposition 209.[16] The declining minority enrollments at UC Berkeley tell the story. Just two years after Proposition 209 was passed, only 3.5 percent of incoming freshmen were African American and 7.5 percent were Latino. These figures were approximately half of what they were the previous year.[17] Affirmative action may not be the perfect fix to California's long history of unequal access, but without an alternative, California's minorities are likely to lose even more ground.

Shame
Tom Brokaw

There were small acts of cruelty to go with the larger violations of constitutional rights. Norman Mineta, later a congressman from California, was just ten years old when his family was loaded onto a train in the San Jose freight yards. He was wearing his Cub Scout uniform and carrying his baseball bat and glove, the American-born son of a prominent Japanese businessman who had lived in the area for forty years. Several of young Norman's schoolmates came to the tracks to say good-bye, just in time to see the armed guards confiscate his baseball bat because, they said, it could be used as a weapon. It was a world turned upside down for these law-abiding, productive, and respectable families.

When Bob Dole of Russell, Kansas, got to know Danny Inouye of Honolulu in the same rehabilitation hospital in Michigan after the war, they had a good deal in common for two young men from such distinctly different backgrounds. Both were trying to learn to live without the use of an arm as a result of combat wounds suffered as Army lieutenants in the mountains of Italy ... [but] Inouye's route to that hospital took a few turns not imposed on the young man from Kansas. Inouye was a Japanese American, raised in Hawaii. On December 7, 1941, Inouye, who was just seventeen, was preparing to attend church when he heard a hysterical local radio announcer explain that Pearl Harbor had been attacked.

Young Inouye was enrolled in a Red Cross first-aid training program at the time, so he went directly to the harbor and began helping with the hundreds of casualties. In effect, he was in the war from the opening moments. He stayed on duty at the Red Cross medical aid facility for the next seven days. In March 1942, the U.S. military repaid Inouye by declaring that all young men of Japanese ancestry would be designated 4-C, which meant "enemy alien," unfit for service. Inouye says, "That really hit me. I considered myself patriotic, and to be told you could not put on a uniform, that was an insult. Thousands of us signed petitions, asking to be able to enlist." The Army decided to form an all-Japanese American unit, the 442nd Regimental Combat Team. Its shoulder patch was a coffin with a torch of liberty inside. The motto was "Go For Broke." Before the war was over, the 442nd and its units would become the most heavily decorated single combat unit of its size in U.S. Army history.

Daniel Inouye went on to become Hawaii's first congressman, and the first Japanese American in Congress.

...

... Nao Takasugi was a junior studying business at UCLA when the Japanese bombed Pearl Harbor. Suddenly, because of his ancestry, he was subject to a strict curfew: he couldn't be out before 6 A.M. and after 6 P.M. He couldn't go five miles beyond his family home in Oxnard, which ruled out UCLA, more than fifty miles away. Then, in his neighborhood, came the posting of Executive Order 9066. "Here I was," he says, "a nineteen-year-old college student full of ambition and ideals. All of that just came crashing down." The Takasugi family—the parents, four daughters, and Nao—were told to prepare whatever personal possessions they could carry in their hands and report to the railroad station in Ventura. The railroad station was bristling with armed guards. The Takasugi family, just days before a respected and productive family of American citizens, boarded for an unknown destination, their most fundamental rights stripped in the name of fear.

Nao Takasugi later earned an MBA at Wharton, became mayor and a member of the city council of Oxnard, and became a California State Assemblyman in 1992.

Senator Inouye and Assemblyman Takasugi are currently on the board of the Japanese American National Museum.

Source: Tom Brokaw, *The Greatest Generation.* Copyright © 1998 by Tom Brokaw. Reprinted by permission of Random House, Inc.

SUMMARY

The struggle for equality in California has not been an easy one. Ever since statehood, communities of color have been subjected to institutional and *de facto* discrimination. The internment of Japanese Americans is but one ugly footnote in California's—and the nation's—past. The landmark civil rights legislation of the 1960s forced leaders to find new ways to break down the barriers to social and economic advancement. From *Bakke* to Proposition 209, affirmative action policies designed to advance equality first came under fire in California. Like many other policy innovations in California, the movement to end affirmative action through direct democracy is taking hold in other states.

Whether California will assertively and affirmatively develop new approaches to ensure equal access in the post-affirmative action era is not yet clear. Without doubt, there is a long way to go. The state's changing demographics may actually solve the problem more quickly than the conflicted policy approaches of the past. California Republicans have already experienced a backlash of their own: In 1998, Latinos and Asians turned out to vote in record numbers against a party that had taken tough anti-immigration and anti-affirmative action positions, prompting fears among Republican leaders that these issues may be damaging in the long run—having alienated too many potential supporters. California's majority white population is expected to slip under 50 percent within the next decade. With no ethnic majority the state's minority communities may fare better. Still, equal protection is about more than race; gender and class remain serious impediments to equality throughout the state. Equal protection and equal access under the law remain a contested terrain in California.

APPENDIX: *KOREMATSU V. UNITED STATES* (1944)

Editor's note: The internment of Japanese-Americans was tested in *Korematsu*. The excerpts below include the Court's majority opinion sustaining the internment, as well as a particularly harsh dissent from Justice Murphy.

MR. JUSTICE BLACK delivered the majority opinion of the Court.

The petitioner, an American citizen of Japanese descent, was convicted in a federal district court for remaining in San Leandro, California, a "Military Area," contrary to Civilian Exclusion Order No. 34 of the Commanding General of the Western

Command, U.S. Army, which directed that after May 9, 1942, all persons of Japanese ancestry should be excluded from that area. No question was raised as to petitioner's loyalty to the United States. The Circuit Court of Appeals affirmed,[18] and the importance of the constitutional question involved caused us to grant certiorari.

It should be noted, to begin with, that all legal restrictions which curtail the civil rights of a single racial group are immediately suspect. That is not to say that all such restrictions are unconstitutional. It is to say that courts must subject them to the most rigid scrutiny. Pressing public necessity may sometimes justify the existence of such restrictions; racial antagonism never can.

In the instant case prosecution of the petitioner was begun by information charging violation of an Act of Congress, of March 21, 1942, 56 Stat. 173, which provides that "... whoever shall enter, remain in, leave, or commit any act in any military area or military zone prescribed, under the authority of an Executive order of the President, by the Secretary of War, or by any military commander designated by the Secretary of War, contrary to the restrictions applicable to any such area or zone or contrary to the order of the Secretary of War or any such military commander, shall, if it appears that he knew or should have known of the existence and extent of the restrictions or order and that his act was in violation thereof, be guilty of a misdemeanor and upon conviction shall be liable to a fine of not to exceed $ 5,000 or to imprisonment for not more than one year, or both, for each offense."

Exclusion Order No. 34, which the petitioner knowingly and admittedly violated, was one of a number of military orders and proclamations, all of which were substantially based upon Executive Order No. 9066, 7 Fed. Reg. 1407. That order, issued after we were at war with Japan, declared that "the successful prosecution of the war requires every possible protection against espionage and against sabotage to national-defense material, national-defense premises, and national-defense utilities...."

One of the series of orders and proclamations, a curfew order, which like the exclusion order here was promulgated pursuant to Executive Order 9066, subjected all persons of Japanese ancestry in prescribed West Coast military areas to remain in their residences from 8 P.M. to 6 A.M. As is the case with the exclusion order here, that prior curfew order was designed as a "protection against espionage and against sabotage." In *Hirabayashi v. United States*, 320 U.S. 81, we sustained a conviction obtained for violation of the curfew order. The *Hirabayashi* conviction and this one thus rest on the same 1942 Congressional Act and the same basic executive and military orders, all of which orders were aimed at the twin dangers of espionage and sabotage.

The 1942 Act was attacked in the *Hirabayashi* case as an unconstitutional delegation of power; it was contended that the curfew order and other orders on which it rested were beyond the war powers of the Congress, the military authorities and of the President, as Commander in Chief of the Army; and finally that to apply the curfew order against none but citizens of Japanese ancestry amounted to a constitutionally prohibited discrimination solely on account of race. To these questions, we gave the serious consideration which their importance justified. We upheld the curfew order as an exercise of the power of the government to take steps necessary to prevent espionage and sabotage in an area threatened by Japanese attack.

In the light of the principles we announced in the *Hirabayashi* case, we are unable to conclude that it was beyond the war power of Congress and the Executive to exclude those of Japanese ancestry from the West Coast war area at the time they did. True, exclusion from the area in which one's home is located is a far greater deprivation than constant confinement to the home from 8 P.M. to 6 A.M. Nothing short of apprehension by the proper military authorities of the gravest imminent danger to the public safety can constitutionally justify either. But exclusion from a threatened area, no less than curfew, has a definite and close relationship to the prevention of espionage and sabotage. The military authorities, charged with the primary responsibility of defending our shores, concluded that curfew provided inadequate protection and ordered exclusion. They did so, as pointed out in our *Hirabayashi* opinion, in accordance with Congressional authority to the military to say who should, and who should not, remain in the threatened areas.

In this case the petitioner challenges the assumptions upon which we rested our conclusions in the *Hirabayashi* case. He also urges that by May 1942, when Order No. 34 was promulgated, all danger of Japanese invasion of the West Coast had disappeared. After careful consideration of these contentions we are compelled to reject them.

... The judgment that exclusion of the whole group was for the same reason a military imperative answers the contention that the exclusion was in the nature of group punishment based on antagonism to those of Japanese origin. That there were members of the group who retained loyalties to Japan has been confirmed by investigations made subsequent to the exclusion. Approximately five thousand American citizens of Japanese ancestry refused to swear unqualified allegiance to the United States and to renounce allegiance to the Japanese Emperor, and several thousand evacuees requested repatriation to Japan.[19]

We uphold the exclusion order as of the time it was made and when the petitioner violated it. *Cf. Chastleton Corporation v. Sinclair*, 264 U.S. 543, 547; *Block v. Hirsh*, 256 U.S. 135, 154–155. In doing so, we are not unmindful of the hardships imposed by it upon a large group of American citizens. *Cf. Ex parte Kawato*, 317 U.S. 69, 73. But hardships are part of war, and war is an aggregation of hardships. All citizens alike, both in and out of uniform, feel the impact of war in greater or lesser measure. Citizenship has its responsibilities as well as its privileges, and in time of war the burden is always heavier. Compulsory exclusion of large groups of citizens from their homes, except under circumstances of direst emergency and peril, is inconsistent with our basic governmental institutions. But when under conditions of modern warfare our shores are threatened by hostile forces, the power to protect must be commensurate with the threatened danger.

... It is said that we are dealing here with the case of imprisonment of a citizen in a concentration camp solely because of his ancestry, without evidence or inquiry concerning his loyalty and good disposition towards the United States. Our task would be simple, our duty clear, were this a case involving the imprisonment of a loyal citizen in a concentration camp because of racial prejudice. Regardless of the true nature of the assembly and relocation centers—and we deem it unjustifiable to call them concentration camps with all the ugly connotations that term implies—we are dealing specifically with nothing but an exclusion order. To cast this case into outlines of racial prejudice, without reference to the real military dangers which were presented, merely confuses the issue. Korematsu was not excluded from the Military Area because of hostility to him or his race. He was excluded because we are at war with the Japanese Empire, because the properly constituted military authorities feared an invasion of our West Coast and felt constrained to take proper security measures, because they decided that the military urgency of the situation demanded that all citizens of Japanese ancestry be segregated from the West Coast temporarily, and finally, because Congress, reposing its confidence in this time of war in our military leaders—as inevitably it must—determined that they should have the power to do just this. There was evidence of disloyalty on the part of some, the military authorities considered that the need for action was great, and time was short. We cannot—by availing ourselves of the calm perspective of hindsight—now say that at that time these actions were unjustified.

MR. JUSTICE MURPHY, dissenting.

This exclusion of "all persons of Japanese ancestry, both alien and non-alien," from the Pacific Coast area on a plea of military necessity in the absence of martial law ought not to be approved. Such exclusion goes over "the very brink of constitutional power" and falls into the ugly abyss of racism.

In dealing with matters relating to the prosecution and progress of a war, we must accord great respect and consideration to the judgments of the military authorities who are on the scene and who have full knowledge of the military facts. The scope of their discretion must, as a matter of necessity and common sense, be wide. And their judgments ought not to be overruled lightly by those whose training and duties ill-equip them to deal intelligently with matters so vital to the physical security of the nation.

At the same time, however, it is essential that there be definite limits to military discretion, especially where martial law has not been declared. Individuals must not be left impoverished of their constitutional rights on a plea of military necessity that has neither substance nor support. Thus, like other claims conflicting with the asserted constitutional rights of the individual, the military claim must subject itself to the judicial process of having its reasonableness determined and its conflicts with other interests reconciled. "What are the allowable limits of military discretion, and whether or not they have been overstepped in a particular case, are judicial questions." *Sterling v. Constantin*, 287 U.S. 378, 401.

The judicial test of whether the Government, on a plea of military necessity, can validly deprive an individual of any of his constitutional rights is whether the deprivation is reasonably related to a public danger that is so "immediate, imminent, and impending" as not to admit of delay and not to permit the intervention of ordinary constitutional processes to alleviate the danger. *United States v. Russell*, 13 Wall. 623, 627–628; *Mitchell v. Harmony*, 13 How. 115, 134–135; *Raymond v. Thomas*, 91 U.S. 712, 716. Civilian Exclusion Order No. 34, banishing from a prescribed area of the Pacific Coast "all persons of Japanese ancestry, both alien and non-alien," clearly does not meet that test. Being an obvious racial discrimination, the order deprives all those within its scope of the equal protection of the laws as guaranteed by the Fifth Amendment. It further deprives these individuals of their constitutional rights to live and work where they will, to establish a home where they choose and to move about freely. In excommunicating them without benefit of hearings, this order also deprives them of all their constitutional rights to procedural due process. Yet no reasonable relation to an "immediate, imminent, and impending" public danger is evident to support this racial restriction which is one of the most sweeping and complete deprivations of constitutional rights in the history of this nation in the absence of martial law.

It must be conceded that the military and naval situation in the spring of 1942 was such as to generate a very real fear of invasion of the Pacific Coast, accompanied by fears of sabotage and espionage in that area. The military command was therefore justified in adopting all reasonable means necessary to combat these dangers. In adjudging the military action taken in light of the then apparent dangers, we must not erect too high or too meticulous standards; it is necessary only that the action have some reasonable relation to the removal of the dangers of invasion, sabotage and espionage. But the exclusion, either temporarily or permanently, of all persons with Japanese blood in their veins has no such reasonable relation. And that relation is lacking because the exclusion order necessarily must rely for its reasonableness upon the assumption that all persons of Japanese ancestry may have a dangerous tendency to commit sabotage and espionage and to aid our Japanese enemy in other ways. It is difficult to believe that reason, logic or experience could be marshalled in support of such an assumption.

That this forced exclusion was the result in good measure of this erroneous assumption of racial guilt rather than bona fide military necessity is evidenced by the Commanding General's Final Report on the evacuation from the Pacific Coast area.[20] In it he refers to all individuals of Japanese descent as "subversive," as belonging to "an enemy race" whose "racial strains are undiluted," and as constituting "over 112,000 potential enemies ... at large today" along the Pacific Coast.[21] In support of this blanket condemnation of all persons of Japanese descent, however, no reliable evidence is cited to show that such individuals were generally disloyal,[22] or had generally so conducted themselves in this area as to constitute a special menace to defense installations or war industries, or had otherwise by their behavior furnished reasonable ground for their exclusion as a group.

Justification for the exclusion is sought, instead, mainly upon questionable racial and sociological grounds not ordinarily within the realm of expert military judgment, supplemented by certain semi-military conclusions drawn from an unwarranted use of circumstantial evidence. Individuals of Japanese ancestry are condemned because they are said to be "a large, unassimilated, tightly knit racial group, bound to an enemy nation by strong ties of race, culture, custom and religion."[23] They are claimed to be given to "emperor worshipping ceremonies"[24] and to "dual citizenship."[25] Japanese language schools and allegedly pro-Japanese organizations are cited as evidence of possible group disloyalty,[26] together with facts as to certain persons being educated and residing at length in Japan.[27] It is intimated that many of these individuals deliberately resided "adjacent to strategic points," thus enabling them "to carry into execution a tremendous program of sabotage on a mass scale should any considerable number of them have been inclined to do so."[28] The need for protective custody is also asserted. The report refers without identity to "numerous incidents of violence" as well as to other admittedly unverified or cumulative incidents. From this, plus certain other events not shown to have been connected with the Japanese Americans, it is concluded that the "situation was fraught with danger to the Japanese population itself" and that the general public "was ready to take matters into its own hands."[29] Finally, it is intimated, though not directly charged or proved, that persons of Japanese ancestry were responsible for three minor isolated shellings and bombings of the Pacific Coast area,[30] as well as for unidentified radio transmissions and night signaling.

The main reasons relied upon by those responsible for the forced evacuation, therefore, do not prove a reasonable relation between the group characteristics of Japanese Americans and the dangers of invasion, sabotage, and espionage. The reasons appear, instead, to be largely an accumulation of much of the misinformation, half-truths and insinuations that for years have been directed against Japanese Americans by people with racial and economic prejudices—the same people who have been among the foremost advocates of the evacuation.[31] A military judgment based upon such racial and sociological considerations is not entitled to the great weight ordinarily given the judgments based upon strictly military considerations. Especially is this so when every charge relative to race, religion, culture, geographical location, and legal and economic status has been substantially discredited by independent studies made by experts in these matters.[32]

The military necessity which is essential to the validity of the evacuation order thus resolves itself into a few intimations that certain individuals actively aided the enemy, from which it is inferred that the entire group of Japanese Americans could not be trusted to be or remain loyal to the United States. No one denies, of course, that there were some disloyal persons of Japanese descent on the Pacific Coast who did all in their power to aid their ancestral land. Similar disloyal activities have been engaged in by many persons of German, Italian and even more pioneer stock in our country. But to infer that examples of individual disloyalty prove group disloyalty and justify discriminatory action against the entire group is to deny that under our system of law individual guilt is the sole basis for deprivation of rights. Moreover, this inference, which is at the very heart of the evacuation orders, has been used in support of the abhorrent and despicable treatment of minority groups by the dictatorial tyrannies which this nation is now pledged to destroy. To give constitutional sanction to that inference in this case, however well-intentioned may have been the military command on the Pacific Coast, is to adopt one of the cruelest of the rationales used by our enemies to destroy the dignity of the individual and to encourage and open the door to discriminatory actions against other minority groups in the passions of tomorrow.

No adequate reason is given for the failure to treat these Japanese Americans on an individual basis by holding investigations and hearings to separate the loyal from the disloyal, as was done in the case of persons of German and Italian ancestry. See House Report No. 2124 (77th Cong., 2d Sess.) 247–252. It is asserted merely that the loyalties of this group "were unknown and time was of the essence."[33] Yet nearly four months elapsed after Pearl Harbor before the first exclusion order was issued; nearly eight months went by until the last order was issued; and the last of these "subversive" persons was not actually removed until almost eleven months had elapsed. Leisure and deliberation seem to have been more of the essence than speed. And the fact that conditions were not such as to warrant a declaration of martial law adds strength to the belief that the factors of time and military necessity were not as urgent as they have been represented to be.

Moreover, there was no adequate proof that the Federal Bureau of Investigation and the military and naval intelligence services did not have the espionage and sabotage situation well in hand during this long period. Nor is there any denial of the fact that not one person of Japanese ancestry was accused or convicted of espionage or sabotage after Pearl Harbor while they were still free,[34] a fact which is some evidence of the loyalty of the vast majority of these individuals and of the effectiveness of the established methods of combating these evils. It seems incredible that under these circumstances it would have been impossible to hold loyalty hearings for the mere 112,000 persons involved—or at least for the 70,000 American citizens—especially when a large part of this number represented children and elderly men and women.[35] Any inconvenience that may have accompanied an attempt to conform to procedural due process cannot be said to justify violations of constitutional rights of individuals.

I dissent, therefore, from this legalization of racism. Racial discrimination in any form and in any degree has no justifiable part whatever in our democratic way of life. It is unattractive in any setting but it is utterly revolting among a free people who have embraced the principles set forth in the Constitution of the United States. All residents of this nation are kin in some way by blood or culture to a foreign land. Yet they are primarily and necessarily a part of the new and distinct civilization of the United States. They must accordingly be treated at all times as the heirs of the American experiment and as entitled to all the rights and freedoms guaranteed by the constitution.

Notes

1. In fact, as early as 1875 a Latino, Romualdo Pacheco, was California's governor.
2. Susan Anderson, "Rivers of Water in a Dry Place—Early Black Participation in California Politics," in Byran O. Jackson and Michael B. Preston, eds., *Racial and Ethnic Politics in California* (Berkeley, CA: Institute of Governmental Studies, University of California Berkeley, 1991), pp. 55–69.
3. Ibid, p. 61.
4. "Jim Crow" refers to the systemic segregation of African Americans in the South following the end of slavery.
5. Murphy, in his dissenting opinion in *Korematsu v. United States* (1944).
6. Quoted by Taylor in his article "The People Nobody Wants," 214 *Saturday Evening Post* 24, 66 (May 9, 1942). See Murphy, dissenting opinion, *Korematsu v. United States* (1944).
7. National Organization for Women web page <http://www.now.org/issues/affirm/talking.html>.
8. National Organization for Women web page <http://www.now.org/issues/affirm/talking.html>.
9. 438 U.S. 265 (1978).
10. See *Wards Cove Packing Co. v. Atonio* (1989); *Patterson v. McClean Union* (1989); *Adarand v. Pena* (1995); *Hopwood v. University of Texas Law School* (1996).

11. As a proposed constitutional amendment, the proposition required 693,230 valid registered voters' signatures—the extra margin of over 1 million would guarantee that it would meet the threshold enforced by the secretary of state's office.

12. Ballot text of Proposition 209 (1996), clause 1, lines 1–3.

13. Ballot text of Proposition 209 (1996), clause 3, lines 5–7.

14. Louis Freedburg, "Connerly Exults at New Affirmative Action Ban," *San Francisco Chronicle*, 5 November 1998, A3.

15. Rachel Gordon, "Supes Extend Affirmative Action Plan," *San Francisco Examiner*, 23 September 1998, A8.

16. Peter Schrag, "Gray Davis: Will There be Affirmative Reaction?" *Sacramento Bee*, 18 November 1998, B6.

17. Ibid.

18. 140 F.2d 289.

19. Hearings before the Subcommittee on the National War Agencies Appropriation Bill for 1945, Part II, 608–726; Final Report, Japanese Evacuation from the West Coast, 1942, 309–327; Hearings before the Committee on Immigration and Naturalization, House of Representatives, 78th Cong., 2d Sess., on H. R. 2701 and other bills to expatriate certain nationals of the United States, pp. 37–42, 49–58.

20. Final Report, Japanese Evacuation from the West Coast, 1942, by Lt. Gen. J. L. DeWitt. This report is dated June 5, 1943, but was not made public until January 1944.

21. Further evidence of the Commanding General's attitude toward individuals of Japanese ancestry is revealed in his voluntary testimony on April 13, 1943, in San Francisco before the House Naval Affairs Subcommittee to Investigate Congested Areas, Part 3, pp. 739–740 (78th Cong., 1st Session):

    "I don't want any of them [persons of Japanese ancestry] here. They are a dangerous element. There is no way to determine their loyalty. The West Coast contains too many vital installations essential to the defense of the country to allow any Japanese on this coast.... The danger of the Japanese was, and is now—if they are permitted to come back—espionage and sabotage. It makes no difference whether he is an American citizen, he is still a Japanese. American citizenship does not necessarily determine loyalty.... But we must worry about the Japanese all the time until he is wiped off the map...."

22. The Final Report, p. 9, casts a cloud of suspicion over the entire group by saying that "while it was believed that some were loyal, it was known that many were not."

23. Final Report, p. vii; see also pp. 9, 17. To the extent that assimilation is a problem, it is largely the result of certain social customs and laws of the American general public. Studies demonstrate that persons of Japanese descent are readily susceptible to integration in our society if given the opportunity. Strong, *The Second-Generation Japanese Problem* (1934); Smith, *Americans in Process* (1937); Mears, *Resident Orientals on the American Pacific Coast* (1928); Millis, *The Japanese Problem in the United States* (1942). The failure to accomplish an ideal status of assimilation, therefore, cannot be charged to the refusal of these persons to become Americanized or to their loyalty to Japan. And the retention by some persons of certain customs and religious practices of their ancestors is no criterion of their loyalty to the United States.

24. Final Report, pp. 10–11. No sinister correlation between the emperor worshipping activities and disloyalty to America was shown.

25. Final Report, p. 22. The charge of "dual citizenship" springs from a misunderstanding of the simple fact that Japan in the past used the doctrine of *jus sanguinis*, as she had a right to do under international law, and claimed as her citizens all persons born of Japanese nationals wherever located. Japan has greatly modified this doctrine, however, by allowing all Japanese born in the United States to renounce any claim of dual citizenship and by releasing her claim as to all born in the United States after 1925. See Freeman, "Genesis, Exodus, and Leviticus: Genealogy, Evacuation, and Law," 28 *Cornell L. Q.* 414, 447–448, and authorities there cited; McWilliams, *Prejudice*, 123–124 (1944).

26. Final Report, pp. 12–13. We have had various foreign language schools in this country for generations without considering their existence as ground for racial discrimination. No subversive activities or teachings have been shown in connection with the Japanese schools. McWilliams, *Prejudice*, 121–123 (1944).
27. Final Report, pp. 13–15. Such persons constitute a very small part of the entire group and most of them belong to the Kibei movement—the actions and membership of which are well known to our government agents.
28. Final Report, p. 10; see also pp. vii, 9, 15–17. This insinuation, based purely upon speculation and circumstantial evidence, completely overlooks the fact that the main geographic pattern of Japanese population was fixed many years ago with reference to economic, social, and soil conditions. Limited occupational outlets and social pressures encouraged their concentration near their initial points of entry on the Pacific Coast. That these points may now be near certain strategic military and industrial areas is no proof of a diabolical purpose on the part of Japanese Americans. See McWilliams, *Prejudice*, 119–121 (1944); House Report No. 2124 (77th Cong., 2d Session.), 59–93.
29. Final Report, pp. 8–9. This dangerous doctrine of protective custody, as proved by recent European history, should have absolutely no standing as an excuse for the deprivation of the rights of minority groups. See House Report No. 1911 (77th Cong., 2d Sess.) 1–2. Cf. House Report No. 2124 (77th Cong., 2d Sess.) 145–147. In this instance, moreover, there are only two minor instances of violence on record involving persons of Japanese ancestry. McWilliams, "What About Our Japanese-Americans?" *Public Affairs Pamphlets*, no. 91 (1944): 8.
30. Final Report, p. 18. One of these incidents (the reputed dropping of incendiary bombs on an Oregon forest) occurred on September 9, 1942—a considerable time after the Japanese Americans had been evacuated from their homes and placed in Assembly Centers. See *New York Times*, 15 September 1942, p. 1, col. 3.
31. Special interest groups were extremely active in applying pressure for mass evacuation. See House Report No. 2124 (77th Cong., 2d Sess.) 154–156; McWilliams, *Prejudice*, 126–128 (1944). Mr. Austin E. Anson, managing secretary of the Salinas Vegetable Grower-Shipper Association, has frankly admitted that "We're charged with wanting to get rid of the Japs for selfish reasons.... We do. It's a question of whether the white man lives on the Pacific Coast or the brown men. They came into this valley to work, and they stayed to take over.... They undersell the white man in the markets.... They work their women and children while the white farmer has to pay wages for his help. If all the Japs were removed tomorrow, we'd never miss them in two weeks, because the white farmers can take over and produce everything the Jap grows. And we don't want them back when the war ends, either." Quoted by Taylor in his article "The People Nobody Wants," 214 *Saturday Evening Post* 24, 66 (May 9, 1942).
32. See notes 4–12, supra.
33. Final Report, p. vii; see also p. 18.
34. The Final Report, p. 34, makes the amazing statement that as of February 14, 1942, "The very fact that no sabotage has taken place to date is a disturbing and confirming indication that such action will be taken." Apparently, in the minds of the military leaders, there was no way that the Japanese Americans could escape the suspicion of sabotage.
35. During a period of six months, the 112 alien tribunals or hearing boards set up by the British Government shortly after the outbreak of the present war summoned and examined approximately 74,000 German and Austrian aliens. These tribunals determined whether each individual enemy alien was a real enemy of the Allies or only a "friendly enemy." About 64,000 were freed from internment and from any special restrictions, and only 2,000 were interned. Kempner, "The Enemy Alien Problem in the Present War," 34 *Amer. Journ. of Int. Law* 443, 444–446; House Report No. 2124 (77th Cong., 2d Sess.), 280–281.

CHAPTER 17

Rethinking California

Featured Reading / Page 195
Philip K. Dick
Do Androids Dream of Electric Sheep?

The Gold Coast

The great gridlock of light.
Tungsten, neon, sodium, mercury, halogen, xenon.
At ground level, square grids of orange sodium streetlights.
All kinds of things burn.
Mercury vapor lamps; blue crystals over the freeways, the condos, the parking lots.
Eye-zapping xenon, glaring on the malls, the stadium, Disneyland.
Great halogen lighthouse beams from the airport, snapping around the sky.
An ambulance light, pulsing red below.
Ceaseless succession, redgreenyellow, redgreenyellow.
Headlights and taillights, red and white blood cells, pushed through a leukemic
    body of light.
There's a brake light in your brain.
A billion lights. (Ten million people.) How many kilowatts per hour?
Grid laid over grid, from the mountains to the sea. A billion lights.

> —Kim Stanley Robinson, describing Southern California in 2027,
> from *The Gold Coast* (New York: Tom Doherty Associates, 1988)

California is at a crossroads. Rebounding from recession, riots, natural disasters, and bitter budget wars, the state once again looks golden. This raises the prospects for government to draw upon its resources to find solutions to public problems before they crest into the next wave of crises. Governor Gray Davis came into office promising to be a centrist activist, riding a wave of rediscovered optimism about the ability of California's people and institutions to chart its own future. The choices that Californians make today will determine the quality of life for future generations of Californians. To get a sense of where those choices might bring us, it is instructive to look back at the consequences of the choices made a generation ago.

In 1971, a group of business leaders, environmentalists, and elected officials published a pamphlet that served up two contrasting visions of California's future. The pamphlet, entitled "The California Tomorrow Plan," quickly attracted the attention of planners and officials around the state and the nation. The plan identified a list of urgent problems facing the state in 1971, a time and place dubbed by the authors as "California Zero." They argued that each of these problems, ranging from preservation of agricultural land to civil unrest, was rooted in four dysfunctional public policy arrangements that needed to be addressed. The four arrangements included: (1) a lack of individual political strength, (2) a lack of individual economic strength, (3) a damaging population distribution, and (4) a damaging pattern of resource consumption.[1] California's social and economic viability would be determined, according to the report, by the willingness of policymakers to act in these four areas during the next three decades (1970–2000).

The plan offered two scenarios projecting what California might be like in the year 2000. "California One" was a nightmarish scenario that the authors predicted would emerge after 30 years of policies that encouraged unrestrained economic growth. In California One, increased urbanization led to massive sprawl and environmental destruction. These problems were exacerbated by governmental policies that subsidized certain economic enterprises while only sporadically enforcing control regulations. In California One, the state budget reflected separate programs of several single-purpose agencies. Because the budgeting and accounting process was not designed to make full assessments of various policy alternatives, the costs of planning and coordination were overstated. Quality of life in California was severely impaired as growth continued unabated. Sprawling cities joined with one another, devouring open space in between. Air pollution increased, despite tougher air quality standards, as more automobiles appeared on the new freeways and roads that connected the proliferating suburbs. Several species, including the remaining salmon population, were lost due to habitat destruction. The state's national parks became severely congested. There was high crime punctuated by occasional periods of civil unrest, encouraging the affluent to seek refuge in the security of private, gated communities. In other words, California One was the logical consequence of three decades of development, while clinging to 1970 methods of solving problems.

"California Two" was an alternative scenario of the state at the beginning of the twenty-first century, which would be expected if policymakers followed the authors' proposed path. In contrast with California One, quality of life was much higher in this near-utopian vision of the year 2000. Coordination replaced governmental fragmentation and the piecemeal policymaking practices of the past were overcome through rational planning. In this vision, agricultural and open space were preserved, as growth was carefully managed and confined to urban boundaries. Energy-efficient mass transit systems moved people within and between urban centers, and wilderness areas and recreational space remained intact. Looking back after three decades, many of the proposals seemed to reveal a pre-Proposition 13 innocence. Roughly formed illustrations of high-speed bullet trains and monorails showed people zipping between urban centers surrounded by open space. Aggressive landscaping transformed inner-city streets into gardens and downtown areas into pedestrian plazas containing schools and cafes.

Even if the authors' unabashed optimism about the capacity of government to improve California's quality of life seems naive by today's standards, the accuracy of their forecast is chilling. Their recommendations went unrealized, and their warnings of what the state would become in 30 years have largely materialized. Californians now face several choices about how the state will be governed and how it will grow over the course of another generation. The example of "The California Tomorrow Plan" hints at the long-term repercussions of choices made—or not made.

Philip Dick's 1968 novel *Do Androids Dream of Electric Sheep?* portrays a nightmarish world in mid-2021, where androids have been employed as slaves on outlying planets, and police assassins search the earth to retire trespassers.[2] The tension between the real and the artificial allows Dick to tease out a logical twenty-first century conclusion to late twentieth century social dysfunction. Set in San Francisco, the book envisions a society where electronic replicas of pets are affordable alternatives to the extremely rare, and extremely expensive, animals themselves. Androids are indistinguishable from humans, both in form and biology, though they differ in emotional capacity. Police powers include summary execution, and due process is reduced to a questionable series of test questions.[3]

The Ridley Scott film *Blade Runner* adapts the Dick novel, placing it in Los Angeles. The film's prologue grimly lays the framework:

Early in the 21st Century, the Tyrell Corporation advanced Robot evolution into the Nexus phase—a being virtually identical to a human—known as a Replicant.

The Nexus 6 Replicants were superior in strength and agility, and at least equal in intelligence, to the genetic engineers who created them.

Replicants were used Off-world as slave labor, in the hazardous exploration and colonization of other planets.

After a bloody mutiny by a Nexus 6 combat team in an Off-world colony, Replicants were declared illegal on earth—under penalty of death.

Special police squads—Blade Runner Units—had orders to shoot to kill, upon detection, any trespassing Replicant.

This was not called execution.

It was called retirement.[4]

That twenty-first century California will emerge this foreboding is unlikely; however, several key issues remain a contested terrain, leaving open several plausible outcomes. Novelist Kim Stanley Robinson examines California's future through three starkly different views of the mid-twenty-first century. One vision, *The Wild Shore*, presents a California in 2047 amid the ashes of nuclear war where daily survival is a battle and within which the blurred distinctions between good and evil are constant morality plays.[5] Alternately, *Pacific Edge* envisions an ecotopia in 2065, where harmony and sustainability are in tension with resurgent greed and exploitation.[6] Finally, and perhaps most salient among the trilogy, *Gold Coast* predicts 2027 suburban sprawl run amok.[7]

The *Blade Runner* metaphor suggests that social evils have become so severe that extraordinary police powers are necessary and appropriate. *The Wild Shore* metaphor suggests that human or natural disasters may usher in a period of moral ambivalence. We should not assume that such extraordinary events are necessarily futuristic—as we have seen with the internment of Japanese Americans during World War II, the Cold War paranoia and Red scare, periodic civil unrest, earthquakes, floods, and fires. The question, ultimately, is of choices made well in advance of the mid-twenty-first century. With this in mind, our current arc of progress is far more likely to arrive at a *Gold Coast*-like scenario then any of the others, "... grid laid over grid, from the mountains to the sea. A billion lights."[8]

When looking into the face of the twenty-first century, several choices appear. Not surprisingly they exist within current policy areas: environment, immigration, education, and civil rights. Environmental degradation is perhaps our most immediate concern, particularly when we include land use, congestion, and urban sprawl. As the state approaches 35 million people, we still insist on land-intensive suburban development. The consequences are severe: continuing reliance on single occupant vehicles, with the associated congestion and poor air quality; less and less open space; greater pressure to develop adjacent to public parks, ridgelines, and the few miles of pristine coastline left.

As California continues to be a gateway for immigration, there is serious potential for greater demonization of new Californians. Anthropologist Fred Krissman[9] observes that immigrants, both documented and undocumented, have historically provided the next generation of citizens. Yet, we provide these new Californians with a civic education grounded in xenophobia and intolerance. Public education will continue to be a contested terrain, particularly as we demand more while providing fewer resources. The civil rights discourse will continue to evolve, as we redefine the notions of inclusion and equity to incorporate the many challenges of twenty-first century statehood. While these pressures will continue to grow, we would be wise to remember Pogo's admonishment: "We have met the enemy and he is us."

"California Two" may yet be possible. The choices discussed throughout the book demand the participation of all stakeholders. The only truism that applies to California's future is, simply, that in a democracy we get the policies we deserve. Greater participation may lead to better choices. This book has explored California politics and policy from a historical, social, and cultural perspective, in an effort to provide a foundation for understanding policy and politics in the Golden State. The rest is up to you.

Do Androids Dream of Electric Sheep?   *Philip K. Dick*

The small beam of white light shone steadily into the left eye of Rachel Rosen, and against her cheek the wire-mesh disk adhered. She seemed calm.

Seated where he could catch the readings on the two gauges of the Voigt-Vampff testing apparatus, Rick Deckard said, "I'm going to outline a number of social situations. You are to express your reaction to each as quickly as possible. You will be timed, of course."

"And of course," Rachel said distantly, "my verbal responses won't count. It's solely the eye-muscle and capillary reaction that you'll use as indices. But, I'll answer; I want to go through this and—" She broke off, "Go ahead, Mr. Deckard."

Rick, selecting question three, said, "You are given a calf-skin wallet on your birthday." Both gauges immediately registered past the green and onto the red; the needles swung violently and then subsided.

"I wouldn't accept it," Rachel said. "Also I'd report the person to the police."

After making a jot of notation Rick continued, turning to the eighth question of the Voigt-Kampff profile scale. "You have a little boy and he shows you his butterfly collection, including his killing jar."

"I'd take him to the doctor." Rachel's voice was low, but firm. Again, the twin gauges registered, but this time not so far. He made a note of that, too.

"You're sitting watching TV," he continued, "and suddenly you discover a wasp crawling on your wrist."

Rachel said, "I'd kill it." The gauges, this time, registered almost nothing: only a feeble and momentary tremor. He noted that and hunted cautiously for the next question.

"In a magazine you come across a full-page color picture of a nude girl." He paused.

"Is this testing whether I'm an android," Rachel asked tartly, "or whether I'm homosexual?" The gauges did not register.

He continued, "Your husband likes the picture." Still the gauges failed to indicate a reaction. "The girl," he added, "is lying face down on a large and beautiful bearskin rug." The gauges remained inert, and he said to himself, An android response. Failing to detect the major element, the dead animal pelt. Her—its—mind is concentrating on other factors. "Your husband hangs the picture up on the wall of his study," he finished, and this time the needles moved.

NOTES

1. The report was later published in book form as *The California Tomorrow Plan: The Future Is Now*, Alfred Heller, ed. (Los Altos, CA: William Kaufmann, 1972).
2. Philip K. Dick, *Do Androids Dream of Electric Sheep?* (New York: Balantine Books, 1968).
3. See excerpt from Philip K. Dick, *Do Androids Dream of Electric Sheep?*
4. Prologue from the Ridley Scott film, *Blade Runner*.
5. Kim Stanley Robinson, *The Wild Shore* (New York: Tom Doherty Associates, Inc., 1984).
6. Kim Stanley Robinson, *Pacific Edge* (New York: Tom Doherty Associates, Inc., 1988).
7. Kim Stanley Robinson, *The Gold Coast* (New York: Tom Doherty Associates, Inc., 1988).
8. Kim Stanley Robinson, *The Gold Coast* (New York: Tom Doherty Associates, 1988).
9. Dr. Krissman is an anthropologist at California State University, Northridge.

Appendix A

California Counties

001 Alameda County
003 Alpine County
005 Amador County
007 Butte County
009 Calaveras County
011 Colusa County
013 Contra Costa County
015 Del Norte County
017 El Dorado County
019 Fresno County
021 Glenn County
023 Humboldt County
025 Imperial County
027 Inyo County
029 Kern County
031 Kings County
033 Lake County
035 Lassen County
037 Los Angeles County
039 Madera County
041 Marin County
043 Mariposa County
045 Mendocino County
047 Merced County
049 Modoc County
051 Mono County
053 Monterey County
055 Napa County
057 Nevada County
059 Orange County
061 Placer County
063 Plumas County
065 Riverside County
067 Sacramento County
069 San Benito County
071 San Bernardino County
073 San Deigo County
075 San Francisco County
077 San Joaquin County

079 San Luis Obispo County
081 San Mateo County
083 Santa Barbara County
085 Santa Clara County
087 Santa Cruz County
089 Shasta County
091 Sierra County
093 Siskiyou County
095 Solano County
097 Sonoma County
099 Stanislaus County
101 Sutter County
103 Tehama County
105 Trinity County
107 Tulare County
109 Tuolumne County
111 Ventura County
113 Yolo County
115 Yuba County

Source: California Geological Survey.

197

Appendix B

California's Constitutional Officers, 2000–2002

Governor Gray Davis
State Capitol Building
Sacramento, CA 95814
Phone (916) 445-2841
Fax (916) 445-4633
graydavis@governor.ca.gov
http://www.governor.ca.gov

Lieutenant Governor Cruz Bustamonte
State Capitol Building
Room 1114
Sacramento, CA 95814
Phone: (916) 445-8994
Fax: (916) 323-4998
http://www.ltg.ca.gov

Attorney General Bill Lockyer
Office of the Attorney General
Department of Justice
P.O. Box 944255
Sacramento, CA 94244-2550
(916) 445-9555
http://caag.state.ca.us

Secretary of State Bill Jones
California Secretary of State
1500 11th Street
Sacramento, California 95814
(916) 653-6814
http://www.ss.ca.gov

State Controller Kathleen Connell
P.O. Box 942850
Sacramento, California 94250-5872
(916) 445-2636
http://www.sco.ca.gov

State Treasurer Phil Angelides
California State Treasurer's Office
915 Capitol Mall
Sacramento, CA 95814
(916) 653-2995
http://www.treasurer.ca.gov

State Superintendent of Public Instruction Delaine Eastin
California Department of Education
721 Capitol Mall
Sacramento, California 95814
(916) 657-2451
board@cde.ca.gov
http://www.cde.ca.gov

Insurance Commissioner Harry Low
California Department of Insurance
300 Capitol Mall, Suite 1500
Sacramento, CA 95814
(800) 927-4357
(916) 322-3555
http://www.insurance.ca.gov

APPENDIX C

California State Senate, 2000–2002

Member		District Number and Office	Capitol Office
Alarcon, Richard	20	6150 Van Nuys Blvd. Suite 400 Van Nuys, CA 91401 (818) 901-5588	State Capitol Room 4074 Sacramento, CA 95814 (916) 445-7928
Alpert, Dede	39	1557 Columbia St San Diego, CA 92101 (619) 645-3090	State Capitol Room 5114 Sacramento, CA 95814 (916) 445-3952
Bowen, Debra	28	2512 Artesia Blvd. Suite 200 Redondo, Beach, CA 90278 (310) 318-6994	State Capitol Room 4040 Sacramento, CA 95814 (916) 445-5953
Brulte, James L.	31	10681 Foothill Blvd. Suite 325 Rancho Cucamonga, CA 91730 (909) 466-9096	State Capitol Room 5087 Sacramento, CA 95814 (916) 445-3688
Burton, John L.	03	455 Golden Gate Avenue Suite 14800 San Francisco, CA 94102 (415) 557-1300 3501 Civic Center / Room 425 San Rafael, CA 94903 (415) 479-6612	State Capitol Room 205 Sacramento, CA 95814 (916) 445-1412
Chesbro, Wesley	02	1040 Main St. / Suite 205 Napa, CA 94559 (707) 224-1990 50 D St. / Suite 120A Santa Rosa, CA 95404 (707) 576-2771 710 E. Street / Suite 150 Eureka, CA 95501 (707) 445-6508 P.O. Box 785 Ukiah, CA 95482 (707) 468-8914	State Capitol Room 3070 Sacramento, CA 95814 (916) 445-3375

Member	District Number and Office	Capitol Office
Costa, Jim	16 2550 Mariposa Mall Suite 2016 Fresno, CA 93721 (559) 264-3078 901 Tower Way Suite 202 Bakersfield, CA 93309 (661) 323-0442	State Capitol Room 5100 Sacramento, CA 95814 (916) 445-4641
Dunn, Joseph L.	34 12397 Lewis Street Suite 103 Garden Grove, CA 92840 (714) 705-1580	State Capitol Room 2068 Sacramento, CA 95814 (916) 445-5831
Escutia, Martha M.	30 400 N. Montebello Blvd. #101 Montebello, CA 90640 (323) 724-6175	State Capitol Room 5064 Sacramento, CA 95814 (916) 327-8315
Figueroa, Liz	10 43721 Mission Blvd. Fremont, CA 94539 (510) 413-5960	State Capitol Room 2057 Sacramento, CA 95814 (916) 445-6671
Hayden, Tom	23 10951 W. Pico Blvd. #202 Los Angeles, CA 90064	State Capitol Room 2080 Sacramento, CA 95814 (916) 445-1353
Haynes, Ray	36 6800 Indiana Ave. Suite 130 Riverside, CA 92506 (909) 782-4111	State Capitol Room 2187 Sacramento, CA 95814 (916) 445-9781
Hughes, Teresa	25 1 Manchester Blvd. Suite 600 Inglewood, CA 90301	State Capitol Room 5050 Sacramento, CA 95814 (916) 445-2104
Johannessen, Maurice	04 410 Hemsted Dr. Suite 200 Redding, CA 96002 (530) 224-4706	State Capitol Room 5061 Sacramento, CA 95814 (916) 445-3353
Johnson, Ross	35 18552 MacArthur Blvd. Suite 395 Irvine, CA 92612 (949) 833-0180	State Capitol Room 305 Sacramento, CA 95814 (916) 445-4961
Johnston, Patrick	05 1020 N St. Suite 504 Sacramento CA 95814 31 East Channel St. Room 440 Stockton, CA 95202	State Capitol Room 5066 Sacramento, CA 95814 (916) 445-2407

Member	District Number and Office	Capitol Office
Karnette, Betty	27 3711 Long Beach Blvd. Suite 801 Long Beach, CA 90807 (562) 997-0794	State Capitol Room 3086 Sacramento, CA 95814 (916) 445-6447
Kelley, David G.	37 11440 W. Bernardo Court Suite 104 San Diego, CA 92127 (858) 675-8211 73-710 Fred Waring Drive Suite 108 Palm Desert, CA 92260 (760) 346-2099	State Capitol Room 3082 Sacramento, CA 95814 (916) 445-5581
Knight, Wm. 'Pete'	17 1008 W. Avenue M-14 Suite G Palmdale, CA 93551 (661) 274-0188 25709 Rye Canyon Rd. / Suite 105 Santa Clarita, CA 91355 (661) 294-8184 15278 Main Street / Suite D Hesperia, CA 92345 (760) 244-2402 128 E. California Ave. / Suite A P.O. Box 1844 Ridgecrest, CA 93556 (760) 371-1640	State Capitol Room 5082 Sacramento, CA 95814 (916) 445-6637
Leslie, Tim	01 1200 Melody Lane Suite 110 Roseville, CA 95678 (916) 969-8232 (916) 783-8232	State Capitol Room 4081 Sacramento, CA 95814 (916) 445-5788
Lewis, John R.	33 1940 W. Orangewood Ave. Suite 106 Orange, CA 92668 (714) 939-0604 Fax: (714) 939-0730	State Capitol Room 3063 Sacramento, CA 95814 (916) 445-4264
McPherson, Bruce	15 701 Ocean St. / Room 318A Santa Cruz, CA 95060 7 John Street Salinas, CA 93901	State Capitol Room 3076 Sacramento, CA 95814 (916) 445-5843
Monteith, Dick	12 1620 N. Carpenter Rd. / Suite A-4 Modesto, CA 95351 (209) 577-6592 777 W. 22nd St. / Suite B Merced, CA 95340 (209) 722-4988 1901 Howard Road / Suite B Madera, CA 93637 (559) 674-2898	State Capitol Room 2048 Sacramento, CA 95814 (916) 445-1392

Member	District Number and Office	Capitol Office
Morrow, Bill	38 27126A Paseo Espada Suite 1621 San Juan Capistrano, CA 92675 (949) 489-9838	State Capitol Room 4062 Sacramento, CA 95814 (916) 445-3731
Mountjoy, Richard	29 500 N. First Ave. Suite 3 Arcadia, CA 91006 (626) 446-3134	State Capitol Room 4052 Sacramento, CA 95814 (916) 445-2848
Murray, Kevin	26 600 Corporate Point Suite 1020 Culver City, CA 90230 (877) 366-8808 (310) 641-4391	State Capitol Room 4082 Sacramento, CA 95814 (916) 445-8800
O'Connell, Jack	18 228 W. Carrillo Suite F Santa Barbara, CA 93101 (805) 966-2296 89 S. Calif. Suite E Ventura, CA 93001 (805) 641-1500 1260 Chorro St. Suite A San Luis Obispo, CA 93401 (805) 547-1800	State Capitol Room 5035 Sacramento, CA 95814 (916) 445-5405
Ortiz, Deborah V.	06 1020 N Street Room 576 Sacramento, CA 95814 (916) 324-4937 5951 Birdcage Center Lane Suite 145 Citrus Heights, CA 95610 (916) 961-1482	State Capitol Room 4032 Sacramento, CA 95814 (916) 445-7807
Peace, Steve	40 7877 Parkway Dr. Suite 1B La Mesa, CA 91942 (619) 463-0243	State Capitol Room 3060 Sacramento, CA 95814 (916) 445-6767
Perata, Don	09 1515 Clay Street Suite 2202 Oakland, CA 94612 (510) 286-1333	State Capitol Room 4061 Sacramento, CA 95814 (916) 445-6577
Polanco, Richard	22 300 S. Spring Street Suite 8710 Los Angeles, CA 90013 (213) 620-2529	State Capitol Room 313 Sacramento, CA 95814 (916) 445-3456

Member	District Number and Office	Capitol Office
Poochigian, Charles	14 4974 E. Clinton Suite 100 Fresno, CA 93727 (559) 253-7122 841 Mohawk St. Suite 190 Bakersfield, CA 93309 (661) 324-6188	State Capitol Room 2054 Sacramento, CA 95814 (916) 445-9600
Rainey, Richard K.	07 1948 Mount Diablo Blvd. Walnut Creek, CA 94596 (925) 280-0276 Fax: (925) 280-0299	State Capitol Room 4090 Sacramento, CA 95814 (916) 445-6083
Schiff, Adam B.	21 35 South Raymond Avenue Suite 205 Pasadena, CA 91105 (626) 683-0282	State Capitol Room 5080 Sacramento, CA 95814 (916) 445-5976
Sher, Byron	11 260 Main Street Suite 201 Redwood City, CA 94063 (650) 364-2080 5589 Winfield Blvd. Suite 102 San Jose, CA 95123 (408) 226-2992	State Capitol Room 2082 Sacramento, CA 95814 (916) 445-6747
Solis, Hilda L.	24 4401 Santa Anita Ave. 2nd Floor El Monte, CA 91731 (626) 448-1271	State Capitol Room 4039 Sacramento, CA 95814 (916) 445-1418
Soto, Nell	32 (909) 984-7741	State Capitol Room 4066 Sacramento, CA 95814 (916) 445-6868
Speier, Jackie	08 400 South El Camino Real Suite 630 San Mateo, CA 94402 (650) 340-8840	State Capitol Room 2032 Sacramento, CA 95814 (916) 445-0503
Vasconcellos, John	13 100 Paseo de San Antonio Suite 209 San Jose, CA 95113 (408) 286-8318	State Capitol Room 5108 Sacramento, CA 95814 (916) 445-9740
Wright, Cathie	19 2345 Erringer Rd. Suite 212 Simi Valley, CA 93065	State Capitol Room 5052 Sacramento, CA 95814 (916) 445-8873

Appendix D

California State Assembly, 2000–2002

Member	District Number and Office	Capitol Office
Aanestad, Sam	03 350 Crown Point Circle Suite 150 Grass Valley, CA 95945	State Capitol Room 4144 Sacramento, CA 95814 (916) 319-2003
Ackerman, Dick	72 305 N. Harbor Blvd. Suite 303 Fullerton, CA 92832	State Capitol Room 4167 Sacramento, CA 95814 (916) 319-2072
Alquist, Elaine	22 275 Saratoga Avenue Suite 205 Santa Clara, CA 95050	State Capitol Room 3120 Sacramento, CA 95814 (916) 319-2022
Aroner, Dion	14 918 Parker Street Suit A-13 Berkeley, CA 94710	State Capitol Room 2163 Sacramento, CA 95814 (916) 319-2014
Ashburn, Roy	32 1200 Truxtun Avenue Suite 120 Bakersfield, CA 93301	State Capitol Room 3098 Sacramento, CA 95814 (916) 319-2032
Baldwin, Steve	77 8419 La Mesa Boulevard Suite B La Mesa, CA 91941	State Capitol Room 4162 Sacramento, CA 95814 (916) 319-2077
Bates, Patricia	73 30012 Ivy Glenn Drive Suite 120 Laguna Niguel, CA 92677	State Capitol Room 4009 Sacramento, CA 95814 (916) 319-2073
Battin, Jim	80 73-710 Fred Waring Drive Suite 112 Palm Desert, CA 92260	State Capitol Room 5158 Sacramento, CA 95814 (916) 319-2080

Member	District Number and Office		Capitol Office
Baugh, Scott	67	16052 Beach Blvd. Suite 160-N Huntington Beach, CA 92647	State Capitol Room 3104 Sacramento, CA 95814 (916) 319-2067
Bock, Audie E.	16	1515 Clay Street Suite 2204 Oakland, CA 94612	State Capitol Room 5144 Sacramento, CA 95814 (916) 319-2016
Brewer, Marilyn C.	70	18952 MacArthur Boulevard Suite 220 Irvine, CA 92612	State Capitol Room 4153 Sacramento, CA 95814 (916) 319-2070
Briggs, Mike	29	83 E. Shaw Street Suite 202 Fresno, CA 93710	State Capitol Room 2111 Sacramento, CA 95814 (916) 319-2029
Calderon, Thomas M.	58	280 North Montebello Blvd. Suite 102 Montebello, CA 90640	State Capitol Room 2148 Sacramento, CA 95814 (916) 319-2058
Campbell, Bill	71	1940 N. Tustin Suite 102 Orange, CA 92865	State Capitol Room 6031 Sacramento, CA 95814 (916) 319-2071
Cardenas, Tony	39	9140 Van Nuys Blvd. Suite 109 Panorama City, CA 91402	State Capitol Room 4005 Sacramento, CA 95814 (916) 319-2039
Cardoza, Dennis	26	384 East Olive Suite 2 Turlock, CA 95380	State Capitol Room 2141 Sacramento, CA 95814 (916) 319-2026
Cedillo, Gil	46	617 South Olive Street Suite 710 Los Angeles, CA 90014	State Capitol Room 5016 Sacramento, CA 95814 (916) 319-2046
Corbett, Ellen M.	18	317 Juana Avenue San Leandro, CA 94577	State Capitol Room 4126 Sacramento, CA 95814 (916) 319-2018
Correa, Lou	69	2323 North Broadway Suite 225 Santa Ana, CA 92706	State Capitol Room 2137 Sacramento, CA 95814 (916) 319-2069

Member	District Number and Office	Capitol Office
Cox, Dave	05 4811 Chippendale Drive Suite 501 Sacramento, CA 95841	State Capitol Room 2002 Sacramento, CA 95814 (916) 319-2005
Cunneen, Jim	24 901 Campisi Way Suite 300 Campbell, CA 95008	State Capitol Room 2174 Sacramento, CA 95814 (916) 319-2024
Davis, Susan	76 1010 University Avenue Suite C-207 San Diego, CA 92103	State Capitol Room 2013 Sacramento, CA 95814 (916) 319-2076
Dickerson, Richard	02 100 East Cypress Avenue Suite 100 Redding, CA 96002	State Capitol Room 3147 Sacramento, CA 95814 (916) 319-2002
Ducheny, Denise Moreno	79 2414 Hoover Avenue Suite A National City, CA 91950	State Capitol Room 6026 Sacramento, CA 95814 (916) 319-2079
Dutra, John	20 39510 Paseo Padre Parkway Suite 360 Fremont, CA 94538	State Capitol Room 6011 Sacramento, CA 95814 (916) 319-2020
Firebaugh, Marco A.	50 7501 Alantic Avenue Suite D Cudahy, CA 90201	State Capitol Room 3126 Sacramento, CA 95814 (916) 319-2050
Florez, Dean	30 1800 30th Street Suite 330 Bakersfield, CA 93301	State Capitol Room 5135 Sacramento, CA 95814 (916) 319-2030
Floyd, Richard	55 One Civic Plaza Suite 320 Carson, CA 90745	State Capitol Room 4016 Sacramento, CA 95814 (916) 319-2055
Frusetta, Peter	28 321 First Street Suite A Hollister, CA 95023	State Capitol Room 5175 Sacramento, CA 95814 (916) 319-2028
Gallegos, Martin	57 15625 Stafford Street Suite 200 City of Industry, CA 91744	State Capitol Room 6005 Sacramento, CA 95814 (916) 319-2057

Member	District Number and Office		Capitol Office
Granlund, Brett	65	34932 Yucaipa Boulevard Yucaipa, CA 92399	State Capitol Room 4164 Sacramento, CA 95814 (916) 319-2065
Havice, Sally	56	16600 Civic Center Drive Second Floor Bellflower, CA 90706	State Capitol Room 5150 Sacramento, CA 95814 (916) 319-2056
Hertzberg, Robert M.	40	6150 Van Nuys Blvd. Suite 305 Van Nuys, CA 91401	State Capitol Room 219 Sacramento, CA 95814 (916) 319-2040
Honda, Mike	23	100 Paseo De San Antonio Suite 300 San Jose, CA 95113	State Capitol Room 5155 Sacramento, CA 95814 (916) 319-2023
House, George	25	3600 Sisk Road Suite 5-D-3 Modesto, CA 95356	State Capitol Room 3141 Sacramento, CA 95814 (916) 319-2025
Jackson, Hannah-Beth	35	101 West Anapamu Street Suite A Santa Barbara, CA 93101	State Capitol Room 4098 Sacramento, CA 95814 (916) 319-2035
Kaloogian, Howard	74	701 Palomar Airport Road Suite 160 Carlsbad, CA 92009	State Capitol Room 4130 Sacramento, CA 95814 (916) 319-2074
Keeley, Fred	27	701 Ocean Street Suite 318 B Santa Cruz, CA 95060	State Capitol Room 3152 Sacramento, CA 95814 (916) 319-2027
Knox, Wally	42	5757 Wilshire Boulevard Suite 645 Los Angeles, CA 90036	State Capitol Room 6025 Sacramento, CA 95814 (916) 319-2042
Kuehl, Sheila James	41	16130 Ventura Boulevard Suite 230 Encino, CA 91436	State Capitol Room 3013 Sacramento, CA 95814 (916) 319-2041
Leach, Lynne C.	15	800 South Broadway Suite 304 Walnut Creek, CA 94596	State Capitol Room 3132 Sacramento, CA 95814 (916) 319-2015

Member	District Number and Office	Capitol Office
Lempert, Ted	21 4149 El Camino Way Suite B Palo Alto, CA 94306	State Capitol Room 2188 Sacramento, CA 95814 (916) 319-2021
Leonard, Bill	63 10535 Foothill Boulevard Suite 276 Rancho Cucamonga, CA 91730	State Capitol Room 2175 Sacramento, CA 95814 (916) 319-2063
Longville, John	62 201 North E Street Suite 205 San Bernardino, CA 92401	State Capitol Room 2196 Sacramento, CA 95814 (916) 319-2062
Lowenthal, Alan	54 115 Pine Avenue Suite 430 Long Beach, CA 90802	State Capitol Room 4139 Sacramento, CA 95814 (916) 319-2054
Machado, Mike	17 31 East Channel Street Suite 306 Stockton, CA 95202	State Capitol Room 5136 Sacramento, CA 95814 (916) 319-2017
Maddox, Ken	68 12865 Main Street Suite 100 Garden Grove, CA 92840	State Capitol Room 4102 Sacramento, CA 95814 (916) 319-2068
Maldonado, Abel	33 1302 Marsh Street San Luis Obispo, CA 93401	State Capitol Room 4015 Sacramento, CA 95814 (916) 319-2033
Margett, Bob	59 55 E. Huntington Drive Suite 120 Arcadia, CA 91006	State Capitol Room 5160 Sacramento, CA 95814 (916) 319-2059
Mazzoni, Kerry	06 3501 Civic Center Drive Room 412 San Rafael, CA 94903	State Capitol Room 3123 Sacramento, CA 95814 (916) 319-2006
McClintock, Tom	38 10727 White Oak Avenue Suite 124 Granada Hills, CA 91344	State Capitol Room 4158 Sacramento, CA 95814 (916) 319-2038
Migden, Carole	13 1388 Sutter Street Suite 710 San Francisco, CA 94109	State Capitol Room 2114 Sacramento, CA 95814 (916) 319-2013

Member	District Number and Office	Capitol Office
Nakano, George	53 1217 El Prado Avenue Torrance, CA 90501	State Capitol Room 2158 Sacramento, CA 95814 (916) 319-2053
Olberg, Keith	34 14011 Park Avenue Suite 470 Victorville, CA 92392	State Capitol Room 4117 Sacramento, CA 95814 (916) 319-2034
Oller, Thomas "Rico"	04 2999 Douglas Boulevard Suite 120 Roseville, CA 95661	State Capitol Room 4208 Sacramento, CA 95814 (916) 319-2004
Pacheco, Robert	60 17870 Castleton Street Suite 205 City of Industry, CA 91748	State Capitol Room 4177 Sacramento, CA 95814 (916) 319-2060
Pacheco, Rod	64 3740 Mission Inn Avenue Suite N-6 Riverside, CA 92501	State Capitol Room 4116 Sacramento, CA 95814 (916) 319-2064
Papan, Louis J.	19 660 El Camino Real Suite 214 Millbrae, CA 94030	State Capitol Room 3173 Sacramento, CA 95814 (916) 319-2019
Pescetti, Anthony	10 9845 Horn Road Suite 150 Sacramento, CA 95827	State Capitol Room 2130 Sacramento, CA 95814 (916) 319-2010
Reyes, Sarah	31 2550 Mariposa Mall Room 5006 Fresno, CA 93721	State Capitol Room 5128 Sacramento, CA 95814 (916) 319-2031
Romero, Gloria	49 1255 Corporate Center Drive Suite PH9 Monterery Park, CA 91754	State Capitol Room 2117 Sacramento, CA 95814 (916) 319-2049
Runner, George	36 709 W. Lancaster Boulevard Lancaster, CA 93534	State Capitol Room 6027 Sacramento, CA 95814 (916) 319-2036
Scott, Jack	44 215 N. Marengo Avenue Suite 185 Pasadena, CA 91101	State Capitol Room 4146 Sacramento, CA 95814 (916) 319-2044

Member	District Number and Office	Capitol Office
Shelley, Kevin	12 455 Golden Gate Avenue Suite 14600 San Francisco, CA 94102	State Capitol Room 3160 Sacramento, CA 95814 (916) 319-2012
Steinberg, Darrell	09 1215 15th Street Room 102 Sacramento, CA 95814	State Capitol Room 2176 Sacramento, CA 95814 (916) 319-2009
Strickland, Tony	37 221 East Daily Drive Suite 7 Camarillo, CA 93010	State Capitol Room 2016 Sacramento, CA 95814 (916) 319-2037
Strom-Martin, Virginia	01 50 D Street Suite 450 Santa Rosa, CA 95404	State Capitol Room 3146 Sacramento, CA 95814 (916) 319-2001
Thompson, Bruce	66 27555 Ynez Road Suite 205 Temecula, CA 92591	State Capitol Room 2160 Sacramento, CA 95814 (916) 319-2066
Thomson, Helen	08 555 Mason Street Suite 275 Vacaville, CA 95688	State Capitol Room 4140 Sacramento, CA 95814 (916) 319-2008
Torlakson, Tom	11 815 Estudillo Street Martinez, CA 94553	State Capitol Room 2003 Sacramento, CA 95814 (916) 319-2011
Villaraigosa, Antonio	45 1910 W. Sunset Bouvlevard Suite 500 Los Angeles, CA 90026	State Capitol Room 319 Sacramento, CA 95814 (916) 319-2045
Vincent, Edward	51 One Manchester Boulevard Suite 601 P.O. Box 6500 Inglewood, CA 90306	State Capitol Room 5119 Sacramento, CA 95814 (916) 319-2051
Washington, Carl	52 145 E. Compton Boulevard Compton, CA 90220	State Capitol Room 2136 Sacramento, CA 95814 (916) 319-2052
Wayne, Howard	78 1350 Front Street Suite 6013 San Diego, CA 92101	State Capitol Room 2170 Sacramento, CA 95814 (916) 319-2078

Member	District Number and Office		Capitol Office
Wesson, Herb	47	5100 West Goldleaf Circle Suite 203 Los Angeles, CA 90056	State Capitol Room 2179 Sacramento, CA 95814 (916) 319-2047
Wiggins, Patricia	07	50 D Street Suite 301 Santa Rosa, CA 95404	State Capitol Room 4112 Sacramento, CA 95814 (916) 319-2007
Wildman, Scott	43	109 E. Harvard Avenue Suite 305 Glendale, CA 91205	State Capitol Room 3091 Sacramento, CA 95814 (916) 319-2043
Wright, Roderick	48	700 State Drive Suite 103 Los Angeles, CA 90037	State Capitol Room 6012 Sacramento, CA 95814 (916) 319-2048
Zettel, Charlene	75	15708 Pomerado Road Suite N-110 Poway, CA 92064	State Capitol Room 5164 Sacramento, CA 95814 (916) 319-2075
Vacant	61		

Appendix E

County Registrars of Voters

Alameda (01)
Bradley J. Clark, Registrar of Voters
1225 Fallon Street, Room G-1
Oakland, CA 94612
(510) 272-6973
(510) 272-6982 Fax
Hours 8:30 to 5:00
www.co.alameda.ca.us/rov/index.htm

Alpine (02)
Barbara K. Jones, County Clerk
99 Water (Fed. Ex. Only)
P.O. Box 158
Markleeville, CA 96120
(530) 694-2281
(530) 694-2491 Fax
Hours 8 to 12, 1 to 5
www.co.alpine.ca.us/dclerk.html

Amador (03)
Sheldon D. Johnson, Registrar of Voters
500 Argonaut Lane
Jackson, CA 95642
(209) 223-6465
(209) 223-0691 Fax
Hours 8 to 5

Butte (04)
Butte County Elections
25 County Center Drive
Oroville, CA 95965-3375
(530) 538-7761
(530) 538-7975 Fax
Hours 9 to 5
elections.co.butte.ca.us/elections

Calaveras (05)
Karen Varni, County Clerk
Elections Dept.
891 Mountain Ranch Road
San Andreas, CA 95249
(209) 754-6376
(209) 754-6733 Fax
Hours 8 to 5
www.co.calaveras.ca.us/ccgc/clerk.htm

Colusa (06)
Kathleen Moran, County Clerk-Recorder
546 Jay Street
Colusa, CA 95932
(530) 458-0500
(530) 458-0512 Fax
Hours 8:30 to 5

Contra Costa (07)
Stephen L. Weir, County Clerk
Hugh Denton, Asst. Registrar of Voters
524 Main Street
P.O. Box 271
Martinez, CA 94553
(925) 646-4166
(925) 646-1385 Fax
Hours 8 to 5
www.co.contra-costa.ca.us/election.html

Del Norte (08)
Vicki Frazier, County Clerk-Recorder
450 H Street, Room 182
Crescent City, CA 95531
(707) 464-7205
(707) 465-0383
(707) 465-4005 Fax
Hours 8 to 12, 1 to 5

El Dorado (09)

Michele MacIntyre, Registrar of Voters
2850 Fairlane Court
P.O. Box 678001
Placerville, CA 95667
(530) 621-7484
(530) 626-5514 Fax
Hours 8 to 5
www.co.el-dorado.ca.us/~edced/

Fresno (10)

Susan B. Anderson, Registrar of Voters
2221 Kern Street
Fresno, CA 93721
(209) 488-3375
(209) 488-3279 Fax
Hours 8 to 5
www.fresno.ca.gov/2850/index.html

Glenn (11)

Vince T. Minto, County Clerk-Recorder
516 W. Sycamore Street
Willows, CA 95988
(530) 934-6414
(530) 934-6485 Fax
Hours 8 to 5

Humboldt (12)

Lindsey McWilliams, County Clerk
3033 H Street
Eureka, CA 95501
(707) 445-7481
(707) 445-7678
Hours 8:30 to 12, 1 to 5
www.co.humboldt.ca.us/election

Imperial (13)

Dolores Provencio, County Clerk-
   Recorder Courthouse
940 West Main Street, Suite 202
El Centro, CA 92243-2865
(760) 339-4228
(760) 337-4182 Fax
Hours 8 to 5

Inyo (14)

Beverly J. Harry, County Clerk/Registrar
   of Voters
168 North Edwards, P.O. DRAWER F
Independence, CA 93526
(760) 878-0224
(760) 872-2712 Fax
Hours 9 to 12, 1 to 5

Kern (15)

Norman Briggs, Chief Deputy Registrar
Elections Office
1115 Truxtun Avenue
Bakersfield, CA 93301
(805) 868-3590
(805) 868-3768 Fax
Hours 8 to 5
www.co.kern.ca.us/elections/

Kings (16)

George Misner, County Clerk-Recorder
Government Center
1400 West Lacey Blvd.
Hanford, CA 93230
(209) 582-3211 EXT. 2486
Hours 8 to 5
kings.ca.us/acr/index.htm

Lake (17)

Diane C. Fridley,
Chief Deputy Registrar
255 North Forbes Street
Lakeport, CA 95453
(707) 263-2372
(707) 263-2742 Fax
Hours 8 to 5

Lassen (18)

Theresa Nagel, County Clerk
Courthouse
220 South Lassen Street, Suite 5
Susanville, CA 96130
(530) 251-8217
(530) 257-3480 Fax
Hours 9 to 12, 1 to 4

Los Angeles (19)

Conny McCormack, Registrar-
Recorder/County Clerk
12400 Imperial Hwy.
Norwalk, CA 90650
P.O. Box 1024
Norwalk, CA 90051-1024
(562) 462-2748
(562) 863-2039 Fax
Hours 8 to 5
www.co.la.ca.us/regrec/main.htm

Madera (20)
Rebecca Martinez, County Clerk-Recorder
209 West Yosemite Avenue
Madera, CA 93637
(209) 675-7720
(209) 675-7870 Fax
Hours 8 to 5

Marin (21)
Michael Smith, County Clerk-Recorder
3501 Civic Center, Room 121
San Rafael, CA 94913-3904
P.O. Box E
San Rafael, CA 94913-3904
(415) 499-6448
(415) 499-6447 Fax
Hours 8 to 4:30
www.marin.org/mc/clerk/elections/index.
    html

Mariposa (22)
Don Z. Phillips, County Clerk
Hall of Records
4982 - 10th Street
P.O. Box 247
Mariposa, CA 95338
(209) 966-2007
(209) 966-6496 Fax
Hours 8 to 5

Mendocino (23)
Marsha Wharff, County Clerk-Recorder
Elections Department
501 Low Gap Rd., Rm. 1020
Ukiah, CA 95482
(707) 463-4371
(707) 463-4257 Fax
Hours 8 to 5
www.co.mendocino.ca.us/acr/index.html

Merced (24)
James L. Ball, County Clerk/Registrar
2222 "M" Street, Room 14
Merced, CA 95340
(209) 385-7541
(209) 385-7387 Fax
Hours 8 to 5
www.co.merced.ca.us/voters/vohome.htm

Modoc (25)
Maxine Madison, County Clerk
204 Court Street
P.O. Box 130
Alturas, CA 96101
(530) 233-6201
(530) 233-2434 Fax
Hours 8:30 to 12, 1 to 5

Mono (26)
Renn Nolan, County Clerk-Recorder
Annex II
Bryant Street
P.O. Box 237
Bridgeport, CA 93517
(760) 932-5241
(760) 932-7035 Fax
Hours 9 to 5

Monterey (27)
Tony Anchundo, Registrar of Voters
1370 B South Main Street
Salinas, CA 93901
P.O. Box 1848
Salinas, CA 93902
(831) 755-5085
(831) 755-5485 Fax
Hours 8 to 5
www.mocovote.org/

Napa (28)
John Tuter, Registrar of Voters
Elections Department
900 Coombs Street, Suite 256
Napa, CA 94559
(707) 253-4321
(707) 253-4390 Fax
Hours 8 to 5
www.co.napa.ca.us/Departments/
    Elections.htm

Nevada (29)
Lorraine Jewett-Burdick, County Clerk-
Recorder
HEW Building, Suite E
10433 Willow Valley Rd., Suite E
Nevada City, CA 95959-2347
(530) 265-1298
(530) 265-7159 Fax
Hours 9 to 4
www.co.nevada.ca.us/coclerk/welcome.
    html

Orange (30)
Rosalyn Lever, Registrar of Voters
1300 South Grand Ave., Bldg. C
Santa Ana, CA 92705
P.O. Box 11298
Santa Ana, CA 92711
(714) 567-7600
(714) 567-7556 Fax
Hours 8 to 5
www.oc.ca.gov/election/

Placer (31)
Jim McCauley, County Clerk, Recorder,
and Registrar
2956 Richardson Drive
Auburn, CA 95604
P.O. Box 5278
Auburn, CA 95604
(530) 886-5650
(530) 886-5688 Fax
Hours 8 to 5
www.placer.ca.gov/clerk/elections.htm

Plumas (32)
Judith Wells, County Clerk
520 Main Street, Room 102
Quincy, CA 95971
(530) 283-6256
(530) 283-6455 Fax
Hours 8 to 5

Riverside (33)
Mischelle Townsend, Registrar of Voters
2724 Gateway Drive
Riverside, CA 92507-0918
(909) 486-7200
(909) 486-7335 Fax
Hours 8 to 5
www.co.riverside.ca.us/election/

Sacramento (34)
Ernest R. Hawkins, Registrar of Voters
3700 Branch Center Road
Sacramento, CA 95827
(916) 875-6451
(916) 875-6516 Fax
Hours 8 to 5
www.co.sacramento.ca.us/elections/index.
  html

San Benito (35)
John R. Hodges, County Clerk, Auditor,
and Recorder
Courthouse, Room 206
440 Fifth Street
Hollister, CA 95023-3843
(408) 636-4029
(408) 636-2939 Fax
Hours 8 to 5

San Bernardino (36)
Ingrid Gonzales, Registrar of Voters
777 East Rialto Avenue
San Bernardino, CA 92415-0770
(909) 387-8300
(909) 387-2022 Fax
Hours 8 to 5
www.co.san-bernardino.ca.us/rov/

San Diego (37)
Mikel Haas, Registrar of Voters
5201 Ruffin Road, Suite I
P.O. Box 85656
San Diego, CA 92186-5656
(619) 570-1061
(619) 694-2955 Fax
Hours 8 to 5
www.co.san-
diego.ca.us/cnty/cntydepts/community/
  voters/

San Francisco (38)
Naomi Nishioka, Director of Elections
City Hall - 1 Dr. Carlton B. Goodlett
San Francisco, CA 94102-4635
(415) 554-4375
(415) 554-7344 Fax
Hours 8 to 5
www.ci.sf.ca.us/election/index.htm

San Joaquin (39)
Larry O. Tunison, Registrar of Voters
212 North San Joaquin Street
P.O. Box 810
Stockton, CA 95201-0810
(209) 468-2890
(209) 468-2889 Fax
Hours 8 to 5
www.co.san-joaquin.ca.us/elect/index.htm

San Luis Obispo (40)

Julie Rodewald, County Clerk -Recorder
1144 Monterey Street, Ste. A
San Luis Obispo, CA 93408-3237
(805) 781-5228
(805) 781-1111 Fax
Hours 8 to 5
www.slocounty.org/Clerk.htm

San Mateo (41)

Warren Slocum, Assessor-County Clerk-
Recorder
555 County Center 1st Floor
Redwood City, California 94063
(650) 312-5222
(650) 312-5348 Fax
Hours 8 to 5
www.care.co.sanmateo.ca.us/

Santa Barbara (42)

Kenneth A. Pettit, County Clerk-Recorder
Courthouse Basement
1100 Anacapa Street
Santa Barbara, CA 93101
P.O. Box 159
Santa Barbara, CA 93102-0159
(805) 568-2200
(805) 568-3247 Fax
Hours 8 to 5
www.sb-democracy.com/

Santa Clara (43)

Kathryn Ferguson, Registrar of Voters
1555 Berger Drive, Bldg. 2
San Jose, CA 95112
P.O. Box 1147
San Jose, CA 95108-1147
(408) 299-8302
(408) 998-7314 Fax
Hours 8 to 5
claraweb.co.santa-clara.ca.us/rov/rov.htm

Santa Cruz (44)

Richard W. Bedal, County Clerk-Recorder
701 Ocean Street, Room 210
Santa Cruz, CA 95060-4076
(831) 454-2060
(831) 454-2445 Fax
Hours 8 to 5
www.co.santa-cruz.ca.us/ele/election.htm

Shasta (45)

Ann Reed, County Clerk
1643 Market Street
Redding, CA 96001
P.O. Box 990880
Redding, CA 96099-0880
(530) 225-5730
(530) 225-5454 Fax
Hours 8 to 5

Sierra (46)

Mary J. Jungi, County Clerk-Recorder
Courthouse, Room 11
P.O. DRAWER D
Downieville, CA 95936-0398
(530) 289-3295
(530) 289-3300 Fax
Hours 9 to 12, 1 to 4

Siskiyou (47)

Coleen Baker, County Clerk
311 4th Street, Room 201
Yreka, CA 96097
P.O. Box 338
Yreka, CA 96097-9910
(530) 842-8086
(530) 842-8093 Fax
Hours 8 to 5
209.232.195.206.clerk/index.htm

Solano (48)

Laura Winslow, Registrar of Voters
510 Clay Street
Fairfield, CA 94533
(707) 421-6675
(707) 421-6678 Fax
www.co.solano.ca.us/elections/

Sonoma (49)

Janice Atkinson, Asst. Registrar of Voters
435 Fiscal Drive
Santa Rosa, CA 95406
P.O. Box 11485
Santa Rosa, CA 95406-1485
(707) 565-6800
(707) 565-6843 Fax
Hours 8 to 5
www.sonoma-county.org/perl/frame.cgi?
    PATH=/main/admin/regvoter

Stanislaus (50)

Karen L. Mathews, County Clerk-
  Recorder
1021 I Street, Suite 101
Modesto, CA 95354-2331
(209) 525-5200
(209) 525-5210 Fax
Hours 8 to 12, 1 to 5

Sutter (51)

Lonna B. Smith, County Clerk
433 Second Street
Yuba City, CA 95991-5595
(530) 822-7120
(530) 822-7214 Fax
Hours 8 to 5

Tehama (52)

Mary Alice George, County Clerk-
  Recorder
633 Washington Street,
Room 33
Red Bluff, CA 96080
P.O. Box 250
Red Bluff, CA 96080-0250
(530) 527-8190
(530) 529-0980 Fax
Hours 8 to 12, 1 to 3

Trinity (53)

Dero B. Forslund, County Clerk-Recorder,
  Assessor
101 Court Street
Weaverville, CA 96093
P.O. Box 1258
Weaverville, CA 96093-1258
(530) 623-1220
(530) 623-3762 Fax
Hours 8 to 12, 1 to 5
www.trinitycounty.org.index1.html

Tulare (54)

Candy Lopez, Chief Deputy–Elections
221 South Mooney Blvd., #G28
Visalia, CA 93291-4596
(559) 733-6275
(559) 737-4498 Fax
Hours 8 to 5
http://tmx.com/tulare

Tuolumne (55)

Tim R. Johnson, County Clerk, Auditor
Controller Administration Center
2 South Green Street
Sonora, CA 95370-4696
(209) 533-5570
(209) 533-5672 Fax
Hours 8 to 5

Ventura (56)

Richard D. Dean, County Clerk-Recorder
800 South Victoria Avenue, L-1200
Ventura, CA 93009-1200
(805) 654-2266
(805) 648-9200 Fax
Hours 8 to 5
www.ventura.org/election/elecidx.htm

Yolo (57)

Tony Bernhard, County Clerk-Recorder
625 Court Street, Room B05
Woodland, CA 95695
P.O. Box 1820
Woodland, CA 95776-1820
(530) 666-8133
(530) 666-8123 Fax
Hours 8 to 5
www.dcn.davis.ca.us/go/election

Yuba (58)

Frances Fairey, County Clerk-Recorder
935 14th Street
Marysville, CA 95901-5793
(530) 741-6341
(530) 741-6285 Fax
Hours 10 to 3 / Telephone hours 8 to 5

Source: California Secretary of State's
Office

Appendix F

California Resources on the Web

California Government

Official California Homepage
http://www.ca.gov

Governor
http://www.governor.ca.gov

Assembly
http://www.assembly.ca.gov

Senate
http://www.senate.ca.gov

State Agencies (by topic)
http://www.ca.gov/search/agency.shtm

California State and Local Government (U.S. Library of Congress resource)
http://lcweb.loc.gov/global/state/ca-gov.html

California County Information

http://www.dof.ca.gov/html/fs_data/profiles/pf_home.htm
http://www.csac.counties.org

California Cultural Resources

California Council for the Humanities
http://www.calhum.org/

California Humanities Network
http://www.thinkcalifornia.net

Japanese American National Museum
http://www.lausd.k12.ca.us/janm/main.htm

Virtual Image of Manzanar Relocation Camp, Owens Valley
http://geoimages.berkeley.edu/GeoImages/QTVR/OwensValley/ManzanarCemeteryS.html

CALIFORNIA STUDIES CENTERS

The Center for California Studies, California State University, Sacramento
http://www.csus.edu/calst/index.html

California Geographical Survey
http://geogdata.csun.edu

California Studies Center, UC Berkeley
http://www-geography.berkeley.edu/californiastudiescenter.html

California Studies Association
http://geography.berkeley.edu/californiastudies.html

Pat Brown Institute, California State University, Los Angeles
http://pbi.calstatela.edu

Institute of Governmental Studies, UC Berkeley
http://www.igs.berkeley.edu:8880

The California Mission Studies Association
http://www.ca-missions.org

California Studies Program, San Francisco State University
http://bss.sfsu.edu/calstudies

Center for Southern California Studies, California State University, Northridge
http://www.csun.edu/~cscs

Southern California Studies Center (SC2), University of Southern California
http://www.usc.edu/dept/LAS/SC2

Center for the Study of Los Angeles, Loyola Marymount University
http://www.lib.lmu.edu/special/csla/csla.htm

An expansive and updated directory of California Studies Centers is located at the California Studies Program, SFSU
http://bss.sfsu.edu/calstudies/cs_directory.htm

Index